Praise for *Ideaflow*

"These authors are masterful at demystifying how any organization can turn creativity into a steady practice."

—Chris Flink, former CEO and executive director of
the Exploratorium and former IDEO partner

"Utley and Klebahn were by far the most transformative professors we had at Stanford. *Ideaflow* finally makes their lessons available to aspiring innovators everywhere. If you've ever wondered whether you have what it takes to put something new out into the world, read this book."

—Maite and Itziar Diez-Canedo, cofounders and coCEOs of Via

"Utley and Klebahn share proven tools and insider tricks from their renowned consulting expertise and best-in-class programs so that these game-changing ideas flow to the rest of us."

—Leidy Klotz, author of *Subtract: The Untapped Science of Less* and professor
of engineering and architecture at the University of Virginia

"A founder's secret weapon. *Ideaflow* is full of tools for everyone seeking to innovate constantly, build thoughtfully, and grow quickly."

—Diarra Bousso, founder and CEO at Diarrablu

"How do you invent what's next? Simply try to learn how to have more and better ideas. *Ideaflow* offers eye-opening techniques combined with practical insights into how anyone can establish creativity as a daily practice in their lives."

—Dr. Frederik G. Pferdt, Google's chief innovation evangelist
and adjunct professor at Stanford's d.school

"Can't imagine where ManiMe would be without Jeremy and Perry. The coolest thing I learned is that we need to have a 'founder's mindset' long before the product is ready for the market. They liberated my thinking, significantly accelerating our launch without unnecessary worry!"

—Jooyeon Song, cofounder and CEO of ManiMe

"The core teaching of *Ideaflow* of getting out into the real world, quickly, is the antithesis to my training as an MBA, but I've since become obsessed with the art of experimenting, iterating, asking, and listening in order to build a massively impactful company that is unique in the marketplace. Founders shouldn't miss this book."   —Aishetu Dozie, founder and CEO of Bossy Cosmetics

"Two masters of the craft provide a road map about how you can develop your creativity practice and help those you work with do the same."
—Linda A. Hill, chair of the Leadership Initiative at the Harvard Business School and coauthor of *Collective Genius*

"Over the last decade, Jeremy and Perry have become my go-to innovation gurus! This book is essential reading for anyone running an organization that desires to enhance and expand innovation. Beware the tidal wave of ideas that will follow once you start reading!"
—Mark Hoplamazian, CEO of Hyatt Hotels Corporation

Ideaflow

Ideaflow

The Only Business Metric That Matters

JEREMY UTLEY

and PERRY KLEBAHN

PORTFOLIO · PENGUIN

Portfolio / Penguin
An imprint of Penguin Random House LLC
penguinrandomhouse.com

Most Portfolio books are available at a discount when purchased in
quantity for sales promotions or corporate use. Special editions, which include
personalized covers, excerpts, and corporate imprints, can be created when
purchased in large quantities. For more information, please call (212) 572-2232
or email specialmarkets@penguinrandomhouse.com. Your local bookstore can
also assist with discounted bulk purchases using the Penguin Random House
corporate Business-to-Business program. For assistance in locating a
participating retailer, email B2B@penguinrandomhouse.com.

Library of Congress Cataloging-in-Publication Data
Names: Utley, Jeremy, author. | Klebahn, Perry, author.
Title: Ideaflow : the only business metric that matters / Jeremy Utley and Perry Klebahn.
Description: New York : Portfolio, [2022] | Includes bibliographical references and index.
Identifiers: LCCN 2022019058 (print) | LCCN 2022019059 (ebook) |
ISBN 9780593420584 (hardcover) | ISBN 9780593420591 (ebook)
Subjects: LCSH: Organizational effectiveness. |
Creative ability in business. | Success in business.
Classification: LCC HD58.9 .U85 2022 (print) | LCC HD58.9 (ebook) |
DDC 650.1—c23/eng/20220815
LC record available at https://lccn.loc.gov/2022019058
LC ebook record available at https://lccn.loc.gov/2022019059

Printed in the United States of America
2nd Printing

Book design by Alexis Farabaugh

PERRY

*To Annie, Parker, and Phoebe for teaching me
that ideas from the heart matter most.*

~

JEREMY

*To Michelle, whose quest for
inspiration first caused me to wonder.*

The truth is that for every good idea, there are a thousand bad ones. And sometimes it can be hard to tell the difference.

—*Marc Randolph, cofounder of Netflix*

Contents

Part One

Innovate

Part Two

Elevate

Foreword

One of the biggest surprises for new students at the d.school—whether they are head of a major company or were head of their high school class—is the idea that quantity creates quality.

Many come to Stanford searching for quality. At the Hasso Plattner Institute of Design (aka the d.school), they hope to learn how to generate world-changing, breakthrough ideas. What we tell them from the get-go is to ignore good and bad in the early rounds and shoot for lots of ideas instead. To go for volume before judgment around quality can set in. This notion of separating idea generation from idea selection can come as quite a shock.

What these students learn, and world-class creators already understand, is that it's hard to distinguish good ideas from bad ones before trying them out to see what happens. Without a reliable process for real-world experimentation, it's hard to know which novel solution is worth pursuing in the first place or how it might be improved later. The surefire approach is to create as many scrappy solutions as possible and then test them rapidly with real people.

As d.school students learn, this means turning creativity into a practice. We don't teach our students to sit on their heels until inspiration hits them and then "sprint" into action. Problems don't wait until the mood strikes. To keep the flow of ideas steady, they learn ways to find diverse and surprising sources of inspiration that will feed a stream of ideas to test. The practice of nurturing this ongoing torrent of ideas is transformative for them. It's as useful in everyday life as it is in creative work.

When it comes to delivering these essential lessons and the habits and practices of exceptional creativity that go along with them, you are in capable hands. Jeremy Utley and Perry Klebahn are gifted teachers who actively assist leaders and their organizations with solving real-world problems. They have been empowering d.school students for over a decade. They are also skilled and prolific creative practitioners themselves. They know how creativity works and, just as important, they explain it lucidly in this book.

Together, Utley and Klebahn have written an essential resource for entrepreneurs, inventors, managers, students, leaders, and anyone else who seeks to reliably develop more and better ideas.

David M. Kelley

Donald W. Whittier
Professor of Mechanical Engineering

Stanford, California

February 2, 2022

Who Needs Ideas?

*I don't need breakthrough results in my
company, my work, or my life.*

—NO ONE (EVER)

You may be wondering if this book is intended for you. It is.

In our teaching and consulting work with entrepreneurs, executives, and other leaders at organizations of every kind, we sometimes encounter an individual who proudly questions the value of, even the need for, creativity in their work.

"Sure," they tell us during one of our presentations or training sessions, "some people in this room need creativity to do their jobs properly. The guys who make the graphics, for example. They should stay to the end. As a leader, however, what I need are breakthrough results."

To judge creativity's true value, not just to designers, writers, or engineers but to everyone who wants to achieve world-class outcomes, we need to define it properly. The best definition we've heard comes from a seventh-grader in Ohio, whose teacher recently shared it with a friend of ours: "Creativity is doing more than the first thing that comes to your mind." In other words, it's the capacity to keep generating ideas after the first one that's "good enough."

What, however, is an idea? We can't proceed without defining this fundamental term next.

One way to think about it is by realizing that your brain never makes anything truly from scratch. It's always working with the raw material of your experiences. Thus, any idea is really just a new connection between two things that were already in your head. Things you've seen, heard, or felt. Take these two:

A. Young families struggle up the hills of San Francisco with overloaded strollers.

B. When you were a kid, your dad had a self-propelled lawnmower.

Zzzt. Did you feel that tiny spark? You got an idea! Self-propelled strollers may not be a billion-dollar business—or even remotely safe—but with the puzzle pieces in place, your brain eagerly snapped them together. That's what the brain does best. Frame a problem, feed it material, and it'll start making connections left and right—if you let it.

Read this book. With our principles and techniques, you will never again feel intimidated by (or skeptical of) the need for more ideas. You'll never wonder where ideas come from, how to find better ones, or what to do with them once they arrive. As you'll learn, there is nothing nebulous or mystical about creating breakthrough results. What happens haphazardly for most of us—creative problem solving—can be learned and mastered like any other skill, both by individuals and the teams and organizations they comprise.

You can't consciously choose to make an idea. (Try it, you'll see.) Instead, ideas start arriving once you've identified a clear problem and gathered sufficient raw material for the brain to do its job. *Zzzt.* It's more helpful to think of yourself as a channel for letting as many ideas through as possible. To clear up another misconception, breakthrough results don't happen by picking the "right" idea from a list but rather by winnowing ideas down through real-world experimentation and iteration until a clear winner emerges.

That's it. That's the formula for success in everything, and we're only on page 2. Of course, you may have more questions than answers at this point, but that's OK. Keep going. Once you fully understand what ideas are, where they come from, and how to separate the winners from the losers, you can finally put that lightning rod down and start *making lightning*.

Introduction

Smart people are a dime a dozen and often don't amount to much. What counts is being creative and imaginative. That's what makes someone a true innovator.

—WALTER ISAACSON

Whether this is the first book about creativity and innovation you've opened or the fifteenth, you're seeking a way to close the gap between creative potential and real-world impact. It doesn't matter whether that gap exists within you, your team, or an entire organization. The fact is, there is so much more that might be accomplished if only you could *activate* creative potential and *enhance* creative performance.

This isn't about a set of tweaks or an incremental improvement. You seek to establish a steady and reliable flow of ideas that results in a torrent of successful products, services, and other solutions. You want to enjoy the tangible benefits of breakthrough thinking by unleashing your own potential and the potential of those around you.

When it comes to achieving these ambitions, picking up this book is one of the better ideas you've had.

It doesn't matter whether you think of yourself as a creative person. In fact, we don't believe there is such a thing. Someone either has or has not developed a robust creative skill set *yet*. Creativity isn't a gift reserved for a precious few. It's learned. If you haven't done so yet, it's simply a matter of knowledge, time, and effort. We'll help you with the first part. The rest is up to you.

Likewise, creative organizations don't happen by accident. They are purpose-built. Nike and Apple were designed by individuals who understood how creativity works. Phil Knight and Steve Jobs deliberately cultivated the environment that creativity needs to thrive. These leaders prioritized creativity's requirements alongside those of profit and growth because they understood that the first one feeds the other two. Innovative powerhouses like these are rare precisely because creative skills are so uncommon among business leaders. That's what makes creativity a superlative leadership trait—it sets you apart like nothing else.

Steve Jobs credited his study of calligraphy at Reed College in the 1970s for the refinement of his aesthetic sensibility. We'd argue that this early experience influenced more than the typography on the first Macintosh operating system. Practicing with pen and ink taught Jobs how creativity works in practice. It gave him a hands-on understanding of the process that made him a far more effective catalyst of creativity and innovation in others.

Leaders who don't understand how creativity works struggle to nurture it in others, let alone leverage its power for the organization. We'll see examples of this blind spot throughout this book. In most cases, the flow of ideas gets disrupted not by the individuals on a team but by the well-meaning, misguided leader who is so fixated on feasibility and relevance that every divergence from the status quo gets immediately quashed. Imagine Steve Jobs saying, "Would you guys stop talking about cellphones already? We're a *computer* company!" He knew in his bones that you go wide and stay there long before you zero in.

Even CEOs who believe in creativity's importance often fail to protect, support, or incentivize it when they don't operate creatively themselves. Despite their good intentions, they simply don't know what robust creativity requires, or how crucial those requirements are. How could they? Traditional leadership and management training that prioritizes error-free efficiency runs counter to creativity, which involves divergence and dead ends. The approach that works everywhere else fails in this one area. It takes a clear understanding of how creativity works to carve out its special place at work. Once you've gotten in the creative habit, your understanding expands. When a student would come to Stanford's legendary Bob McKim for feedback on an idea, he'd refuse: "Show me three first." As an engineer himself, McKim understood how ideas work on a fundamental level. That's what made him so good at inspiring creativity in others.

All of this is very good news for those who don't think of themselves as creative. Creativity can be learned and, in learning it, you learn to properly support the creative efforts of others. This means that you, too, can build or lead an organization capable of world-class creativity and innovation. To get there, however, you will need to let go of any mythology about creativity you may have picked up along the way. Creativity is the craft of problem solving. Painting and poetry call on it, but so do mergers and acquisitions. In business, creativity is as foundational and practical as double-entry accounting. It magnifies and accelerates all your other efforts.

We find it helpful to think of it in this way: If you already knew how to solve a problem, it wouldn't be a problem at all. Not the way we think of problems, anyway. A problem you know how to solve is really just a task, an action that requires a given amount of time and effort to complete. A trunk full of groceries to unload isn't a problem per se. A tub in need of a scrub isn't, either. "Solving" problems like these is simply a matter of doing them as quickly and efficiently as possible. It's only when the usual approach fizzles that you're forced to think of something new. What do you do when you discover that the power in the house is out and the fridge is lukewarm? Now those groceries are a *problem*. A true problem responds to only one thing: ideas. From this perspective, **every problem is an idea problem**. Therefore, creativity isn't just about "new tagline" or "new product." It's about "how do I close this deal?" or "how do I frame this important email?" Ultimately, creativity is the way your contribution goes from incremental to exponential.

With the system of innovation we've developed, which is trusted and relied upon by top organizations around the world, you will know exactly how to tackle any problem effectively, minimizing the risks and maximizing the odds of success. Even better, you will be able to communicate and catalyze this system with groups of all sizes, integrating a rigorous approach to innovation into your team or organization and consequently multiplying everyone's efforts.

What truly distinguishes our approach to creativity is its relentless focus on a concept we call "ideaflow." We'll define that term more specifically in the next chapter, but the gist is that *quantity drives quality*. More output equals better output. Talent, genius, and luck have less to do than you might think with the quality and consistency of real-world outcomes.

In the long run, methods beat muses.

The beauty of ideaflow as a concept and an approach to creativity is that in increasing the number of ideas we generate, we dramatically reduce the pressure and stress involved in the entire process of idea generation, all while increasing the odds of success and lowering the costs and risks to an absolute minimum.

Whether you seek to develop your own creative capacity or establish a full-scale innovation lab at a Fortune 500 organization, this book will help you solve the problem of solving problems for good.

~

This all sounds good, certainly, but why should you believe any of it?

The two of us, Jeremy Utley and Perry Klebahn, teach innovation, leadership, and entrepreneurship at Stanford's Hasso Plattner Institute of Design. The Institute, known colloquially as the d.school, is an extraordinary place. It's what brought the two of us together and continues to give us the opportunity to learn from and collaborate with an unparalleled array of world-class practitioners and educators. Our amazing colleagues and students, current and former, are a big piece of what made it possible for us to write this book. (Thanks to all of you.)

Perry started teaching product design at Stanford in 1996 while running a snowshoe company he'd founded. Even as he moved on to leadership roles at Timbuk2 and Patagonia, Perry continued to make time for teaching and, in 2006, he took a leave of absence to cofound the d.school.

In 2010, Stanford asked Jeremy, who was just completing a fellowship there, to scale up the d.school's executive education program. Though excited by the opportunity, Jeremy couldn't help but notice that the other d.school programs were led by complementary pairs. He asked for a collaborator. Perry had recently stepped down as CEO of Timbuk2 to teach at Stanford full-time, and the two of us clicked right away. Together, alongside an incredible team of world-class design educators and practitioners, we've built the executive education program at the d.school into the best in the country.

In addition to our work with Stanford's graduate students, we've spent the last decade showing entrepreneurs, managers, and leaders at organizations of every size and across industries how to drive disruptive innovation. We use the word "disruptive" here in a very specific sense. To be disruptive, the new way of doing something must upend the old one. Designing a vacuum tube that burns out less often is a regular innovation. Designing the transistor, which ultimately makes vacuum tubes obsolete, is a disruptive innovation. To be clear, this is scary—if you happen to be a vacuum-tube manufacturer. Once you get *really* innovative, it starts to feel like you're always on the verge of putting yourself out of business. In a good way.

Today, every business is building horse-drawn carriages in turn-of-the-century Detroit. Innovations as disruptive as the transistor don't happen just every decade or so as they once did. We have entered an era of *continual disruption*. The skills we teach at Stanford are no longer just crucial for Silicon Valley entrepreneurial success but for any organization's ongoing survival. As technology sprints forward, companies must adapt and evolve at a much faster pace than ever before. The pace will only accelerate.

At Stanford, we place our students at real organizations to lead innovation efforts. This program provides a robust source of insights. Likewise, our work teaching innovation to executives at multinational corporations offers us an unrivaled laboratory for exploring teaching methods and learning styles. Finally, we run an incubator program, Launchpad, whose alumni have raised over $1.1 billion in venture capital. This, too, has proven to be a well of real-world outcomes to study. Today, sixty-five Launchpad companies are active in the marketplace, and we learn as much from those that fail as we do from the many that have succeeded. Across all these disparate experiences, we are only confirmed in our fundamental belief that creativity works pretty much the same way for everybody and in every context. This means that the best practices we've developed apply to you and your organization, whether you're bootstrapping a start-up or leading a team of hundreds.

Part of our success as collaborators stems from a serendipitous opportunity early on in our work together. The legendary management professor Bob Sutton invited the two of us to join him for a corporate advising gig in Singapore. Our plates were full, but you don't say no to Bob Sutton. As it turned out, the two of us enjoyed teaching executives how to solve real-world idea problems more effectively. Before we knew it, we were circling the globe: Russia, Taiwan, New Zealand, Malaysia, Israel.

For a decade now, we've run one innovation effort after another at organizations of every description. What a gift this has turned out to be. As fun as our Stanford programs can be, the learning cycle is restricted. We have only so many at-bats to try new things. Unlike a classroom environment, where professors are expected to arrive with a fixed curriculum, a corporate setting allows for a more fluid approach. Leaders understand that each company's needs are unique, so there is no expectation that everything we try works perfectly. This gives us permission to take risks. Thus, we experiment with our clients, changing up the methods we teach to see what sticks with different teams and in different scenarios. Then the discoveries we make in the field feed back into the d.school's flagship programs. (As you read further, you'll see how this arrangement combines all the elements of an effective innovation lab.) It's in the field that we get all our best material. Most of the examples in this book are drawn from our personal experiences working on real-world projects with students, managers, leaders, and founders.

On campus, we teach innovation not only to executives but to everyone from aspiring lawyers and doctors to budding journalists and computer scientists. Though their future professions couldn't be more disparate, all these learners see the value in the creative tool set now offered in this book. Our programs don't exist in a vacuum. If our approach didn't translate into breakthrough results, students would turn to Harvard or Princeton. Yet our programs are packed; major banks, manufacturers, and retailers keep knocking on our door; and our online courses are among Stanford's most popular. We mention this not out of ego but as proof that there is nothing mystical or random about creativity. With the right techniques, it can be mastered by anyone. Including you.

~

Chapter by chapter, this book will teach you the habits and techniques required to generate, test, and implement breakthrough ideas. Though you can dip in and out of the material, it works best to read *Ideaflow* from cover to cover and follow our advice in order. The book is divided into two parts: Innovate, where we explain the entire pipeline from ideation through experimentation, and Elevate, where we offer our most powerful techniques for improving creative outcomes. Regardless of your profession or industry, reading both parts of this book will transform your approach to creativity and problem-solving. More important, it will help you organize, direct, amplify, and enhance the efforts of peers, colleagues, and direct reports. Ultimately, this system can be scaled up to magnify the innovation output of an entire organization. Creativity is never truly a solitary feat, even if you work primarily alone. We always make our greatest impact working in tandem with others. A key benefit of our system is the way it helps us bring out the best in one another and combine our unique contributions toward a greater goal.

"I'm blown away by how excited these people are," Robb Webb, Hyatt's chief human resources officer, whispered to Jeremy during a session. "I can't remember the last time I saw a team so enthusiastic about the projects they've been working on." Years later, when we followed up with Robb to make sure we recalled this remark correctly, he had more to say with the benefit of hindsight: "This tapped into a need we all had. We'd unintentionally been sucking the humanity out of our daily work. I realized how important creativity was when one of our hotel GMs said she felt reminded of why she first fell in love with hospitality."

It begins with you. Whether you are a collaborator or a leader, talk is cheap. Changing your own behavior drives lasting, meaningful change in others like nothing else. Recommending this book at the next all-hands meeting won't move the needle. Nor will a company-wide email urging people to read it. (Feel free to do both these things, of course!) To make a change, walk the walk. Based on our years of experience watching change succeed—and fail—within teams and across organizations, we ask you to make a commitment, here at the start, to adopt these methods yourself before asking your colleagues to do so. If people don't see you investing in the hard work of innovation, they won't put in the requisite effort themselves. Set an example. Lead the charge. Demonstrate your willingness to face the fear. Yes, fear, because fear is what actually stands in the way of improvement. Would you hesitate to try something new if its success was guaranteed? Of course not. That's never the case in real life, however. Any new product or service can fail with customers. Any improvement to a process can have unforeseen consequences. Ideas are inherently risky. If you don't learn to weigh the risks of trying new things against the dangers of stagnation, fear will always hold you back from your greatest achievements.

The riskiest move is no move at all. Conditions are always changing. If you're too scared to leap to the next patch of ice, the one you're standing on will end up melting anyway. Of course, if you see innovation as something that demands huge amounts of effort, poses enormous risks, and delivers underwhelming results, you will only ever choose mediocrity. This book will show you, however, what the world's most successful entrepreneurs and organizations already understand: an effective approach to creative problem-solving *reduces* effort, *minimizes* risk, and *magnifies* results. If you don't believe us, compare a list of the world's most innovative companies with a list of the world's most profitable companies. Other than fossil-fuel companies—which could use some disruptive innovations of their own—you'll be looking at essentially the same roster of organizations. That's no coincidence.

Let go of your preconceived notions about how creativity works, the risk that ideas represent, or the value that new approaches can offer. Today's challenges demand innovation on a level never previously required. From your organization. From you. Roll up your sleeves, and let's get to work.

Part One

Innovate

1.

Measure Tomorrow's Success in Today's Ideas

One resists the invasion of armies; one does not resist the invasion of ideas.

—VICTOR HUGO

I t was a chilly April morning in Ventura, California, when Perry realized he'd run out of ideas.

Getting out of his car at Patagonia headquarters, fleece pullover zipped to the chin and piping hot coffee in hand, Perry felt large and in charge. The year was 2002, and he was responsible for a good chunk of sales and operations at the beloved outdoor clothing company founded by iconoclast climber and blacksmith Yvon Chouinard. It had been an incredibly stressful few months for the entire world since the tragic events of September 11, but at least here and now, things were starting to feel normal again. Perry was lucky enough to work at a great company with outstanding values, and his colleagues were terrific. That morning, it felt OK to breathe deeply of the salty ocean air and welcome spring.

Perry's feeling of optimism cooled faster than his coffee, however, as he thumbed his way through the newly arrived racks of clothing for the following year's spring season. *This* funereal assortment would be sent to Patagonia's stores and countless other retailers around the country? *These* drab, colorless garments were Patagonia's idea of vernal exploration and renewal? Perry forced down a sip of now-lukewarm java.

Trying (and failing) to seem casual, Perry turned to the senior merchandiser busily organizing everything for the product team's review.

"Good morning, Adrienne," he said, forcing himself to breathe. "The product line looks a little . . . dark for a spring line, don't you think? Where are the new colorways?" There was an uncomfortable silence before she responded.

"*New* colorways?"

Perry smiled harder and inclined his head at the dispiriting racks of black and gray clothing as if to say, *The colorways that aren't here yet, but must certainly be on the way.* At that moment, Adrienne's face showed some of that missing color.

"Perry," she said, "you told us we have to focus on the winners."

Perry bit off a retort. It was true. He *had* said that. Somehow, playing it safe had made a lot of sense at the time. Now that Patagonia's spring lineup resembled a mortician's closet, however, not so much. Looking at rack after rack of black and gray clothing, he could just imagine the jarring effect these garments would have on Patagonia's bright and welcoming stores. Talk about a downer. This was the consequence of a decision that had been made, above all, to avoid risks. By narrowing his options in pursuit of "security," however, Perry had taken a terrible risk instead.

"How quickly do you think we can get some variety in here?" Perry asked, keeping that fake smile plastered to his face. "Things are getting back to normal. Customers are coming back to the stores. I think they'll be ready for a little color by next spring."

"You're kidding, right?" Adrienne replied, making no effort to match Perry's smile. "You know our standard lead time is eighteen months."

Eighteen months! Perry thought. *How do I get today's ideas into yesterday's company so we still have a tomorrow?* He dumped his cold, half-finished cup in a wastebasket. Time to get to work.

THE DANGEROUS BUSINESS OF NEW IDEAS

As we've said, an idea is simply a new connection between two things that were already floating around in your head. When you give your brain a problem to solve, it goes to work, way in the background, by jamming disparate pieces of knowledge and experience together in different ways until a light bulb goes off. "Does this work?" Maybe, maybe not, but you don't want to cut off the flow of ideas yet, so you say: "Good job, brain! What else have you got?"

A problem, as we've said, is anything you don't already know how to do. It can be anything from "How do we meet next quarter's revenue target?" to "What colors should we offer for this season's snow pants?" The real-world effectiveness of any potential solution is unknown until it's tested, so every single idea represents a risk. Forget the possibility of catastrophic failure—in many cases, it simply won't work.

Thus, tackling an unfamiliar problem—or seeking out a better solution for a familiar one—requires not just ingenuity but courage and vulnerability. A willingness to put things out there and make the occasional mistake. The irony of the creative process is that we limit our creativity just when we need it the most, as illustrated by Perry's experience at Patagonia. When we're under pressure, we default to the known and familiar approach even when it clearly won't suffice. It feels safer to fail by doing the expected thing than risk looking foolish by trying something new.

Through the system in this book, you will unlearn this defensive instinct so that you can maintain a steady flow of new ideas through adverse circumstances. You must learn to trust in your ingenuity. If you can keep the pipeline of potential solutions flowing in both good times and bad, you can overcome any challenge. Abundant creativity and the capacity to execute on it represent an extraordinary competitive advantage. To understand why, let's go back to Patagonia.

There are tough times, and then there are catastrophes. After the tragic events of September 11, 2001, no one knew how to react. Beyond the sense of existential threat to the United States felt by many at the time, beyond the psychic shock of the unprovoked murder of thousands of civilians, the attacks disrupted everyday life for all Americans. Everything came to a halt. A sky without aircraft was just the most visible aspect of this collective paralysis. In the days and weeks after the fall of the Twin Towers, "normal" started to feel like a distant memory. People operated in a state of ceaseless vigilance. Who was responsible for the attacks? Would there be more? What would happen next?

Naturally, discretionary spending after the attacks sputtered. Businesses worldwide faced one hard choice after another. The slowdown might last years, especially if there were more attacks. How would they survive the next quarter, let alone meet their existing goals and targets? At Patagonia, Perry and the rest of the leadership team faced pressure to take decisive action. The company was on track to buy millions in raw materials for the upcoming season. Betting on the future seemed, well, *risky,* so, like nearly all their competitors that fall, Perry had cut the order for raw materials by a large percentage to match the drop in demand. As for where to make those cuts, he offered clear guidance to the merchandisers: "Keep the winners we know we can sell."

It doesn't require a wave of terrorist attacks to inspire short-term, self-defeating decision-making. Most of us try something new only when we're desperate. We weigh potential losses far more heavily than potential rewards. This so-called loss aversion exists for a good reason. If a prehistoric human mistook a bush for a lion, it was good for a laugh. Mistaking a lion for a bush, however, wasn't good for anyone but the lion. Deepseated instinct tells us it's safer to stay the heck away from the bushes in general, even if some might hide tasty fruit. To attempt something new, you're fighting against the brain's bias. The problem when it comes to our ideas, however, is that we're terrible at distinguishing the winners from the losers until we've tried them. We will see many, many examples of this throughout the book. In our experience, the more experienced and successful the innovator, the less they trust their own capacity to pick the winners on sight. Never pick when you can test.

For an outdoor clothing company like Patagonia, black and gray basics are the "safe" options. When the creative team was told to pick the winners, that meant nothing new, nothing colorful. Dozens of new products under development were shelved. A rainbow of colorways was bleached away. At the time, this strategy made sense. What if people didn't want puce next spring because of the national climate of anxiety? Or what if they wanted puce, but not cerulean? Everyone can agree on black.

Can't they?

By the time the new spring line arrived for review, however, life in America was returning to normal. More important, many people were ready to pull on hiking boots and venture back into the outdoors to escape the doldrums of the new War on Terror. When these customers entered Patagonia's stores to outfit themselves for these much-needed excursions, however, they would encounter an array of options as dismal as the world they were trying to leave behind. Racks of black rain jackets as far as the eye could see. Nothing could have been further from the vibe of rebirth and renewal people would be seeking that spring. Patagonia's safe bet had proven to be anything but.

Realizing the extent of his overcorrection, Perry discovered that by turning off the designers' creative spigot—a decision that made perfect business sense in itself—he had left himself without options. He had no way to adapt to an unexpected situation. By narrowing the flow of the creative pipeline running from inspiration to ideas to experiments to products, Perry had ensured it would take a painfully long time to get a more vibrant array of clothes into stores. Of course, he had needed to take steps to protect the company in adverse circumstances, but, as we'll see, he could *also* have left himself options in anticipation of more than one possible turn of events. (If only he'd had this book at the time!) Luckily, while store traffic was low that spring, Patagonia was saved by the fact that its major competitors had fallen into the very same trap. Had Patagonia left themselves some options, they might have left those competitors in the dust.

As we'll discover, it's never safe to stopper the flow of new ideas entirely, regardless of outlook and external conditions. Pausing innovation for even a moment has a lasting effect. Since we weigh risks more heavily than rewards, discouraging creativity is effortless compared to encouraging it, which requires steady and patient work. You can't get ideas overnight. You need to keep them flowing in good times and bad. Ideas are solutions to future problems. They represent tomorrow's profits. No ideas, no tomorrow. That's why gauging the organization's capacity to innovate is the best way to measure success before it happens.

EVERY PROBLEM IS AN IDEA PROBLEM

How creative are you? How creative is your team or organization? On the surface, this might seem like a Zen koan, an esoteric puzzle along the lines of "What is the sound of one hand clapping?" But creativity is concrete. When presented with a problem—whether it's "What should the product's tagline be?" or "How are we going to save next quarter?"—either you have new ideas or you don't. Good or bad doesn't enter into it yet. In most cases, you can't really judge the merit of an idea until you've tested it in the real world. At the start, you just need lots and lots of ideas. When it comes to creativity, quantity drives quality.

The most useful measure of creativity we've found is as follows: the number of novel ideas a person or group can generate around a given problem in a given amount of time. We call this metric *ideaflow*. An organization with low ideaflow is in trouble because it's running out of an essential resource. Its leaders know there's a problem, they can see that progress is stalling, but they can't quite pinpoint the scarcity starving it of its potential. While the proper execution of ideas is crucial, ideaflow is the foundation, the essential force that drives *all* future success.

You might wonder whether it's practical to pay so much attention to the raw generation of new ideas versus, for example, a more "bottom-line" metric like patents issued or new initiatives launched. The problem is, those lagging indicators tell you there's a problem long after you should have solved it. No measure is as useful as ideaflow at diagnosing innovation issues in time to address them. Tracking new products and services won't flag the flaws in your innovation process until it's too late. Think of that eighteen-month lead time at Patagonia. Also, results manifest in different ways. Some companies launch new products or services all the time: record companies, toy manufacturers, start-up incubators. Others— car companies, law firms, banks—continually refine a handful of core offerings. To get a clear and consistent sense of when creativity needs a boost, move upstream and observe the source.

Ideaflow is a useful proxy for measuring overall innovation capacity because the ability to generate a flood of ideas on demand correlates with overall creative health. It's a barometer—it doesn't tell you where every cloud is, but rather that a storm is on the way. When ideaflow dips, as when Perry's decision to "keep the winners" stifled contributions at Patagonia, it tells you there's a larger problem with your creative culture. For example, sensing the drop in ideaflow among the design team, Perry could have gone to them and asked them for new ideas on how to react to falling orders. Defaulting to an all-drab spring lineup was one approach, but there might have been many more to consider.

Ideaflow should be a key performance indicator on every leader's radar. Taking stock of personal and organizational ideaflow is a quick and easy way to determine a creative baseline and chart progress.

For many years, Amazon's profits bore little resemblance to the market cap of AMZN. Wall Street was betting on the future Jeff Bezos wanted to build. We'd argue that Amazon's stock price reflected the company's off-the-charts ideaflow. For a publicly traded company, that projected value took an unusually long time to manifest in its traditional business metrics. The earthshaking potential, however, was visible from the beginning in its extraordinary flood of ideas and its relentless commitment to experimentation. As always, the creative mindset of a company spreads from the top. Even before he founded Amazon, Bezos was "constantly recording ideas in a notebook he carried with him, as if they might float out of his mind if he didn't jot them down." He wasn't precious about these ideas, either. As a leader, Bezos "quickly abandoned old notions and embraced new ones when better options presented themselves." Modeling good creative habits yourself is the most effective way to cultivate and energize a creative team or organization. As CEO, Bezos modeled an approach that propagated throughout the company as its ambitions proliferated beyond selling books on the World Wide Web.

You might be thinking, *the comparison doesn't work for me because disruption is expected in something like e-commerce.* So, is your situation different because your industry *isn't* facing any disruption? If your business is somehow immune from the tidal forces affecting the rest of the world economy, tell us about it and you'll have our résumés in the morning.

Clearly, Jeff Bezos has demonstrated enormous prescience in his career. However, don't ascribe to talent or luck what was driven by skill and effort. You don't have to be able to see the future to build a successful one for your organization. A randomized, controlled trial involving over a hundred Italian start-ups demonstrated that entrepreneurs trained in a rigorous approach to generating and validating business ideas—like the mindset and method we advocate in this book—outperformed their counterparts in a control group. Based on our experience working with hundreds of entrepreneurs in Stanford's Launchpad incubator, this finding is no surprise.

Even if you accept that ideaflow drives innovation, you still may not see the need for it yourself. You may be wondering whether this book is intended for you at all, and not better off in the hands of some up-and-comer in a "creative" role. An intern in the design department, maybe. Only a few people in a typical organization are explicitly called upon to draw things, name products, coin slogans for ad campaigns, or otherwise "be creative" in a conventional sense. For the rest of us, there is no literal drawing board to go back to. Whether you're a director of marketing or the director of NASA, whether your start-up just got its first funding round or your real estate development just entered its first phase of construction, much of your day consists of emails, meetings, and calls. Sure, you make decisions, but how often do you need new ideas per se? How often do you find yourself stretched out on a couch in the office in a state of creative contemplation, fiddling with a Rubik's Cube or something? That's not you. That's not most of us. *But that's not creativity, either.* True creativity is both less dramatic and more universal than you believe.

The thick black line between creatives and everybody else in a company is based on a profound misunderstanding of what creativity is, how it works, and what it's for. Every time a new cohort arrives at Stanford's d.school, we begin by disabusing incoming students of all their counterproductive notions about creativity. The executives in particular arrive with the idea that creativity is a skill reserved for artists and writers, not upper management. As discussed in the introduction, we call on our creativity every time we solve a problem.

How do you know when you've got yourself a problem, not a task?

Problems keep you up at night. You stew about them during your commute. They take you out of the moment when you're supposed to be enjoying your weekend with the family. If you keep rereading the same sentence of an article you've been trying to finish, you've got yourself a problem, and a problem responds to only one thing: Not hard work. Not long hours. Not a can-do attitude. *Solutions*—each of which starts life as an idea. One of many. This brings us to the simple but profound insight driving our work at Stanford's d.school, the insight at the heart of this book: **Every problem is an idea problem.**

Why is this so important? Why do the ramifications get us out of bed each morning to teach and write and work with leaders at major companies around the world? Because learning how to systematically generate, test, refine, and implement ideas makes every aspect of life and work easier. It's the skeleton key, the meta-skill that unlocks hidden potential. If you don't see that frustrating email or scary conversation as an idea problem in need of creative thinking, you dread facing it. You procrastinate when you don't know how to proceed—and mistakenly think that you should have an answer in hand. Once you identify these as problems that demand new thinking, as *idea problems,* you realize you have a toolbox. You know what to do next: Get creative. It takes practice to recognize a knot in your stomach as a cue to unleash creativity, but once you get the hang of it, it becomes the ultimate aha moment even though you haven't technically solved anything yet. What a relief to know you don't know.

Until now, your creative toolbox has contained a haphazard assortment of tips, tricks, and techniques assembled over a lifetime of trial and error. You will finish this book with an organized and comprehensive set of problem-solving tools, a unified system for innovation used by top entrepreneurs and C-suite leaders around the world to methodically seize opportunities and demolish obstacles.

If every problem is an idea problem, it might follow that you don't need help. After all, you must be pretty good at this idea business already.

You solve problems every day of your life, right? They say practice makes perfect. Not if you're practicing the wrong things, however. Bring to mind a problem you're grappling with right now, something pulling your attention away from this book. It could be anything: a misunderstanding with the bank, a conflict with your boss, a job search, a presentation, a negotiation. How does it feel when you contemplate the dilemma? Try for a moment. Do you feel excited to tackle it? Do you know exactly how you're going to approach solving it, step by step? Now, be honest with yourself. Are your creative juices flowing—or is that knot in your stomach bigger than ever?

If you're like most people, your instinctive response to a problem is avoidance. There's a desire to withdraw, to avoid. Even when you push through and solve a thorny problem successfully, the path to that solution feels uncertain and accidental, with lots of fruitless stumbling and wheel reinvention along the way. Without a true and tested creative skill set, "practice" only means we get better at procrastination, writer's block, and decision paralysis—not effective and enjoyable creative problem solving. Thankfully, a lifetime of counterproductive reflexes can be unlearned and replaced. That's what the study of Italian start-ups found—if you teach people an innovation method, outcomes improve dramatically. It just takes a little technique.

MEASURING IDEAFLOW

So how, exactly, does one measure ideaflow? No need to stick any electrodes to your scalp. As a metric, ideaflow is a simple gauge of the *relative* health of your creative engine or that of a team. The only value in measuring it lies in comparing your current score to previous and future ones. It looks like this:

$$ideas / time = ideaflow$$

Measuring your ideaflow is easy. Take out a pen and piece of paper. Next, select an email in your inbox, preferably an important one, that needs a response. (It's OK if you've sent an actual response already.) Now, set a timer on your phone for two minutes. For the span of that time, write down as many different subject lines for your response as you possibly can, one after the other. No deliberation, no pausing, no judgment or revision of the subject lines you've already written. Don't give yourself time to think. Just write down every subject line that comes to mind as quickly as your hand can move. These subject lines can be serious, informal, humorous, even absurd. Variations on the same approach count. Focus only on quantity, not quality. Come back when the time runs out.

Done? Now count them up. How many distinct subject lines were you able to generate? Divide that number by two and you have a rate of ideas per minute that, for the purposes of this exercise, represents your ideaflow. To be clear, you could spend five minutes generating ad slogans or ten coming up with product ideas. The important thing is that you take the same measurement regularly, using the same duration and a similar prompt, ideally the same kind of idea generation you'd benefit from in the normal course of your work. That way, you can gauge the waxing and waning of your ideaflow throughout a day or measure the effect of a specific technique from this book.

Ideaflow may seem simplistic, but think of the deceptively simple yardsticks and heuristics in your own area of expertise. A physical therapist, for example, might learn quite a bit about a client's overall fitness from something as simple as an attempted toe touch. Likewise, a simple metric updated frequently is much more helpful to any practitioner than a complicated diagnostic that can be performed only once in a blue moon. Whether or not you found yourself brimming with possibilities, your initial score means something. As you learn and adopt the skills in this book and watch your own number change, that relevance will become more apparent.

What ideaflow isn't is a measure of intelligence or talent. Instead, you might say it assesses your state of mind. Rapidly generating divergent possibilities requires you to suspend self-consciousness. To operate without fear of failure or embarrassment. Unleashing the full measure of your ideaflow demands what Harvard Business School professor Amy Edmondson calls *psychological safety*. When we feel safe enough to take intellectual and emotional risks, "the rewards of learning from failure can be fully realized," she writes. Your brain opens the floodgates only once the social and financial costs of trying new things—and potentially making mistakes—are outweighed by the potential benefits. If the thought that people might laugh at one of your suggestions scares the heck out of you, psychological safety is sorely lacking.

You can't just snap your fingers and "activate" creativity when you don't feel safe, whether because of your own faulty beliefs or because of the conservative mindset of people in your organization. If your own ideaflow is low, you must adopt a creative mindset and develop the necessary internal resilience. If ideaflow is low among those you lead, it's not their problem. It's yours. Improvements at the profitable end of the creative pipeline—problems solved, plans executed, products shipped—requires a sense of safety across the entire team at the start of that pipeline.

Ideaflow is a spectrum, but from the outside it can look as though someone's either got "it" or they don't. One member of the team will fire off a ton of contributions when presented with a problem while others sit silent. Don't fall into the trap of seeing creativity as an inborn talent. Instead, use ideaflow to identify and address bottlenecks on the team. Rather than let a single star performer carry the creative load— which, if nothing else, results in a more narrow and less interesting set of possibilities—help the other members unleash their own creative potential using these techniques. This deepens your bench of talent and opens up the creative floodgates to an unprecedented degree. Unlike a fixed metric like IQ, ideaflow fluctuates based on context. Raising it is not just possible but necessary. This is the driving purpose of both our work and this book.

Make a note of your own ideaflow here at the start and check it regularly as you progress. While your score will vary depending on factors like sleep and stress, you should see an overall upward trend correlating with the effort you invest in implementing these habits, behaviors, and techniques. To boost ideaflow, you will become input-seeking and curiosity-driven in ways you'd never previously imagined. Once you've seen the benefits of this shift in mindset yourself, you'll be far better prepared to help elevate the creative output of others.

FLIP THE SCRIPT

Failure to innovate isn't the only way to derail a company. That said, an organization with low ideaflow will inevitably falter. That's because ideas are future profits. No matter how stable your industry or secure your market position, tomorrow eventually becomes today. Without ideas, you won't have a tomorrow.

When the creative well runs dry, it's the rare leader who points the blame toward something as squishy as psychological safety. Yet creative risk-taking demands it. If people don't feel safe, they won't take risks. Nothing ventured, nothing gained. In fact, the usual interventions in a crisis—more ambitious targets, shorter time frames, rounds of layoffs—have the most chilling effect on creativity. In their scramble for security, leaders often inspire the very fear that kills innovation. (If you have an example of a company pulling out of a nose dive by torpedoing creativity among its employees, we'd love to hear about it.) Time and again, organizations weather disruption through unbridled, fearless creativity.

It's understandable that leaders end up blocking the one resource that might rescue their business. When they fail to prioritize the true needs of creativity, it's simply because they don't understand its needs. Creativity doesn't *look* creative when you're doing it. A simple afternoon walk around the neighborhood, for example, can reveal the path to profitability. In tough times, however, we're praised for staying at our desks and burning the midnight oil. How are you supposed to see the horizon with your nose pressed against the grindstone? Thanks in large part to the factory mentality of modern workplace culture, organizations discourage the very behaviors that can save them.

Ultimately, leaders who truly understand how to build and nurture a high-ideaflow organization—at companies like Netflix and Tesla, for example—wield an enormous advantage over their competitors. What do they know that the rest of us don't? For one thing, they understand that creativity is the lifeblood of *any* business, not just those in "creative" industries like advertising and design, industries where "eccentric" behaviors like doodling and naps are encouraged. It's easy to downplay the need for innovation in sectors that experience long stretches of stability. Leaders allow themselves to believe, falsely, that they can take risks and invest in innovation only when required to do so by the occasional disruption. This mentality frees them to focus exclusively on minimizing risk and maximizing short-term gains the rest of the time, leading to the toxic, next-quarter-focused thinking that has poisoned corporate America for decades.

Companies, unlike people, have no natural life-span. When an established brand descends into irrelevance, it isn't something inevitable but rather the result of creative stagnation. To thrive, an organization must continually renew and reinvent itself. Its people must be encouraged and incentivized to try new things and take risks. If innovation isn't an integral part of the company's approach, it isn't standing still but falling behind. If the innovative spark stays lit, on the other hand, age is meaningless to a corporate entity. Elderly organizations from Siemens (1847) and Goodrich (1870) and Nintendo (1889) to Procter & Gamble (1837) and Ball Corporation (1880) continue to deliver profits through continuous, relentless reinvention. For individuals, ideaflow is a competitive advantage. For companies, it's the fountain of youth.

If you are in a traditionally creative role, or you pursue a creative hobby on the side, you're probably nodding your head. You know from experience that ideaflow is a muscle that must be exercised regularly. The more consistently you create, the easier it is to do so when you really need ideas. On the other hand, if you've never thought of yourself as a creative person and have never really been called on to drive breakthrough thinking in your job, this book is going to change everything you think you know about solving problems. The creative mindset you develop here will make all your work both more enjoyable and less frustrating than you ever thought possible.

At its heart, a creative approach to problem-solving demands a shift in mindset, a flip. When you reframe a real headbanger of a dilemma as an idea problem, you flip the usual, counterproductive approach to problem solving on its head. Instead of struggling to come up with a single perfect solution, you go from:

- Quality to quantity

- Precious to scrappy

- Perfection to practice

- Done to doing

- Your perspective to someone else's

- Isolation to collaboration

- Relevance-requiring to randomness-embracing

- Focused to mind-wandering

- Order to chaos

- Your expertise to unfamiliar territory

- Output-focused to input-obsessed

Some of these flips are undesirable in an ordinary business context. As we'll see, however, succeeding with creativity begins by recognizing its special status. Like the medieval carnival, creation is an arena where the usual rules get turned upside down. Factors crucial to the functioning of a business—focus, efficiency, quality, hierarchy—only hinder your efforts. The more quickly and completely you can make these flips when transitioning into innovation, the more effective your use of that time will be.

Since we do most of our work with organizations, we're going to have plenty to say about helping others make the flip. If you win over your peers or even your organization, you will enjoy the exponential benefits of creative collaboration and serendipity. That said, you can benefit from flipping your approach even if no one else on your team understands the need to do so. Keep these payoffs in mind as we walk through the habits, behaviors, and routines underlying a creative mindset.

IDEAFLOW IN ACTION

Boosting ideaflow requires sustained effort over time. To begin, however, you simply need to commit to the process. To become willing to step outside the accepted modes of doing business in search of breakthrough ideas. Are you ready to make a commitment to creativity? Or are you always going to judge the creative process from the outside, sabotaging the greatest possible contributions you'll ever make?

It's worth the plunge into the deep end of the pool. By increasing ideaflow, you and your team will perform better on a quantitative basis even as the qualitative experience of being at work improves. You'll experience greater ease, enjoyment, and engagement—and at the end of the day, your bottom-line results will look better than ever.

If you've never been inside a creative organization before, this new way of working can look . . . a little weird on the surface. Be prepared for differences that may rub you the wrong way at first. For example, people operating creatively tend to be away from their desks more frequently. They talk to one another more, hold lengthy, formal meetings less. (When you know how to tackle problems effectively, the waste of time most meetings represent becomes too obvious to endure.) The meetings that do get held tend to be either quick and spontaneous or highly focused, with a specific, action-oriented outcome in mind. People at creative companies get together for energy and inspiration, or to solve a problem they couldn't solve alone, not to collectively review results that could have been sent around in an email. Also, when people do congregate, it will usually be in the afternoon, after the hard thinking of the day is done, and outside a stuffy conference room.

Finally, yes, in a creative organization people will occasionally stare off into space or, the ultimate cliché, doodle. Leave them be. For the leaders and managers reading this, it's crucial to relax your ingrained sense of what work "should" look like. To stop insisting on the performative rituals of the modern workplace and cut some creative slack for the team. It's also important to protect your people from others in the organization who might undercut your efforts to establish psychological safety. The results of greater ideaflow will more than justify any odd behavior— eventually. But it will take time, effort, and trust to normalize these new behaviors across the organization.

Just as professional athletes develop a highly accurate awareness of their physical needs and limits, members of a creative team learn how they think and perform at their best. They develop greater introspection, a deeper and subtler sense of their mood and energy levels. This helps them make the best possible use of their time. When ideaflow is high, they go all-out on generating fresh possibilities. When their energy wanes, they crank on mundane tasks and recover. To recharge, they take a walk, make a coffee run, get some fresh air and sunlight. The specifics will differ but, as a manager, you serve people best by letting them calibrate their own performance. At every desk in a creative org, mindless and ceaseless busyness is replaced by deliberate, results-oriented effort alternating with restorative rest. Every member of the team learns to respect their brain as a high-performance idea engine that demands careful maintenance to deliver optimum results.

In a creative organization, the work is no longer about keeping bosses happy or mollifying shareholders. Getting the job done right—effectively, elegantly, ambitiously—is motivated first and foremost by the pride of accomplishment. People learn that firing on all creative cylinders feels good. Innovating, collaborating, and experimenting are intrinsically rewarding. When you incorporate creativity into everything you do, you experience a profoundly gratifying sense of mastery and self-actualization, the highest level of Abraham Maslow's hierarchy of human needs. This is what work should be for all of us. In a creative organization, employee satisfaction rises in tandem with business results.

~

Innovation is only getting harder. According to a paper from a team at Stanford, research productivity—the pace of innovation you can expect based on the resources you invest—has been on the decline for decades. A century ago, a small team could still achieve a huge advance like the telegraph or the steam engine. In a wildly complex world with many fundamental innovations already established, it now takes vast effort to deliver even incremental improvements. According to the paper, the economy must double its research efforts every thirteen years to maintain the same rate of growth. These global trends apply to both individuals and organizations. It's on all of us to amplify our innovation efforts. History will not be kind to those who ignore this imperative.

We hope we've convinced you of the merits of investing effort in ideaflow. If you're a leader, you can stop wondering how to help your team improve. It's simple. Change begins with you. If you don't cultivate your own creative practice and learn to approach every problem as an idea problem, you'll never inspire that attitude in others. Ideaflow in your organization will remain a feeble trickle. Everyone will keep banging their heads against the wall, waiting for the universe to deliver a solution rather than generating one themselves.

In the next chapter, we will lay out a simple but effective creative practice that will boost your ideaflow while setting a robust example for everyone in your orbit.

2.

Amplify Ideaflow

The sole substance of genius is the daily act of showing up.

—MARIA POPOVA

Increasing ideaflow doesn't begin with a better brainstorming technique but at the very moment you wake up. The way you invest your limited time has an enormous impact on your creative output. To illustrate this, let's spend a day with Jen and Jim, composites of leaders we've known. Jen and Jim have similar roles but achieve very different results.

Jim heads up the marketing department of a software development shop. The company has been on a growth trajectory since the launch of its first mobile app early last year. Between growing his team and responding to one urgent demand after another, Jim approaches each day as triage. When his phone alarm goes off in the morning, a barrage of notifications awaits his review. From that point forward, Jim glances up from his screen only when absolutely necessary: to shower, while driving to work (except at red lights), to receive his egg sandwich and coffee at the drive-through. In a kind of trance, Jim puts out fires over email and work chat until he pulls into the company parking lot.

By 9 a.m. Jim is running on fumes. Irritable and anxious, he still faces an inbox brimming with issues to resolve and a calendar packed with meetings. Reacting all day, every day, feels like being stuck on a treadmill, but while there are proactive actions that might drive growth, trying anything new means carving out precious bandwidth. With time and energy so scarce, it feels too risky to invest effort in anything that isn't guaranteed to pay off.

How is Jim supposed to know in advance which new marketing initiative might succeed? He could set aside an hour or two here or there, but he'd never be able to sustain effort for weeks or months without knowing for sure that something will deliver results. Big ideas will have to wait until he clears up a correspondingly large chunk of uninterrupted time. As soon as he does that—any day now!—he'll sit down and dream up something *huge*.

Everything Jim busies himself with is undeniably relevant. He adds value in meetings, answers questions over email, and manages his growing team. Sure, he hasn't pushed any boulders uphill, but the company is scaling up incredibly quickly. There's no need for new ideas when the ones they already have are working so well. Jim can worry about the future when this breakneck pace flags. For now, he will race from meeting to meeting until his calendar clears up and he can finally head out. In fact, he'll do some planning after dinner.

(Of course, by the time Jim gets home each night, he is physically drained, mentally blank, and emotionally unfulfilled. With nothing but an hour or two to recover before doing it all over again tomorrow, working on new ideas is the last thing he'd do. This undeniable fact never stops him from making the same promise to himself over and over.)

As Jim consigns himself to another day on autopilot, the founder calls an all-hands meeting to inform everyone that an anticipated venture capital round hasn't panned out. They're going to have to get profitable earlier than expected. This shift will require bold thinking, primarily from marketing.

"Anything relevant in the pipeline, Jim?"

Noticing the sudden silence in the room, Jim looks up from his phone, only to realize that every eye is on him. The founder repeats his question.

Pipeline? No one gives me time to work on a pipeline. Jim knows better than to say that thought out loud, of course. "Tons," he says. "Let's take this offline and I'll walk you through our latest ideas." That should buy him a couple of hours. More than enough time to come up with . . . something.

A TALE OF TWO LEADERS

Does Jim's situation sound familiar? Though your day may look different on its surface, chances are you spend much of your time at work in a headlong rush, too. Like Jim, you may also find yourself wishing you could be more proactive, creative, and productive. You've probably observed that the people who rise quickly, both in your organization and across your industry, are the ones who go above and beyond. They come up with big new ideas and follow through on them in a highly visible way, all on top of their regular duties.

You just can't figure out how.

What do high-performing innovators know that you don't? Do their calendars contain a couple of extra hours yours doesn't? You're always waiting for that mythical time when things will quiet down long enough to think up and execute on something significant. For real this time. Amid the usual chaos, however, you wouldn't even know where to begin with something genuinely new.

Creative problem-solving and innovation are primarily collaborative. Solving new problems is something you usually do with others, whether as a manager, a CEO, or even a start-up founder, as we'll see. In the coming chapters, we will walk you through the entire innovation pipeline in a way that will be relevant regardless of your particular perspective, from gathering raw inspiration to generating divergent possibilities to validating potential solutions in the real world. *Every* step at *any* level of *all* organizations, however, rests on an all-too-neglected foundation: you. Metaphors about inspiration aside, you are not some sort of antenna. Ideas don't exist somewhere out in the universe for you to catch them. They come from *inside your head.* A chef keeps their knife razor-sharp. A musician takes exquisite care of their instrument. In this chapter, we will show you how to keep your own tools in tune.

Since you've experienced a good flow of ideas at least once in your life, you know you have the capacity to create. So you blame your workload. Or your family life. Or fill in the blank. If the reason for your lack of creative output is your ever-multiplying to-do list, it follows that you'll be more creative as soon as you're less busy. So you wait. And wait. If you're lucky, you really will experience a slow period at work. If you're even luckier, you'll get unexpectedly laid off. Lucky because that's the only way you'll finally accept the truth: *nothing happens anyway.* There is no pent-up deluge of great ideas. No rush of motivation and excitement to pursue the ideas you already have. You're still stuck, just without an excuse to make. Then and only then will you question your assumptions. *Maybe you were wrong about how ideas work all along.*

Ultimately, we all want to make measurable, meaningful advances toward our goals. If you keep operating the way Jim does, however, that day will never come. When the hoped-for lull arrives, it does so without warning, and it doesn't spur leisurely reflection. A lull is usually an emergency in itself. Think of when orders stalled at Patagonia after 9/11. A slowdown in your business is the last time you're going to start planning for tomorrow.

If most of us approach creativity the way Jim does, what's the alternative? How, in fact, does anything big ever get conceived, let alone implemented? In our experience, major accomplishments at most organizations rest on the work of a handful of star creators, the rare few who consistently deliver in significant ways. Regardless of their specific expertise, they share the same behaviors and characteristics: Massive ideaflow. Patient testing and refinement. Steady implementation of validated ideas. These people work deliberately, stewarding their time and energy in order to drive through high-value efforts. They optimize for *effect* (accomplishment) over *affect* (looking busy). If joining their ranks appeals to you, understand that this way of working isn't driven by productivity tips or motivational slogans but by a profound shift in mindset, an entirely new way of approaching problems.

What does a star creator look like in action? Cut back to the all-hands meeting. Pan a few chairs to Jim's left for a close-up of his colleague Jen, director of sales at this suddenly shaky software start-up. Her team is as large as Jim's, her responsibilities just as pressing, but Jen handles her workload in a relaxed yet purposeful manner. She never makes a big show of being harried the way Jim always does. She doesn't furrow her brow, brandish her phone to send a text while talking to someone, or power-walk between meetings to prevent people from questioning her importance to the company. She just delivers on one initiative after another.

Crucially, this isn't because Jen ignores her day-to-day responsibilities. Like any department, sales has plenty of fires to put out of its own, but they get resolved promptly and without undue fuss. This is because Jen— and, by extension, the sales team she leads—approaches work *strategically*. She plans ahead, batches similar tasks, and prioritizes the needs of the future alongside the demands of the present. This frees the time and energy required for innovation. Over time, her direct reports have learned to do likewise. Despite what Jim secretly suspects, Jen has the same twenty-four hours in her calendar. Let's see how differently she uses them.

Morning arrives. Having disabled unnecessary notifications on her phone, Jennifer glances at the device only long enough to shut off the alarm. Next, she spends an hour preparing her mind and body for sustained mental effort: meditating, exercising, and completing a period of quiet reflection and journaling. She thinks of this as getting in tune with herself. Intensive preparation is necessary because she intends to act on, not simply react to, the demands of the day. Feeling calm and clear, she enjoys a nutritious breakfast while reading a book from a field unrelated to her job to warm up her brain and spur new thinking.

Before leaving for the office, Jen reviews her notes, which she keeps in a large notebook that never leaves her side. Following no particular system of organization, the notebook is simply an unfussy place to jot next actions from meetings, ideas about current and potential projects at work, and the occasional doodle. It's where Jen thinks on paper. As she reviews yesterday's ideas, they jog new ones, which she dutifully records without judgment. Primed for creativity and brimming with possibilities, Jen heads to work, eyes on the road the entire drive.

Arriving at the office rested and refreshed, Jen confirms that the first hour on her calendar is clear, as it is nearly every morning. Jen defends her team's mornings against external intrusions. Aside from unavoidable emergencies and the occasional all-hands meeting, that first hour is for planning, writing sales copy, preparing presentations, sometimes just thinking. The air of quiet stillness in the sales department draws curious looks from new hires who can't help but notice the contrast with the general chaos elsewhere in the office. It almost looks like another company is leasing space. Newcomers quickly learn, however, that sales is the beating heart of the organization. It's a department that delivers what you need when you need it. Even better, it delivers what you don't realize you'll need tomorrow.

When you deal with the marketing department, every request seems to run into unexpected delays and unforeseen complications. It's never strictly anyone's fault, but problems always crop up despite the endless sprints and stand-ups and other performative productivity efforts. You learn to keep bugging them if you want to get anything you need from them, which only wastes everyone's time and wears everyone down. Yet, though Jim and his team make a lot of noise about everything else on their plates that's more important than your request, all this busyness never leads to anything tangible. Plenty of surface churn, nothing visible beneath. (Remember this the next time someone suggests another hackathon to solve a problem. "Be regular and orderly in your life," Gustave Flaubert, author of *Madame Bovary,* advised a friend, "[so] that you may be violent and original in your work.")

Thanks to the reliability and responsiveness of the sales department, people have learned not to nag them or otherwise squander their valuable bandwidth by including them on every email chain and meeting invite. Sales is quiet, they understand, because it's working on stuff that matters. Jen's department isn't just looking to the future of the company, it's building it. They're the ones making sure everyone else has a job next year and people respect that.

To be clear, Jen didn't achieve Flaubert's orderly regularity overnight. Unlike Jim, she invests time in delegating and prioritizing her work rather than pouncing on whatever issue feels most urgent in the moment. She creates systems and processes to save time on repeated tasks. She steadily increases her efficiency because she needs the lion's share of her time to effectively address the needs of tomorrow. This forward-thinking mindset explains why Jen, though she faces the occasional crisis and holds the odd morning meeting, experiences nothing like the chaos that Jim always does.

After Jim freezes in the headlights at the all-hands meeting, Jen opens to a page in her notebook. When the founder turns his attention to her, she's ready with several possibilities her team has been actively testing in anticipation of this shift. Jim and Jen both knew that the company would start charging for its app sooner or later. Jen bet on sooner. The founder gives her the go-ahead to devote more resources to experimentation as well as put one of the validated ideas into action. Jen and her team get to work on tomorrow's challenge. Jim goes back to putting out yesterday's fires while fretting helplessly about tomorrow.

Though Jen and Jim are only composites, they are firmly based in our experiences working with hundreds of leaders at companies around the world. They should each resonate with you if you've spent any time working within an organization of any size. You've worked for Jim at some point. You might even *be* Jim. If you're lucky, you've also worked for Jen, though that's less likely. There is no real reason, however, that we can't all be Jen in our professional endeavors. If that notion appeals to you, keep reading.

~

The moment progress stalls, panicked leaders demand solutions on the spot. When an avalanche of creativity fails to materialize, they start blaming people instead of the counter-creative culture they've established. If this is you, it's time to stop thinking of creativity in terms of its output. By focusing on solutions, you're looking through the wrong end of the telescope. Creation is a process, not a product. Effective innovators don't just go out of the room for an hour and magically return with a bunch of ideas. They deliver creative thinking when it's needed only by establishing and maintaining a creative practice. With a steady investment of time and energy in creativity, the output takes care of itself.

Like a tomato, an idea needs fertile soil and plenty of time to grow. Unlike a tomato, you can't just pick up a new idea at the grocery store on your way home from work. A red, ripe tomato of an idea represents the bounty of a garden you've already been tending with care. How can you expect to grow anything when you haven't tilled the soil or planted any seeds? Inspiration may feel mysterious, but ideas don't just pop into existence at the grocery store. It only seems that way when we're oblivious to the path they took: A seed was planted. A rich compost of experiences and information helped that seed form roots—valuable connections with other ideas, facts, and concepts. Only then does a sliver of green appear in your conscious awareness. To draw on steady and abundant ideaflow whenever you need it, you must go from plucking the odd stalk of sidewalk grass to cultivating the fruits of a lush, well-tended garden.

It's time to change your mindset from one of problems and projects to one of process and practice. There is nothing episodic about innovation. Creativity is a capacity you train and develop like physical strength or flexibility. Without proper technique and regular effort, generating ideas is exhausting and often unproductive. That's why the foundation of a creative practice is a light, daily warm-up.

THE IDEA QUOTA

Loosening up your stiff creative muscles every morning helps you make the crucial flip from a mindset of *quality* to one of *quantity* when it's time to come up with ideas. Making the following Idea Quota a part of your day will lighten the subconscious pressure for perfection that stymies creative exploration.

Every morning from now on, you will write down ten ideas. (We'll get to what kind of ideas in a moment.) The quality of these ideas isn't the point. Contrary to what you might believe, you can't judge the merit of an idea while it's still inside your head. Idea *validation* is as crucial to the creative process as idea *generation*. But that happens later. For now, our aim is just to freshen up stale thinking.

Performing an Idea Quota is a simple, three-S process:

1. **Seed.** Select a problem and study it.

2. **Sleep.** Let the unconscious mind process the problem.

3. **Solve.** Flood the problem with ideas.

Let's see how each step works in detail.

Seed

You never generate ideas in a vacuum. Whether you're aware of it or not, the brain is always processing problems in the background. You can always generate a list of ideas "at random," but they will inevitably be informed by whatever has been nagging at the brain's attention. These tend to be petty annoyances, however. Brooding on them is not a valuable use of your problem-solving capacity. Since your subconscious mind can't distinguish between urgency and importance, you must consciously steer its efforts. Otherwise, your thoughts will snag on whatever is top of mind, not necessarily what matters most to your long-term ambitions.

From now on, you will feed your brain high-importance problems, pointing it toward areas where new thinking will contribute meaningfully to your goals. Instead of ruminating on something rude a stranger said or untangling a plotline from a show you've been bingeing, your brain will puzzle away at a stumbling block on a work project, an interpersonal issue at the office, or even a lack of vision for your career. Remember, a *task* is something you know how to do, even if you'd rather not do it. A *problem* is something you don't even know how to approach. A true problem responds only to new ideas. Before you go to bed every night, you will seed your mind with a worthwhile problem to sleep on:

- How am I going to cut costs this quarter?

- Where are we going to take the kids for vacation this year?

- How do I ask my boss for that raise?

- What's the best way to start my presentation at sales conference?

Don't worry about identifying the perfect problem, and don't spend more than a couple of minutes choosing. If you mark someone's email unread after reading it because you *just can't deal with it right now,* that's a classic sign of an idea problem. If you keep clearing your inbox to avoid a piece of work that brings up feelings of dread, ditto. Instead of waiting until bedtime, mark it down. If you have more than one pressing idea problem, create a Problem Queue. (You can never have too many good problems to work on.)

As you unwind for sleep, select a problem from your Problem Queue and let your mind play with it in a relaxed and unfocused way. You might even spend a few minutes doing some related reading. Don't force solutions, though. What you're doing here is luring the interest of your subconscious. Ponder the relevant details, but don't try to make everything fit together yet.

Sleep

Though you're unconscious at night, your brain stays busy. Research shows that sleep is essential for both cognitive performance and routine brain maintenance. While the conscious mind rests, the brain processes what you've experienced during the day in a looser, more intuitive way that can be incredibly powerful. Why let that extraordinary capacity go to waste?

Great insights arrive in dreams. Famously, the chemist August Kekulé claimed to have deduced the circular shape of a benzene molecule after dreaming of a snake swallowing its own tail. Likewise, Nobel laureate Otto Loewi proved that nerve impulses are transmitted chemically, not electrically, in the brain, after arriving at the correct approach in a dream. That said, people rarely dream up complete solutions. Instead, they wake from sleep to find stale thinking replaced with fresh.

Research shows that sleep improves our ability to solve difficult problems during the day. Thus, poor sleep is a double whammy: It doesn't deliver new insights, and it doesn't prepare you to innovate effectively while you're awake. What's more, sleep deprivation "impairs attention and working memory" and "affects other functions, such as long-term memory and decision-making."

If you struggle with sleep, there are the tried-and-true remedies: cutting down on alcohol, avoiding large meals before bed, and supplements like magnesium. For more serious sleep problems like sleep apnea or insomnia, see an expert. One way or the other, you should be sound asleep at a reasonable hour and remain asleep throughout the night to operate at your best.

Solve

In the shower, while making breakfast, on your morning run—during any lightly distracting physical activity, noodle on the problem in a relaxed manner. Then, before leaving for work, spend a few minutes jotting down possible solutions. Aim for a minimum of ten but count all iterations and variations. If you're coming up with colors for a new logo, for instance, aquamarine and cornflower blue both count.

While generating ten ideas every morning sounds intimidating, the average participant in one of our training programs routinely learns to do so in under three minutes by not trying to come up with "good" ones. If you let notions of quality cloud your mind, you can agonize over a blank page for half the day. The process of idea generation should always revolve around quantity, not quality. A morning Idea Quota boosts ideaflow by desensitizing you to the discomfort of expressing "bad" ideas. Remember, we're no good at distinguishing bad ideas from promising ones at first. Once you've let go of the need to be "correct," possibilities flow more quickly. Once you've hit the ten-idea minimum, mark the feat as accomplished and move on with your day.

We work with a Singaporean technology executive who told us that she always finds the Idea Quota excruciating—at the start. The first few ideas tend to be banal and obvious, as though her brain is clearing gunk out of the pipes. But then richer and more interesting possibilities well up. As soon as she gives herself permission to write something truly outrageous, ridiculous, or just plain illegal, the floodgates open. It's like that moment during a run when the endorphins kick in. Inevitably, the last two or three she generates turn out to be the most valuable.

STOP KILLING YOUR IDEAS

Refuse the temptation to judge which ideas are keepers. As you'll see, the biggest obstacle to ideaflow isn't a lack of ideas. It's your internal censor. As good as the brain is at generating possibilities, it's far better at nixing them. That's the muscle you've been training for most of your adult life, after all. In fact, you'll sometimes second-guess a promising idea before you're even fully aware you've had it. A daily Idea Quota is the first step toward relaxing that instinctive response.

Self-censorship is a useful cognitive reflex. Experiencing an uninhibited, ceaseless flow of new ideas throughout the day would make it pretty hard to focus, let alone finish anything you start. The problem is that this "no" muscle gets overdeveloped—think Popeye's bulging forearms. The tendency to second-guess yourself gets encouraged right from elementary school. Observe any classroom and you will see children scolded for suggesting something out of the ordinary, or even asking a difficult question that doesn't yield a clear yes or no answer. Don't blame teachers, blame the system. Ideas are disruptive when you're trying to keep things "on track." Optimum efficiency means pruning divergent thinking whenever it arises. Efficiency is counterproductive when it comes to creativity, however, particularly in times of crisis and disruption. To increase ideaflow, we're going to have to unwind these extraordinarily strong and swift inhibitions against original thought.

Dr. Charles Limb is a doctor and musician who combines his divergent pursuits in fascinating ways. He has studied jazz musicians and hip-hop artists using MRI scans to understand exactly what happens in the brain during the act of spontaneous creation. During improvisation, Limb has found, the parts of the brain that activate when we are self-aware grow quiet. Whether we're composing a melody, performing a free-style rap, or jotting down ten ideas for a new tagline, creativity requires the brain to stop monitoring its own activities so closely. "If, as a jazz musician, you're continually thinking about what could happen if you make a mistake," Limb told an interviewer, "you take fewer risks, and so reducing self-inhibition is a necessary ingredient to actual generation of musical novelty." Notably, Limb sees a parallel between the creative and dreaming states. "[When] you're dreaming you're also dealing with unplanned outcomes and free associations," he said. "One of our most creative times is when we're dreaming—we're not inhibited and so we have the capacity to be incredibly imaginative."

Over time, the Idea Quota will develop your capacity to release new ideas on demand. Practiced diligently, it will undo your counterproductive conditioning against novelty and train you to relax the inhibitive part of your brain on cue. You will get comfortable expressing *all* the ideas that come to mind, no matter how silly or outrageous they feel.

By priming the pump in the morning, you will notice richer and swifter creative thinking throughout your day. Catherine Allan, head of the NICU at Boston Children's Hospital, experienced this effect recently. "This morning," she told us, "I was thinking about how to solve the problem of impediments to care at the head of the patient's bed—multiple cords, pieces of large equipment, et cetera." Her Idea Quota included some potential solutions, but then, as she passed through the hallway on her way out of the house, she noticed the wall hooks where she hangs her keys and realized a similar setup might be ideal for patient beds: "Bingo!"

Laura D'Asaro, founder of the cricket-protein start-up Chirps, challenged herself to generate a new business idea every day for a year. Regular practice of this tool over weeks and months sharpened her entrepreneurial acuity. "I'm hyperaware of problems," she told us. "Every time I'm annoyed, every time I feel that little 'Oh, *this* is annoying,' I'm, like, '*Oh*. If I'm having this problem, maybe other people are having this problem.'" At Halloween that year, she noticed that pumpkins in California rot quickly after carving. She developed a salt-based spray that could preserve newly carved pumpkins. And that was just one day out of 365.

Unresolved problems make us anxious. Anxiety is the brain's way of drawing conscious attention to something it can't yet solve. Rather than obey this warning signal, however, we tend to let this very useful emotion inhibit the very creative output a solution would require. When a problem makes us nervous and we don't see a clear path toward solving it, we use distractions to *avoid* thinking about it, postponing the uncomfortable feeling until later. A moment of relief spent scrolling through social media only strengthens the underlying anxiety, unfortunately. This habit of avoidance creates a negative feedback loop that feeds procrastination and leaves us mentally and emotionally exhausted. We're fighting with ourselves instead of with the problem itself. Once we have a trusted method for problem-solving that tells us exactly how to proceed in the face of uncertainty, it becomes so much easier to harness anxiety and use its power properly.

THE DISCIPLINE OF DOCUMENTATION

At the d.school, we have a saying: "If you don't capture it, it didn't happen."

Memory isn't as reliable as you might think. People chronically underestimate how much they'll remember about something after even a few minutes have passed. This is even more true of our own ideas than simple facts like where we parked the car, or what our spouse wants from the take-out place.

Simply walking through a doorway is enough to cue the brain to dump working memory. This is why you enter a room to fetch something only to realize you don't remember what you'd wanted in the first place. This forgetting doesn't happen by accident, either. Remembering takes cognitive effort, and that effort can get in the way of, for example, quickly and accurately processing where everything is in a new environment. Thus, the brain abandons information that is no longer useful, and it pretty much assumes information isn't useful when you don't act on it immediately. Swish, into the dustbin.

If you want to remember something, write it down now, right in the moment. Show the brain what matters to you by taking out that pen. Otherwise, even if you retain the core of an idea later, you will have lost the context and detail that made it such a vital and interesting one when you had it. Getting things down right away is a central creative habit we call the *discipline of documentation*. It's the first thing we teach at the d.school because it underpins all the rest. Every professional who works with ideas regularly learns to take the integrity of their notes seriously. After all, if you lose your wallet, you can get more cash at the ATM. Money is fungible—some ideas come only once. And how are you going to earn money in the first place without ideas? They are your most valuable currency. Scientists, engineers, mathematicians, writers, musicians, and designers tend to become fanatical and obsessive about their notes. According to one of Victor Hugo's sons, the great writer would transcribe nearly everything he heard people say. Much of this dialogue found its way into Hugo's novels. "Everything ends up in print," his son reported. There are even waterproof notepads that suction-cup to the shower wall. To a creator, being able to take notes at *any* time matters.

In your notes, document not only your own ideas but also interesting quotes, facts, stories, statistics, and other inputs that might be relevant down the line. The nature of what you collect will be dictated by what you create. And vice versa: Our creations are shaped by our collection habits. Film director David Lynch uses an audio recorder to collect interesting and evocative sounds that might be useful in future projects. He gathers this "firewood," as he calls it, not with a specific scene or even a particular film in mind but simply to stock a reservoir of sonic possibilities. Whatever sparks your interest should get saved for later.

In the sciences, you're required to follow a specific approach to note taking. For most of us, however, there is no standard, which means you'll have to enforce your own discipline of documentation. Here are some guiding principles.

Go big. A limited writing surface limits your thinking as well. Whenever we generate ideas in a group, we seek out the largest writing surface in the building. Ideally, we corral a row of whiteboards for the session. In your home or office, you can use special paint to turn a wall into a whiteboard or blackboard surface. Some of our grad students have done this in their dorm rooms. If an entire idea wall isn't an option, wrap a table in butcher paper. The more blank space you have, the more your mind will create to fill it. To capture what you write, just snap a photo with your phone.

At your desk, aim for a letter- or legal-size notepad at minimum—bigger if possible, of course—and use smaller pads only for your pockets.

Go analog. While you can take notes on your computer, phone, or tablet, there will inevitably be a moment when your device is off at the very instant you have a great idea, or an insight when it's inappropriate to fiddle with your phone. During an important client meeting, for example. You don't want to give others the impression that you're surreptitiously checking emails. Paper is safer, if only as a backup for note-taking software.

More important, your goal when generating ideas is to flip from convergent to divergent thinking. Rather than zeroing in on The Answer, you're trying to generate as many directions as possible. This is hard to do when you're caught up in day-to-day minutiae. A Scottish sales executive we advise was surprised to discover that a physical notebook, while less convenient than the note-taking app on his phone, was much better for getting into the right frame of mind. He told us how freeing it was to not be interrupted by a constant stream of notifications. Also, he explained, the phone keeps him tethered to what is, whereas the notebook lets him explore what might be.

~

All of this may seem unnecessary or even juvenile, but if you've ever experienced the agony of losing a great idea for lack of a pen, you know the value of being prepared. Blanketing a room with writing materials also has a way of encouraging creativity for everyone who enters it. People feel the difference and get fired up. We can't help but want to fill a blank space.

THE RIGOR OF REVIEW

The entrepreneur and venture capitalist Henrik Werdelin—more about him in a later chapter—fills his primary notebook every ten days or so. At that point, he'll go through it and transcribe the best bits onto the first pages of the next one. "That way," he told us, "I end up with a distilled version of all the thoughts in the last book." Transcribing an idea from one notebook to another proves his own enthusiasm about it. As we'll see, enthusiasm is a crucial metric in the creative decision-making process. You can start only so many businesses in one life. Regularly distilling ideas in this way highlights the ones that are most aligned with Henrik's interests, values, and goals.

It isn't enough to write every idea down. Pair the discipline of documentation with the *rigor of review.* An old saying goes, "The faintest ink is better than the sharpest memory." But that's not true if you never go back to read what you wrote.

Naturally, you'll review project-specific notes throughout that project and perhaps again at the end as part of a postmortem. If an idea doesn't apply to an active endeavor, however, or if it never gets used during a project but still has merit, hold on to it. You might transcribe the keepers to a single digital file or, like Henrik, move them into subsequent notebooks in a process of continual distillation. This reservoir of ideas will serve as a resource for future thinking.

"A link between a problem and a solution," Stanford business professor James G. March told *Harvard Business Review,* "depends heavily on the simultaneity of their 'arrivals.'" With ideas, timing is everything. The you of tomorrow who returns to an idea will be different from the you of today who writes it down. Depending on the experiences and problems you've faced in the interim, that idea may strike you very differently. Last month's "aha" may lose its zing. On the other hand, an offhand notion from last year might be exactly what your current dilemma demands. Review your notes regularly to leverage the serendipitous intersection between your past and present selves.

If you have a method of note taking and review that works for you, tinker with it judiciously. What we advise at Stanford is a weekly review of all the notes you've generated where you transfer anything interesting to a permanent record, whether analog or digital. Then, dedicate time on your calendar every quarter to sit down and review this archive. Use this opportunity to seek connections between what you were thinking before and what you've learned since then. Don't hesitate to build on an idea when it suggests intriguing new avenues of thought.

Yes, ten or twenty minutes each week and a couple of hours each quarter represent a time commitment for a busy professional, but not an onerous one, and we find it offers an extraordinary ROI.

In addition to your quarterly review, pull out your file whenever you face a new project, particularly one that lies outside your comfort zone. An unfamiliar challenge can be intimidating because you don't even know where to begin. Writers aren't the only ones who get blocked this way. Leafing through your notes can warm up the synapses. As the rigor of review becomes a routine part of your creative practice, you'll come to rely on your prior self as an essential source of advice and inspiration.

PAD YOUR SCHEDULE

What are the chances you'll make an interesting discovery doing something in the exact same way you always have? To learn something new, you must try new things, and experiments always have a risk of failure. To take that kind of risk regularly, you can't chase 99 percent efficiency every moment of your day. Maximizing every minute works great on an assembly line, but it doesn't leave room for creative exploration. Give yourself room to take valuable risks.

Keller Williams CEO Carl Liebert sets aside every Friday as a buffer: "It's a wide-open space to explore," Liebert told us. On a Friday, he might read a book, study one aspect of the organization in detail, or just go on a ride with a Keller Williams agent and watch them in action with customers. "I reserve material that I don't have time to address during the week," he said. "Stuff I want to do, learn from, and get through." Liebert doesn't attend meetings on Fridays and takes only emergency phone calls. Above all, Friday is an opportunity for him to think, process, and stock the pond—gathering the inputs necessary for breakthrough thinking.

Carving time out isn't easy for any CEO, but Liebert has learned that it's worth the effort to defend his buffer at all costs. When a call or meeting keeps getting pushed ahead, he'll shift it to the following week rather than let it settle on Friday, as hard-to-schedule events tend to do. In a pinch, he'll even sacrifice weekend time. "I've found that a call with a potential candidate is better on a Saturday anyway," he told us, "since they're working somewhere else." One way or the other, Friday is sacred. "That's my creative day," he said. "I'll work to protect it."

Perry came to a similar realization when he was CEO of the bag manufacturer Timbuk2. During a turbulent period, board member and Timberland COO Ken Pucker told Perry to take all his Fridays off. Since the company was in trouble, this struck Perry as an odd suggestion for a member of the board to make to the CEO.

"Sure," Perry said. "I get it, Ken. Take time to think. I'll stay off email that day and focus."

"No," Pucker replied. "I mean don't come to the office. Don't work at all. You'll never achieve this turnaround if you don't have time to process what you've learned the other four days of the week. How will you bring fresh ideas into this place if you're always putting out fires? Don't work *at all* on Fridays." That's exactly what Perry did, and the time alone helped him distinguish the problems that deserved his attention from the million others that didn't. That crucial perspective gave him the clarity to steer Timbuk2's turnaround.

Google famously gives its employees "20% time" to pursue ideas that interest them personally while at work. For decades more, 3M has offered its employees a smaller but still substantial 15 percent to work on pet projects. Stanford gives every member of the faculty a chunk of discretionary time, too. We've always invested this buffer in our advising work with companies. Though it amounts to only forty days or so out of every year, we consistently learn the most during that time. In fact, nearly every story in this book comes from this buffer. Even a small dose of divergence delivers big payoffs.

PUTTING YOUR CREATIVITY
PRACTICE INTO PRACTICE

When you *act* like a creative person, you begin to *feel* more comfortable being creative in your work and encouraging creativity in others. What's more, the people we advise, no matter their role or industry, experience greater satisfaction and fulfillment in all areas when they adopt these habits. They learn to delight in—instead of dread—the creative challenges life brings. Creating regularly, you develop the confidence that a better solution can always be found. The anxiety of encountering an unfamiliar problem is replaced by the excitement of playing a game you really enjoy.

When you're out of practice with creativity, it's natural for ideas to feel scary. Every idea represents a risk of failure. While ignoring problems is ultimately riskier than attempting a new remedy, you can't be blamed for the wrong move if you don't make one at all. When a leader puts today's needs ahead of tomorrow's inevitabilities, they can blame the economy, technological disruption, and hungry competitors when their shortsightedness catches up to them. Look at the quarterly earnings report of any struggling public company for examples of this passive evasion. Championing an ambitious idea that fails, on the other hand, leaves the consequences squarely on your shoulders.

The solution isn't to avoid innovation but to double down on it. Innovative organizations don't just forgive failure—they expect plenty of it. If you aren't failing frequently enough, it's a sign that you need to fill your pipeline of possibilities. More ideas, more experiments, more iteration. Striking out is a natural consequence of stepping up to the plate, but if you warm the bench all day, you'll never hit a home run. As the home runs stack up in parallel with the strikeouts, you'll free yourself from your aversion to big swings.

Ideaflow grows slowly at first, particularly if you've thought of yourself as a noncreative person for most of your life. Be patient with yourself and get these foundational habits in place *before* you suggest them to others. If your peers and direct reports don't see you capturing your own ideas, they aren't going to feel safe taking their own pencils out. Show, don't tell.

~

With a personal practice in place, we can turn our attention to the one creative technique nearly all of us have employed: the brainstorm. With rare exceptions, everyone dreads them, and for good reason. In fact, some experts argue that generating ideas together will never outperform what the same group of individuals can achieve working alone at their desks. As we'll see, however, brainstorming together properly can be an extraordinarily effective way to generate an enormous array of divergent possibilities.

3.

Flood Your Problem
with Ideas

A multitude of bad ideas is necessary for one good idea.

—KEVIN KELLY, FOUNDING EXECUTIVE
EDITOR OF *WIRED* MAGAZINE AND
AUTHOR OF *THE INEVITABLE*

A vague calendar event appears in your inbox. There's an urgent need for breakthrough thinking and you're invited. It's got something to do with the big sales conference next week. Or a major new client. Or that recent wave of negative Yelp reviews. Doesn't matter. The important thing is that you show up. An organization's desperate, last-minute scramble for ideas is always democratic. Everyone is welcome to contribute solutions—as long as they sound feasible and involve zero risk to anyone with power at the table.

It's time to brainstorm.

Inevitably, the big session gets squeezed into an awkward afternoon slot, when everyone is running on empty. Or, worse, near the end of the day, when people are anxious to head home. *Why am I here?* they all wonder to themselves, grimacing at increasingly bleak rush-hour traffic reports on their phones.

If anybody knew how to solve this—stalling sales, escalating costs, a PR disaster—it wouldn't *be* a problem. It would just be a project, delegated to the appropriate individual or team. You call everyone together only when you *don't* see a clear path to a resolution. Forget answers. No one's even sure of the question. Ultimately, the corporate brainstorming session is an act of desperation: "Somebody's got to know how to handle this—I sure don't!"

Is anything more demoralizing than being forced to "innovate" this way? Considering the odds of looking foolish or ignorant while weighing in on an unfamiliar problem, it feels risky to say anything either ambitious or unusual. Safer to stay quiet and take a free ride on the contributions of others.

If you're *really* eager to catch your train, your best bet is to point out the lack of perfect and complete data on every aspect of the entire situation and its five-year outlook. This is a classic delaying tactic that can prompt leaders to punt the problem back to some poor soul for More Research. That'll be the last anyone hears about this particular problem for a while.

If freeriding or delaying don't work, you're out of luck. You're on the spot. You're going to have to generate a bunch of ideas if you ever want to see your loved ones again. Buckle up.

Rule one of the corporate brainstorm: nothing negative. You know better than to point out the flaws in an idea or say what *can't* be done. The CEO is wildly allergic to the word "no." Never say out loud what the company can't do no matter how many times it has failed to do it in the past.

Rule two: nothing ambitious. None of the people who will have to follow through on your idea want some big new headache. So don't scare them with a pie-in-the-sky Hail Mary that sounds like a lot of effort. Aim for quick and inexpensive. You score the most points in a brainstorming session by elegantly slicing the Gordian knot: "Why don't we just do X and call it a day?" Drop the mic. Your work is done here. There's something palpable about the relief that sweeps the room when someone suggests an easy way out of a fix. *Whew! Guess we won't need all these Post-it notes after all.*

According to brainstorming logic, a good idea is (a) simple to execute and (b) can't possibly fail—even if the bar is set low enough to cross with ice skates. As soon as a suggestion meets these cheerless criteria, the meeting is essentially over. Sometimes, leaders will keep soliciting suggestions for a few more minutes as a show of good faith. Deep down, however, everyone knows that the time for big thinking is over.

If this seems like an exhausting and ineffective way to generate a handful of timid ideas, well, it is. In our experience, however, it remains standard practice at many, if not most, companies. We haven't even begun to list all the other ways brainstorming goes south, either. Hierarchical wrangling and turf wars. Preexisting agendas. Pet ideas that people refuse to drop. Negative Nancy/Nathan. On and on. Without effective guardrails and guidelines, group brainstorming brings out everyone's worst creative tendencies.

Is there any alternative? If you need more heads working on a problem, you must bring them together, right?

Decades ago, advertising executive Alex Faickney Osborn popularized brainstorming in several books on creative thinking, pitching the technique as a way to generate more and better ideas than the same participants could ever accomplish alone. The brainstorm was intended to remove bottlenecks by getting everyone's knowledge, experience, and authority in one place and watching the serendipitous sparks fly. Yet studies of group brainstorming have been hit-or-miss. For example, a 1987 meta-analysis of brainstorming studies published in the *Journal of Personality and Social Psychology* found little hard evidence for a positive effect.

If brainstorming underperforms, why do people still do it? An hour-long meeting of a team represents a significant investment of company resources. Chewing through everyone's time for lackluster results makes little sense, yet this is how most teams respond to an urgent need for ideas. Could it be the desire for moral support? A group session may blunt the creative output of a team, but it also diffuses accountability. Better to fail as a group than shoulder the risks alone. It's a depressing notion, but one that's all too understandable considering the prevailing mindset toward creativity and risk at most organizations.

It's possible to reap Osborn's promised benefits. The method of group idea generation we teach at the d.school and at organizations around the world leads to very different outcomes than those you've probably experienced. With the approach laid out in this chapter, each participant becomes an atom of uranium-235 in a nuclear reactor. When one person fires off an idea, it collides with the knowledge and experience of everyone else, sparking additional ideas in them. Contributions start pinging back and forth. Before you know it, you have a chain reaction, creative fission. Organized and run properly, an hour in a conference room delivers a payload of divergent thinking well in excess of the time and energy invested.

If it's true that brainstorming can be conducted effectively, which works "best"—group or solo? Both. As it turns out, maximizing a team's creative output means alternating between individual and collaborative idea generation. A study comparing solo work, group brainstorming, and a hybrid model alternating the two found that this last approach produced the most ideas. In fact, Osborn said as much in his own books, although clearly the message was lost over time. For best results, use an innovation sandwich: Bring people together for all the benefits of serendipity and shared knowledge. Send them back to their desks for quiet contemplation of what they've discussed. Finally, gather them together once more to share their thoughts and strike even more sparks.

One of the pitfalls of creativity is the psychological need for what social psychologist Arie Kruglanski dubbed "cognitive closure." It's increasingly uncomfortable to postpone judgment and keep thinking up new possibilities when there are one or more viable answers on the table. There is a strong instinct to run with what you've got as soon as you've got *something*. Consequently, people cut off the flow of divergent possibilities far too early. By interrupting the group process to give everyone a chance to noodle alone, you disrupt that tendency to prematurely converge.

The innovation sandwich works better even if you're a freelancer, an entrepreneur, or otherwise face idea problems alone. You'll never arrive at the same breadth of possibilities without the help of other people. Just as teams should incorporate periods of solitary reflection, individuals should seek out opportunities to bounce their ideas off others as part of their creative process: friends, peers, spouses. When you need ideas, call in reinforcements.

Do you actually need so *many* ideas, though? Must you keep going after the first good suggestion gets made? In the end, a problem needs only one solution. Why not stop as soon as you've got one?

THE IDEA RATIO

Contrary to popular opinion, successful creators aren't just people who come up with great ideas. Any single idea generated by a top performer is usually no more or less viable or interesting than one generated by anyone else in the room. The "equal-odds rule," put forward by psychology professor Dean Keith Simonton, states that the number of one's creative successes correlates to the total number of works created. More symphonies, more great symphonies. More mathematical theorems, more groundbreaking theorems. The equal-odds rule appears to apply to a staggering array of fields.

What set the winners apart in Simonton's research—and our own experience—is *volume*. World-class innovators routinely generate many more possibilities than average. If you want better outcomes, fill the top of your innovation funnel with many, many more ideas for achieving them. Just as important, gather your ideas from as far across the spectrum of possibilities as you possibly can.

How much more is "enough"? How many ideas does it actually take to arrive at a great one? In our experience, the answer is something on the order of *two thousand*. Yes, that's a two with three zeros after it—2,000 to 1. We call this the Idea Ratio.

To be clear, we're not telling you to go into a room and think up two thousand ideas on the spot. Creativity is iterative. When we suggest a ratio of 2,000 possibilities to 1 delivered solution, we're counting every combination, variation, and refinement along the entire innovation pipeline.

Credit for the Idea Ratio goes to our colleague Bob Sutton, who first saw evidence of it in his work at the design consultancy IDEO. Collaborating with a toy manufacturer, he learned that the company's inventors went through four thousand product ideas to get to two hundred working prototypes. Of those, a dozen or so were released commercially and two or three became legitimately successful. Once he identified this pattern, he started to see it everywhere creators get consistently great results.

We can divide these numbers in two and do a little rounding to make it easier to remember: To arrive at a single successful product, 2,000 ideas become 100 working prototypes. Those 100 prototypes become 5 commercial products. Of the final 5, 1 will succeed. To truly grasp the implications of 2,000:100:5:1, however, forget the fact that we're talking about toys, or even products in general. What we've found working with innovators of every kind is that the *scale* of this approach applies universally.

The Idea Ratio appears again and again in case studies of successful innovation. For example, Taco Bell's Insights Labs developed the category-annihilating Doritos Locos Tacos by starting with thirty or so core recipes and spinning those out into "untold variations," each of which required sampling. How many variations did product development manager Steve Gomez have to eat before landing on the game-changing product? "If I said a couple thousand shells," Gomez told a journalist, "it probably sounds like I'm exaggerating." Taco Bell is an acknowledged innovation juggernaut in fast food because of its ideaflow. "I write 50 concept ideas a month," senior marketing manager Kat Garcia told the journalist. (Among other accomplishments, Garcia invented the beloved Double Decker Taco.) "We do 300-500 ideas a year in the drawing phase. Cull that down to maybe 20 or 30 ideas that actually get in-market. A lot of things get tossed aside."

How is volume like this even possible? Process. A robust innovation process explains why companies like Apple, Pixar, and, yes, Taco Bell remain consistent even as very talented employees come and go. Meanwhile, other companies struggle to deliver wins regularly even as they invest in hiring and retaining top talent. (Remember Quibi?) Instinct combined with experience can accomplish magnificent things, but it's brittle. You can't rely on it. Process makes the Idea Ratio not just possible but sustainable.

The right process involves not just generating as many possibilities as you can without judgment but continually feeding them through a winnowing and validation pipeline, something we cover in the next chapter. The *movement* of ideas is key. We want ideaflow, not an idea pond. By using what you learn from experimentation to generate even more possibilities, raw ideas intersect with concrete data to spawn insights you never would have had sitting in a conference room. Follow this approach methodically and you'll easily hit two thousand variations by the time you're through.

Is there something magical about the number 2,000? Not necessarily. In some industries, it's even higher. According to our friend Wolfgang Ebel at the Japanese pharmaceutical company Eisai, the number of candidate compounds at the top of the solution funnel is more like 10,000 to 20,000. According to the inventor and entrepreneur Sir James Dyson, it took 5,127 *prototypes* to create his namesake bagless vacuum cleaner. (We don't even want to think about how many ideas went into creating that many actual prototypes.) In other arenas, the right ratio of ideas to successful outcomes might be "only" 500 or 1,000 to 1.

What the right number *isn't* is two, ten, or twenty. The secret to coming up with *good* ideas is coming up with many *more* ideas. With practice and experimentation, you'll arrive at an Idea Ratio that works best for your context. In the interim, begin by generating ideas for much longer than you usually do. As you test and validate those ideas, you will quickly learn that *any* idea is just a starting point, a spark. Some ideas that sound completely feasible fall flat in the real world. Others appear wildly impractical, even silly. Then you try them and discover that a few tweaks are enough to make them work.

It's worth repeating: for quantity to soar, relax expectations around quality. As you're learning from your Idea Quota, generating lots of ideas requires a no-judgment zone. You'll find that much of the value in any new idea lies in the additional ideas it sparks in others. Remember, the goal is creative fission.

In *Bird by Bird,* author Anne Lamott urges writers to accept that first efforts tend to be terrible. A lousy first draft is how writers get to "good second drafts and terrific third drafts." This is normal. Rookie writers get stuck because they expect to write it right, right away. The need for iteration isn't unique to the arts, either. Thomas Edison famously churned through ideas to arrive at a final product. "I have not failed," he is often quoted as having said. "I've just found 10,000 ways that won't work."

Edison's actual words were slightly but notably different. He'd been working for months developing a new battery. A friend found him surrounded by the debris of countless failed efforts.

"Isn't it a shame that with the tremendous amount of work you have done you haven't been able to get any results?" Edison's friend said. The inventor replied, "Results! Why, man, I have gotten a lot of results! I know several thousand things that won't work." Edison framed his failed attempts as *results*. Getting to thousands of ideas requires persistence, but Edison didn't get there through iron discipline as much as a sense of play and enjoyment. He *liked* generating and testing possibilities. He would never have persevered to a solution by banging his head against the bench every time an idea didn't pan out. It was this mindset that led to so many commercially successful products. He interpreted each iteration not as a failure but as a victorious step forward.

WHY PEOPLE STOP TOO SOON

In our experience, the typical brainstorming session results in a handful of ideas at best. Once there are even a couple of feasible options on the table, the enthusiasm to continue quickly dwindles. Before you know it, the discussion has shifted to implementation. One minute, everyone's spitballing. The next, they're drawing up a budget and delegating subtasks.

Otherwise intelligent and successful leaders consider this paltry amount of ideation sufficient even in the case of ambitious, large-scale projects. In their view, spending an hour coming up with eight or nine possibilities is sixty minutes well spent. One team at a major bank asked us, "Which of these six new ventures should we present to the board?" Six! Each of these ventures would involve months of effort by a large team and a seven-figure investment. Think of what the seventh idea might have been, if only they'd persisted a few more minutes? Instead, they confidently called it a day at six.

If the right starting number isn't six but the far side of six hundred, how do we bridge the gap between what people *think* they need and the scale of output that drives world-class results? It would help to use all the time available, for one thing. In our work at Stanford, we've found that even professional creatives tend to stop generating ideas before the allotted time. In most cases, people anchor on the first good idea the moment it's been suggested and, once that happens, the energy in the room changes. The group spends the rest of the time effectively reassuring itself that the idea they've latched on to is a good one. *I really think we've got ourselves a winner here, folks!*

You won't get to a company-saving strategy or an era-defining product by coming up with eight possibilities and then circling back to #3, which has been your favorite since, heck, way back at #4. Yet this is what always happens in the absence of a rigorous brainstorming process. There are a few factors at play here:

Pressure. Even if your problem isn't a true emergency requiring immediate resolution, every minute of the group's time constitutes a significant investment. If people aren't aware of the correlation between quantity and quality, persisting past the first good idea can be interpreted as perfectionism. Wasteful. People get annoyed when one contributor keeps throwing out new ideas when the majority is forming a consensus. If you value the opinion of your peers, you learn to zip your lip once a good-enough idea has been suggested. With a viable option on the table, the anxiety of not knowing is alleviated. Everyone relaxes. They may half-heartedly suggest additional possibilities, but as the meeting continues there's a clear tilt toward that early idea. Call it the urge to converge.

The creative cliff. Another cognitive bias at play here is the "creative cliff illusion," a phenomenon identified by psychology professors Brian Lucas and Loran Nordgren. In their research, Lucas and Nordgren found that people in a brainstorm sense that their creativity is getting "used up" when they generate ideas. However, unlike other cognitive resources like patience and willpower that may get depleted over time, creativity remains stable or increases as you use it.

Because of the creative cliff illusion, people don't persist in generating ideas for nearly so long as they could. In fact, they quit just as they're getting to their most interesting ideas. The ideas that arrive after ignoring the internal imperative to stop tend to be the best of the lot.

This isn't a talent thing. It's an expectations thing. Lucas and Nordgren found that people's beliefs about creativity— for example, whether they (incorrectly) believed that your best ideas arrive first—correlated with how long they persisted at creative tasks. In other words, understanding the creative cliff illusion helps dispel it.

Knowledge without a process isn't enough, however, because these biases are stubborn. In the same way that a trainer helps you push through your perceived physical limitations, a creative process helps you push past the creative cliff. As you'll see, it's only after you've contributed all the obvious suggestions that come to mind that your best ideas start to arrive. Your most unexpected, unusual, and unprecedented contributions are all waiting beyond that imaginary precipice.

Anchoring bias. A third limiter on the flow of ideas is the anchoring bias, first proposed by Amos Tversky and Daniel Kahneman, two key progenitors of behavioral economics. When making decisions, people tend to latch on to an initial reference point, or anchor. For example, if you ask a group of people to estimate the size of an object, the remaining estimates will cluster around the first guess—even if that first guess is way off base. That initial number becomes a focal point, an event horizon that's cognitively difficult to escape for the other participants. Worse, the effect can be observed in the pattern of guessing even if everyone is aware of the anchoring bias.

Both powerful and subtle, the anchoring bias plays a substantial role in creative problem-solving. The first few suggestions in a brainstorming session will inevitably steer what follows. Even experienced creators fall prey to anchoring, unconsciously positioning all their suggestions in relation to earlier suggestions instead of letting the development process diverge across the full spectrum of possibilities. That's why we need a process that systematically prevents anchors from forming in the first place.

The Einstellung effect. Assuming you withstand the pressure long enough to push past the creative cliff and soar, anchors and all, you still have one last obstacle to overcome. Observed by psychologists for decades, the Einstellung effect occurs when one possible solution prevents you from seeing any others. Simply thinking of one direction to approach a problem can blind you to the full range of alternatives.

If you've ever played a word-search game and found yourself noticing the words you've already spotted over and over, you're familiar with the power of this bias. Once your brain sees a path through the maze, it becomes very hard to unsee, to consider alternate routes.

Merim Bilalić and Peter McLeod used eye-tracking cameras to demonstrate this in a novel study of chess players. Even as players insisted they were scanning the whole board for a solution to a chess problem, their eyes kept following the same pattern, one they'd been primed to see by solving a previous, similar problem. The previous approach to a solution didn't work for this new problem, but they couldn't break free of it. These players were completely unaware that they were going in circles.

The Einstellung effect explains why solo idea generation underperforms. To comb the full spectrum of possibilities, we need others to push us out of the ruts we don't even know we're in.

A SIMPLE METHOD FOR SOLVING COMPLEX PROBLEMS

If we're going to bring a group together to tackle a problem, we want to walk away with the greatest possible volume *and* variety of ideas in return for the investment of time and energy.

The output of a brainstorming session should reflect the full range of experiences, backgrounds, and thinking styles in the room. It should engage every participant fully, not just the folks who enjoy the sounds of their own voices.

The following guidelines have proven effective with organizations of every size and across industries. For remote and hybrid work, you can now choose from among a robust array of online tools designed specifically for facilitating virtual sessions. This approach adapts surprisingly well to digital whiteboards and pixelated Post-its, and the best part is, you're never distracted by that one guy wandering around the conference room with a bag of chips instead of staying put at his table.

Assemble the right mix

Leaders often invite people to a brainstorming session indiscriminately: the more, the merrier. We'll see in a later chapter how bringing diverse perspectives together can spur divergent thinking, but it must be done thoughtfully. A well-calibrated roster helps ensure the success of the session. If you're not careful, you can end up with the core team on one side and a group of outsiders unable to offer relevant contributions on the other. The outsiders who lack any context then either distract the core team with completely unfeasible ideas or remain silent out of fear of doing so.

Resist the urge to CC the whole company the next time you need ideas. Small is good. Three people with insight into a problem are enough to reap the benefits of brainstorming. With more than six participating, you'll just end up at a long conference table with each person interacting with a handful of others in earshot. (If more than six people are coming together to brainstorm, divide them up into teams of three to six as indicated below.)

Everyone in the room should have enough relevant experience and expertise to offer grounded contributions. This doesn't mean that everyone must come from the same department, of course. As we'll see in chapter 7 on mining perspectives, inviting someone with a very different function *who still has visibility into your problem* can be incredibly useful.

Nor is this to say that novice viewpoints can't be helpful. To welcome a fresh perspective into the discussion, just do so deliberately and with a specific end in mind rather than sprinkling in a bunch of interns as an afterthought.

Navistar ran into trouble with its electric bus fleet that required break-through thinking. Unfortunately, the employees most familiar with the issue operated defensively, suggesting only incremental improvements. Too much familiarity with the problem had become a handicap. To combat this, leaders assembled a group of employees from across the organization, briefed them on the problem, and gave them a day to generate as many ideas as they could. These novices had no vested interest in the project, and in this case that left them free to think bigger. They generated sixty discrete ideas, which eventually led to a solution.

There will be more in chapter 7 on using novice perspectives as an advanced tactic for overcoming inertia. In most cases, you'll want to take full advantage of experience and expertise when you assemble the group.

Gather initial suggestions

Expecting people to spitball in a group setting favors the extroverts. It also leaves everyone vulnerable to anchoring—the first few suggestions will steer every contribution that follows, limiting the eventual scope. Before bringing everyone together, give the participants a prompt related to the problem at hand and ask them to submit at least two contributions in advance. These initial suggestions will serve as seeds for idea generation and a hedge against the insidious anchoring bias, ensuring that the widest spectrum of possibilities gets explored.

A good prompt will usually take the form of a "How might we?" question, as in: "How might we help customers find products more easily on our mobile app?" (More on creating helpful prompts in chapter 9.) For this and many other purposes at the d.school, we will create a "scaffold," a template that can be reused whenever we run that particular exercise. A group brainstorming scaffold might have the "How might we?" question at the top followed by a cue: "Leveraging your own unique experience and perspective, what new solutions might you recommend?" If participants lack some context, basic details here might help. Below that, leave ten or more blank spaces to encourage more than the minimum of two suggestions.

Distributing a printed scaffold with clear instructions will boost participation compared with an email. Also, since an effective scaffold can be adapted and reused, be sure to save the document.

In an ideal situation, give each participant the evening before the group convenes to work on the scaffold. In a pinch, however, a lunch hour is enough to jot down a few possibilities. Anything is better than "on your mark, get set, go."

Get everyone in the right mindset with warm-ups

Spend the first ten or fifteen minutes warming up as a group just as you might with a tennis partner before a game. Warm-up exercises help participants clear away the cobwebs—along with any preexisting agendas and pet ideas they may be holding in mind. Warm-ups also shift the group out of the conventional, convergent mindset they rely on at work.

When we're doing our jobs, we're primed to notice mistakes, minimize risk, organize chaos, and stay on point. Generating ideas together requires a different mode of operation. Instead of converging on a path forward— eliminating variability, reducing risk, making decisions—we want to diverge as widely as possible, generating as many potential directions to explore in the time we have available.

After we explained this distinction to a group of executives from Japan, one high-ranking participant offered a novel interpretation: "When we are diverging, it's OK to suggest anything," she said. "When we are converging, we have to think *responsibly*." A native English speaker probably wouldn't have implied that creative thinking is somehow irresponsible, but this interpretation felt exactly right. It *does* feel irresponsible to throw out a wild or risky idea at work. We want to be good stewards, whether of the company's resources or simply our own reputations. In a creative context, however, we need new thinking that would never arise in the normal course of a day. This means allowing yourself, just for this window of time, to think "irresponsibly." When you adopt a divergent mindset, there are no longer mistakes. Only, in the words of the great creativity expert and landscape painter Bob Ross, "happy little accidents."

A good warm-up exercise sets the tone, implicitly establishing creative rules of engagement such as deferring judgment, going for quantity, keeping each contribution brief, and building on the ideas of others. You're probably familiar with the usual icebreakers, like people mirroring one another's movements or a rock-paper-scissors tournament. Anything that gets things moving physically and mentally will do. In our experience, however, the best warm-up is doing the same thing you'll be doing during the session but with lower stakes.

For example, if you're looking for ways to convince customers to switch from buying each new version of your app to paying for a monthly subscription, give the group a parallel challenge: "How might we convince Alan's kids to eat their vegetables?"

For a group that is relatively new to this method, begin with a rule that everyone has to say no to each idea:

"Maybe we could blend the vegetables into a smoothie?"

"No, that won't work. You have to roast them."

"No, roasting takes too long. Smother them in salad dressing instead."

Once the participants have done this for a minute or two, ask them to affirm and build on one another's ideas instead, using the improviser's mantra, "yes, and . . . ":

"Yes, and use a low-calorie, organic salad dressing for even more health benefits."

"Yes, and you could even give them a choice of two different salad dressings so they feel more in charge."

And so on. At the end of the warm-up, ask everyone if they noticed the improvement after the switch from "no" to "yes, and." Saying no is unnecessary—we're not winnowing ideas yet—and it interrupts the flow. Saying "yes, and" encourages the participant to use the other person's output as a divergent input to spur a new direction. Again, the idea is to tune participants into the right mindset.

Split into teams and assign facilitators

If you've got a group of unwieldy size, split it into teams of three to six people. Think like a wedding planner approaching a seating chart: break existing connections up wherever possible to create the greatest possible diversity of viewpoints (and minimize any distractions). Think diversity not only in terms of age, race, and gender but role, department, and place in the hierarchy. Map it out on paper or use a spreadsheet and shuffle things up. Once you're all in teams, assign one member of each team as its facilitator and, if necessary, take a minute to instruct the facilitators in the following approach.

The team's facilitator begins the session by distributing Sharpies and Post-it pads to each team member. Ideally, use different-colored pads so that each person's contributions can be identified. It also helps to position everyone within arm's reach of the whiteboard. The physical arrangement of the group emphasizes that each member of the team is an equal author with equal opportunity to contribute.

Importantly, the facilitator is not a boss. This is true even if they are, in fact, the boss. (Roles and hierarchy go out the window when we're generating ideas, and if that requires removing badges, stripes, or other visible signs of rank, do so.) The facilitator simply runs the session, making sure everyone is participating fully and minding the energy level.

The facilitator reviews the team's scaffolds and selects five or six seeds to spur idea generation. Since we're looking to generate the broadest possible diversity of solutions, we want at least one idea from each member of the team. Beyond that, look for a balance between novelty and feasibility. Anything completely untethered from reality will generate possibilities that are too frivolous or off-the-wall to be useful. Anything too obvious or pedestrian will keep the discussion in low orbit.

Once the seeds have been written on the whiteboard, each at the top of a separate column, it's time to begin in earnest.

Set the pace

Typically, we'll devote an hour to a group session like this, including that ten- or fifteen-minute warm-up. If more time would be helpful, break it up into multiple sessions of an hour or less, leaving five minutes at the end of each hour to collect ideas and hold a quick postmortem discussion.

When the timer starts, the facilitator invites ideas inspired by the seed in the first column on the whiteboard. To contribute, a participant (a) writes their idea down, (b) says it out loud to the team, and (c) sticks it in the appropriate column. As the session progresses, the facilitator contributes their own ideas while cheering everyone else on—always in terms of quantity, not quality.

You can't evaluate your own ideas too closely if things are moving quickly, so keep it light and lightning fast so that no one has time to second-guess themselves. Throughout the session, the facilitator should continually encourage the other team members to defer judgment and build on one another's ideas. Keep pushing back against any tendency to converge on a "winner" or anyone's effort to steer the group's output in a certain direction. It's not what we think of any particular idea that matters but what each idea helps us think of next.

As the columns fill up, keep an eye on the colors: "Bill, I don't see any green Post-its on the board, make sure you add some stuff, too." You want to get as close to complete participation as possible to take full advantage of the diversity of the team. If one or two participants keep dominating, assign an order and solicit contributions one at a time. This heavy-handed tactic usually isn't necessary, but sometimes, particularly in virtual sessions, people won't speak up unless they know they're next in line. Likewise, keep reminding people to use their Sharpies. If you don't write it down, it didn't happen, remember? "That's a great idea, Bill, but put it on a Post-it and get it up on the board!" (You may have to say this *a lot*.)

Generating ideas is like microwaving popcorn. At the start, a couple of straightforward ideas will "pop" in quick succession. This will be followed by steadier, and steadily more divergent, popping as the obvious directions are exhausted and the creative cliff is surpassed. Before the ideas stop popping altogether—typically, this takes five or six minutes—the facilitator directs the group's attention to the next column, both to keep the energy up and to get the group through all the columns in the given amount of time. With six columns and six minutes to a column, you'll have sufficient time for the warm-up at the start and the wrap-up at the end in a given hour.

Capture, marinate, and reassemble

At the end of a session, bring all the teams together and spend five minutes talking through the results and their implications. Be sure to snap photos of all the whiteboards. Above all, don't even try to decide which ideas are most promising. As we'll see, that's just not something people do very well, especially right away.

Next, send the group out with a clear mission: "We'd like you to continue to reflect on the prompt, as well as the solutions we've imagined together," you explain. "Some of your freshest thinking will happen after this meeting is over. When we reconvene to make decisions about how to move forward, everyone can share the insights and ideas that arrived in the interim."

Before dispersing, tally the total number of ideas generated by each team. Knowing that the group produced, for example, a few hundred ideas over the course of sixty minutes can be incredibly motivating for everyone who participated. It helps highlight the ROI of the hour they spent.

Over time, you will develop a sense of the right Idea Ratio for the kind of work you're doing. That ratio becomes a target to hit every time. Remember that the creative cliff illusion keeps telling our brains we're out of ideas when we're not. The metrics help show us otherwise, shifting our expectations and making it that much easier to persist longer next time.

~

With this simple and systematic method, one hour will accomplish more than you ever thought possible. You won't get to two thousand ideas, but you will generate dozens or even hundreds to start with, and you'll begin to see how the data generated by experimentation might spark the remainder.

To supercharge your results, make things competitive (in a good way). With multiple teams, see which one can generate the most possibilities. Or challenge each team to beat its previous tally of ideas with each new column. Make it fun. Think fundraising marathon, not Cold War U.S.-Soviet chess showdown.

Our friend Dan Klein, head of the Stanford Improvisers, offers a final piece of advice: Don't try to be creative. Dare to be obvious instead. What feels "obvious" to one person will strike others as novel, even inspiring. Make the tacit explicit. Nothing ever "goes without saying." Remember those creative neutrons flying around the nuclear reactor? Rather than try to dream up something outside your own reality, say what comes to mind immediately and watch the chain reaction begin. Dare to be obvious and trust the team to be fantastic.

This is the core advantage of working in a group. It's a process of steel sharpening steel. It's why we don't simply retreat to our desks to generate ideas alone. In a group, no single person bears the burden of being the creative hero. We can all relax and let loose, striking sparks off one another as we coast forward.

When a session ends, excitement gives way to pragmatism. Quantity without judgment is fun, but what about the quality it's supposed to drive? The inevitable question we hear from participants is, "How do we know whether any of these is a *good* idea?" The next chapter begins to answer this question. As you establish an innovation pipeline for validating ideas in the real world, you'll see how experimental results inspire even more creative thinking. Instead of charting a path and following it blindly, the trick is to feel your way forward.

Group sessions are an invaluable tool for solving idea problems, but generating ideas isn't a discrete event that happens at the beginning of a project. The cycle of testing, refinement, and further exploration continues throughout the innovation process. It ends only once you've achieved your aim—or abandoned it to mine an even richer vein of opportunity.

4.

Build an Innovation Pipeline

We are trying to prove ourselves wrong as
quickly as possible, because only in that way
can we find progress.

—RICHARD FEYNMAN

S ilicon Valley Bank is a large commercial bank headquartered in
Santa Clara, California. Since its founding in 1983, SVB has specialized in a local commodity: high-tech start-ups. Today, SVB is
one of the largest banks in the country, with operations worldwide. For
all its scope, however, technology and venture capital—innovation—still
play a vital role in its success. Eager to drive growth, CEO Greg Becker
brought us in to work with high-potential leaders at the bank in 2016.
Becker assembled nine teams from around the organization and gave each
one a strategic area of opportunity to explore.

Working with a new group, we'll usually introduce a hypothetical
project for teaching purposes. Since we already had Becker's nine strategic
areas, we decided to start with one of those. Debt financing for start-ups

struck us as an ideal demo, one with plenty of relevance to SVB's core business. That team would be looking at how founders borrow money to launch new businesses. What kinds of terms do these customers expect? What problems do they commonly face? How might SVB make its debt-financing offerings more compelling? The answers might have major ramifications.

After explaining the idea-generation process described in the previous chapter, we divided the group into nine teams and set them to work. For three days, each team generated ideas, prototyped concepts, and gathered user feedback. At the end of the third day, the entire group gathered to share results. The team tasked with eventually tackling this problem would act as a jury, selecting the most promising suggestions for testing and validation.

Though the portfolio review got off to a good start, it became increasingly clear that the jury was prioritizing risk avoidance over upside. At the end of the presentation, they went to the front of the room and announced their choice. As we'd feared, it was the one we'd seen as the least risky, interesting, and promising option. Realizing that the audience wasn't reacting as expected, the jury faltered. We asked for a show of hands. "Outside of the jury," we asked, "who would have voted for this particular idea?" After a pause, two hands out of forty went up.

"Are you *serious*?" one of the jury members exclaimed.

"Are *you*?" someone called from the back.

Everyone on the jury thought they'd picked the obvious winner. Everyone else thought otherwise. What happened?

WHY PICKING IS DIFFICULT

We all know someone who shouts the "right" plays at the screen during the Super Bowl. You find armchair quarterbacks in every arena. Some of us love second-guessing a decision . . . when we face none of the consequences of making the wrong one.

This isn't necessarily a bad thing. Knowing that you'll be the one to face the consequences of a decision can't help but shape your thinking about it. With skin in the game, your options look different. If you'll have to follow through, you will instinctively narrow the scope and shorten the horizon. It may be obvious from the outside that your friend needs to quit that toxic job driving them to an early grave. When it's your own lousy job, however, the picture isn't as clear. The effort and risk involved in leaving a job or even changing careers are far more intimidating. Maybe your boss isn't so crazy after all. It's tough to think big when you're the one carrying the load.

The showdown at Silicon Valley Bank illustrates this tension. If you don't have to worry about logistics, bandwidth, or risk, why think small? There were more than a handful of genuinely novel ideas put forward that piqued everyone's curiosity. Validating any idea requires real-world experimentation, but these ideas brimmed with potential. Even if they weren't viable, exploring them would have led in interesting directions.

The jury group at SVB steered to the lowest-potential idea because it was the most feasible one on the list. We are hardwired to evade sabertooth tigers, not maximize the growth potential of debt-financing programs at Bay Area banks. This is the cognitive bias known as loss aversion showing up once again. When our necks are on the line, risks outweigh rewards. Under pressure, the mind relies more heavily on instinct. Then it justifies these intuitive decisions retroactively, adding a gloss of logic and reason to choices that were driven by cognitive biases.

The safest, least interesting idea genuinely seemed like the right choice to the people on the jury. That's why they were surprised by the audience's reaction. On an emotional level, they had latched on to a sure thing: a manageable amount of effort required with a clear line of sight to the goal and alignment with the status quo. Only then had their rational minds entered the picture to make the business case. As our good friend at Stanford Professor Baba Shiv says, "The rational part of the brain is excellent at rationalizing decisions made elsewhere."

Since perceived effort and risk stymie the capacity to think big, it helps to lower the pressure. We do this by establishing a testing pipeline for ideas. A validation process gives ideas an outlet, someplace to go other than two buckets labeled Yes and No. When you hear testing, forget the expensive and bureaucratic corporate "pilot program." Instead, think rapid, scrappy tests straight out of high school science class. Hypothesis to results in an hour and then off to lunch.

When you select ideas for testing, as opposed to full-on implementation, all you're committing to is a quick, scrappy test. This mindset frees you to evaluate your ideas on their merits alone. Creating a pipeline to validate your ideas is crucial to maintaining ideaflow. When an expensive and scary green light is the only option, most ideas seem too risky and resource-intensive to even consider. That's why your most ambitious ideas tend to stagnate as you keep reaching for ones that are easier and less risky to implement. Once your creative mind recognizes this logjam, it usually stops generating more big ideas.

Where Israel's Dead Sea is famously salty, the freshwater Sea of Galilee, ninety miles to the north, supports a diverse ecosystem. Though both bodies of water are fed by the Jordan River, the Dead Sea has no outlet while the Sea of Galilee supplies 10 percent of Israel's water needs. *Flow* is essential to life and vitality. A low-stakes outlet for ideas restores the flow of creativity. If we get stuck in the mindset that we must generate a ton of ideas at the start and then pick the "right" one, the pressure of perfection leads to sterile and safe choices. With the binary approach, we don't try things out, let alone use what we've learned to adapt our thinking.

Reality is an excellent source of creative input. Through experimentation, your ideas will benefit from the lessons of costs, clients, and customers.

This is why you don't generate a mountain of ideas in a vacuum, decide which one wins, and go make it happen. From now on, you will test ideas in the real world, using the data you gather to refine the ones you have and spark better ones along the way. This is how we move, step by step, down the path from inspiration to conviction.

In this chapter, we will show you how to establish a pipeline for ideas.

NEVER STOP TESTING

Even if you're an acknowledged expert in your field, you simply aren't qualified to decide which ideas to pursue in the absence of real-world data. Nobody is! There are too many unknowns. Without real-world testing, you're leaving the success of your pursuit to luck to one degree or another. Innovation without validation is the equivalent of pointing your car in the direction of home, closing your eyes, and hitting the gas pedal. You might make it back to the house, but chances are you'll end up in a ditch. It makes no sense, yet companies routinely drive home blindfolded, throwing barrels of money and time into engineering solutions before even validating desire. When it turns out that nobody wants whatever the product or service is, blame falls on the sales department, or on changing market conditions. Never on the faulty innovation process where it belongs. Thus, the cycle begins again.

General Motors saw early traction when it deployed its car-sharing service, Maven, in 2016. Thousands of people signed up for the pilot effort in New York City to rent GM cars for hourly or daily use. The right next step would have been to expand Maven to the surrounding area or, even better, try a different locale altogether. A second pilot program in Phoenix, Arizona, would have tested GM's assumptions in a very different way. Instead, eager to stake a claim in the space, GM burned through millions in a misguided effort to expand Maven to more than a dozen cities at once. What GM's leaders discovered too late was that there were critical gaps in the concept that hadn't been exposed by its Big Apple test run. Those flaws became obvious only in other markets with different conditions on the ground. Unfortunately, scaling up meant addressing all these problems simultaneously to keep the concept afloat. As it turned out, there was no time to fix everything before the initiative hit the end of its runway. GM shuttered Maven only four years after its promising launch.

A similar thing happened when a bold new concept was proposed at Keller Williams, according to our friend John Keller, the company's head of transformation. As Keller explained to us, local insights are currency in real estate. Anyone can put up a shingle and list some properties. Coming to know a place well takes time and effort. It goes far beyond doing a Yelp search for good coffee shops. The best real estate agents amass encyclopedic knowledge about their areas, and this hard-earned expertise becomes a competitive advantage. People learn to trust in an agent's knowledge of school districts, noise pollution, residential streets that get used as shortcuts by commuters, and other relevant factors. Over time, this expertise gets rewarded with loyalty and referrals. When a real estate agent saves you from buying the wrong house for a reason you would never have spotted on your own, you remember.

Collectively, Keller Williams agents possessed an enormous reservoir of local knowledge. However, they had no way of sharing this knowledge among themselves. To better leverage this valuable resource, the company wanted to create an internal database. Keller Williams agents would share their knowledge. In return, they could draw on that database whenever they needed answers. For example, they would be able to get up to speed much more quickly when moving to a new area themselves. Onboarding would also be easier with all that collective knowledge in one place. You wouldn't have to keep explaining the same local quirks to each new agent.

The database idea was promising, but it raised questions. What kinds of information would qualify as local insights: Dining options? Good pediatricians? Reliable contractors? In terms of implementation, would off-the-shelf software work, or would the company need to invest in a pricey custom solution? When it came to using the database, how easy would it be to contribute and find information, particularly on a mobile phone? Good real estate agents aren't known for sitting still.

Every idea comes with a set of questions attached. The only way to proceed is to make assumptions about what the answers might be. You won't know whether you've guessed right, however, until you've tested your assumptions in the real world. Leaving that testing process to the public launch of a completed product or service is a critical error made by far too many organizations. Keller Williams was savvy enough to start with a pilot version of the database, opening it up to agents in a single area. Within a short time frame, thousands of insights were entered into the new repository. The participants seemed happy with it. What had threatened to be a hassle was actually easy to use and fairly valuable in practice. The rate of adoption exceeded the company's expectations.

As with Maven at GM, the right next step would have been to expand the offering to a very different area in order to test the same assumptions from another angle. And again, that isn't what happened. If the institution doesn't have a culture of testing and an established innovation pipeline, it's just too tempting to run with promising ideas rather than "waste time with endless tests."

As Keller ruefully admitted to us years after the fact, Keller Williams rolled the database out nationally after that one successful test. But leaders hadn't grasped that scale magnifies complexity. Making an idea even a little bigger can make it a lot more complicated. During the pilot, real estate agents could easily police the database, educating one another about best practices and clearing out any low-quality contributions cluttering up search results. On a national scale, the database was suddenly flooded with contributions at a pace that far exceeded the users' capacity for self-moderation. Once the database had ballooned to half a million entries, sifting valuable insights from the accumulated dross became impossible. The best contributors grew tired of watching their carefully written insights get diluted by a sea of one-sentence remarks. The software hadn't yet been optimized for sorting vast amounts of data, either. Finding anything at all became difficult as the overloaded database grew buggy and slow. The database seemed to run into a brick wall as tens of thousands of users almost simultaneously stopped using the product. Attempts to fix the system failed. When all the frustration threatened to become a distraction from the work of selling properties, leaders canceled the project. In its eagerness to reap the benefits of a promising idea, Keller Williams had killed the golden goose.

John Keller sees this as the biggest innovation flop in the company's history because the core concept had held such potential. If the company had taken the time to validate its assumptions through multiple stages of iteration and testing, it might have homed in on a workable approach, avoiding what Keller called "a hectic scramble that came from not having a plan in place." Once an idea goes south at scale, however, there is rarely any institutional willingness to wind it back down and start refining it from an earlier stage of development. By the time Keller Williams had pulled the plug on its insights database, users had lost interest in investing time in this voluntary, unpaid activity. This project's failure illustrates the danger of going all-in on an idea, even one with a successful test behind it.

The right validation process is cyclical. You don't just generate a bunch of ideas, test one, and then scale it up like crazy if it works. Instead, you go through stages: test, analyze results, refine, test again. Our observation, confirmed many times over, is that organizations are so eager to scale promising ideas that they compulsively skip this effort. In their hurry to score a win, they unwittingly undermine their efforts. This is doubly true of companies that are perennially starved for innovation. Be particularly cautious of the urge to run with promising ideas when ideaflow is just ramping up in an organization. There are *always* problems that must be resolved at each stage of growth before you can move forward. Pace yourself. People blame poor execution when a project goes off course, but even great drivers can't steer blind. The sooner you let go of the delusion that you can "eyeball it" or "do it on the fly," the more consistent your success will be. *Test before you invest,* not once but at every stage. Testing is forecasting. It's how you see your success before you achieve it.

There are several reasons for the institutional reluctance to test, false incentives chief among them. If you don't know any better, testing seems like lots of work for little reward. The innovation process generally begins with a mandate from a leader to make or fix something. No one rises in the ranks of an organization by telling leaders something *won't* work, just as scientists don't win Nobel Prizes for publishing a lack of positive results. If testing is seen as simply ruling something out, a binary act ending in either victory or defeat, the stakes are too high. If you're going to risk defeat, you might as well aim for the moon. That's why most people are reluctant to look at any viable-sounding idea too closely before implementing it. Meanwhile, leaders tend to interpret caution and curiosity at the developmental stage as skepticism and procrastination. No one wants to be seen as a momentum-killer.

This resistance fades once everyone understands what testing actually entails. A rapid, scrappy test should take hours, tops. Not weeks, and certainly not months. As we saw with Thomas Edison's efforts to develop a long-lasting light bulb, experiments aren't for killing ideas. They're for filtering the best from the rest. He succeeded so frequently by cramming as many scrappy tests as possible into every twenty-four-hour period. When you boost ideaflow, test-based filtration becomes a necessity. There are too many ideas to consider and, as we've seen, our biases tend to steer us from the winners even if it was possible to identify them without real-world data. A good test rules out lots of options that won't work while homing in on the ones that might, vastly reducing the risk of failure. Reframing testing as a scrappy process of learning, refinement, and validation is the key to circumventing the reluctance to experiment.

As for the effort required, running a test can and should be quick and easy relative to implementing the idea in its final form. You're going to be testing a lot, so you're always looking for the biggest bang for your experimental buck. When we design tests, whether for boot-strapped start-ups or multinational corporations with massive R&D budgets, we always optimize for **experimental efficiency**. The best experiments return lots of actionable data in exchange for a minor investment of time and energy. Why invest months and millions in a new product when a few days and a few hundred dollars might reveal that nobody wants to buy it as currently envisioned? In fact, why pursue *any* new idea seriously if you don't have credible evidence of desire?

Test, refine, and test again until you've zeroed in on a solution that works. With the right validation process, you'll know whether an idea has wings long before you hit the end of the runway. In the case of a product, you'll even know things like how much to charge and how much inventory to keep on hand before you go to market. In this way, you can leverage the full value of your ideas while minimizing the uncertainty and risk involved in making them real.

CREATE A PORTFOLIO OF EXPERIMENTS

Stop trying to predict winners. Research by our colleague Justin Berg at the Stanford Graduate School of Business found that "participants tended to under-rank their highest-potential idea." For best results, test every single possibility and compare outcomes. Daunting as it sounds, testing everything you've got is more feasible than you think. Though the list of possibilities you've generated may be intimidatingly long, there usually aren't that many distinct *directions* to pursue once you've combined similar ideas. You can compare the merits of stripes and polka dots before worrying about the precise width of each stripe. By testing each main branch, you build conviction among the stakeholders that you're headed the right way. From there, you let real-world data steer you by testing increasingly specific possibilities leading from that main branch.

To create the bagless vacuum cleaner, Sir James Dyson tested at least one variation a day for four years, fastidiously documenting the impact of each incremental change to the design. "It was fascinating," he said. "I'd do an experiment and sometimes it would get better, sometimes it would get worse. But because I only made one change at a time, I knew exactly what it was that had made it better or exactly what it was that made it worse." Let data decide for you to the greatest extent possible. Revise your idea based on what you learn from your tests and proceed in one direction only once the results indicate a clear winner.

Unlike Sir James, most people can't spend years working through thousands of variations one test at a time. Test an array of ideas simultaneously by creating a *portfolio* of ideas and then prototyping them in parallel. As with financial investments, the key to a successful portfolio is diversity: include a "sure thing," a handful of promising bets, and a moon shot or two. The number of tests you can run at once will depend on the nature of the ideas you're testing, and we'll have much more to say about effective testing in the next two chapters. Think like an investor hedging their bets in volatile market conditions. Committing everything to one approach, even a completely reasonable one, can easily fail, while a small bet in an unlikely direction can pay off handsomely. Aim for as large and diverse a portfolio as you can manage. The wider you cast your net, the greater the likelihood you'll snag a trophy. Preserve as much of the creative potential you generated for as long into the innovation process as possible. Keep the excluded ideas, too. Even after you've created a portfolio and run a series of tests, you can always return to the original list of possibilities and reconsider them through the lens of the lessons you've learned.

A portfolio approach to your experiments makes sense once you accept that innovation is an inherently low-yield activity. Every individual attempt carries a high risk of failure. That's not just OK but an essential attribute of trying new things. Innovation works differently than other areas of business. Rather than trying to lower the failure rate, minimize the costs and risks of each test and aim to rack up as many failures as you can. That's how you'll know you're setting the bar high enough.

Don't let concerns about resources or bandwidth enter the picture as you select which ideas to test. If an experiment reveals enormous potential in an idea that requires a major investment of time and energy, you'll have hard data to justify the additional resources. What seems intimidating when alone at your desk looks very different with a seven-figure budget and a large team attached. Successful experiments win internal support or the attention of outside investors. In our experience, decision-makers prefer real-world data to any elevator pitch.

To construct a truly diverse portfolio, get help from people who won't be involved with implementation. At Logitech, CEO Bracken Darrell makes this a company policy. "[Outsiders] can think much more radically about solutions," Ehrika Gladden, a senior leader at the company, explained to us. Remember how the other teams at Silicon Valley Bank could weigh the potential of different ideas more accurately than the jury team. Being freed from the expectation of implementation provides valuable perspective.

If you're a solo entrepreneur, tapping into an unbiased viewpoint this way is more difficult. You may not be comfortable outsourcing your decision of which business idea to pursue to someone else. After all, they can't know as much as you do about your strengths, skills, and interests. Again, however, the point isn't to choose the idea to pursue but to make an array of small bets. There is no question that another person will help you devise a more diverse portfolio of options than you can on your own. As an entrepreneur, you can ask a friend, associate, or former colleague for their input without surrendering your fate to their whims. Getting an unbiased outside perspective is too important to skip.

When testing every idea isn't possible, build the most diverse portfolio of experiments you possibly can. Depending on the number of ideas you start with, even this can be an overwhelming task. That's when a rock-solid winnowing process comes in handy.

WINNOW BY EXCITEMENT

The larger the pool of ideas, the stronger the lure of low-hanging fruit. When the company solicits employee suggestions, for example, a massive spreadsheet of results ends up in someone's inbox. Scrolling through hundreds or thousands of rows of random ideas trying to pick the "best" submissions, you're going to settle on the quick and easy wins that catch your eye.

To sidestep this, establish criteria to winnow the list down *before* reviewing it. If you consider the options and then decide on selection criteria, you will inevitably design criteria that steer toward your subconscious preferences. Instead, you might start by sorting the list along a few different axes: time to implement, potential cost, etc. Use that approach to filter things down to a manageable size. At that point, you can establish a formal array of requirements based on a well-researched understanding of the organization's complex business needs. Take your goals for the next few quarters into account. Work up some charts and graphs. Rigorously sift all the ideas through one filter after another: ROI, EBITDA, Effort/ Value, and on and on.

At a large organization, the charts and the graphs are sometimes necessary to make the case for which ideas to test. However, if you have the flexibility, as a solo entrepreneur, for example, you can use a single question to remove the chaff more effectively than any bureaucratic, metric-driven process ever could:

"Is this exciting?"

Remember how entrepreneur Henrik Werdelin painstakingly copies over the most promising ideas to a fresh notebook whenever he fills his current one? He's measuring his own excitement. Excitement is the fuel of innovation. In our experience, the key to achieving world-class results is *expecting* delight. Most people at most companies don't even look for it. When you've gotten fired up by a new idea only to watch it sputter a few times in your career, you get jaded. Indifference becomes a survival strategy at big companies that don't know how to innovate. We don't want to get emotionally invested in ideas because we don't see a clear path toward making them a reality. This sense of inevitable failure around innovation becomes a self-fulfilling prophecy.

Your early-morning insight will never be realized exactly as you imagined it. Compromises are unavoidable. Therefore, if you're not excited now, don't take another step forward. As Justin Berg's research showed, we may put our best ideas in second or third place, but they still end near the top. Bias or no bias, the losers still end up at the bottom. There is no way you're going to reach a great outcome at the end of a process that begins from a place of indifference. If you're not curious to find out whether an idea will work, don't try to find out! Whether it's a new business, an improvement to an internal process, or a solution to a nagging customer problem, what ultimately matters is stakeholder delight. Not just the stakeholders in upper management or the CEO, but *all* the stakeholders: customers, vendors, partners, employees. Anyone whose problem the idea will address. If you're not excited by the potential of an idea to delight everyone involved, trust in your creativity and cut it from the list.

Yes, we're going to make a great business case based on hard data. Before that, however, we need ideas that provoke wonder, excitement, and joy. This is pure pragmatism. Boring ideas lose money and sap momentum. Whatever was going through the jury's minds in our exercise with Silicon Valley Bank, it wasn't excitement. They weren't aiming to delight anyone. They saw a way to make something concrete happen with a minimum of fuss. Fundamentally, we're all built like the jury team. To achieve better results, learn to demand them. You will profit the most from the ideas you can't stop thinking about, the ones you're genuinely excited to pursue.

Great outcomes never start with a shrug.

THE CORKBOARD R&D DEPARTMENT

Innovation powerhouses have a robust creative culture and an established research and development process. If you don't have a framework for evaluating ideas, employees learn that it's easier to just keep doing things the way they've always been done. Even if there's an obvious opportunity for improvement, it simply isn't worth the effort of pursuing it. If you stick to the status quo, the bosses can't blame you for messing something up.

To restore the flow of ideas, create a pipeline for them. Once water starts flowing through a body of water again, life returns. A pipeline encourages people to create by giving them a place to route possibilities. It also takes the pressure off. In most organizations, if someone suggests a promising-sounding idea, the typical response is: "That sounds good— why don't you run with that?" Nobody's sitting around wishing they had a new boulder to push uphill alone. Nor does anyone want management getting excited about an idea that might not work out. Shift the emphasis from "run with that" to "let's see if anyone would be interested in this and go from there."

You can establish a quick-and-dirty idea pipeline with little more than a large corkboard. (If some of your team works remotely, use a virtual whiteboard tool along the following lines instead.) Position it in a prominent spot—a well-traveled corridor, for example—and leave a generous supply of index cards, markers, star stickers, and pushpins within easy reach.

This is your corkboard R&D department. Whenever anyone has an idea to share with the team, they will pin it on the board. No byline. Each idea should stand on its own. Other members of the team can review the cards on the board in passing, scribbling comments or suggestions and adding stars to express enthusiasm. As cards accrue, don't let an idea pond form. On a weekly basis, move the card with the most comments and stars to the right side under the label "Testing." This indicates that the team will run a quick, high-efficiency experiment that week.

You now have a functional R&D lab for under a hundred bucks.

Running a test every week may seem like a lot of work, but is there a better use of scarce resources than trying out exciting ideas with the potential to delight stakeholders? By giving your organization, or just yourself, a designated place to put possibilities, a pipeline that feeds into a validation process, you will inevitably boost ideaflow. Once one of those ideas successfully becomes a reality, company-wide creativity will rise even higher. A prominent corkboard R&D department makes the value of experimentation visible to everyone.

Some friends of ours at DIRECTV did something similar out of necessity. They wanted to establish a user-centered innovation lab but couldn't secure a dedicated space at company headquarters. So they got creative, commandeering a stretch of hallway. The impact of this rogue maneuver was incredibly positive across the organization. People who weren't "supposed" to be involved with innovation ended up getting hooked as they passed the board in the hallway, voluntarily contributing to the lab's efforts with their own ideas. They couldn't help it, passing by all those interesting projects on their way to the coffee machine. Visibility and enthusiasm are tightly linked.

Whether you have a corkboard R&D department or a hallway innovation lab, you're never committing to anything more than a quick and dirty test with any idea. If the experiment conclusively fails, you never have to let it nag at you again. At least, not in its current form. Like Thomas Edison, you've successfully identified another thing that won't work. If the idea shows promise, on the other hand, it will be that much easier to justify a little more effort to develop it further. Over time, you will clear the bottleneck of untested ideas and restore a steady flow of fresh creativity.

Bob McKim, one of the progenitors of Stanford's d.school, advocated for keeping a "bug list." The things that bug us tend to spark the best contributions. For example, Bette Nesmith Graham was a secretary at a bank when she first switched to the new IBM electric typewriter. It bugged the heck out of her that the keys were so sensitive they led to more typos. Since she painted signs on the side, a novel solution suggested itself: a tiny bottle filled with white tempera paint for quickly covering up mistakes. Graham patented Liquid Paper in 1958, eventually selling the business she built around it to Gillette for $47.5 million.

Paste this useful prompt right at the top of the corkboard to kickstart contributions: "It bugs me that . . ." You may find that your colleagues have great ideas for making your workplace culture more energizing and creative. An idea can be something as simple as "No more morning meetings." It would be easy enough to test that notion before making it company policy. If everyone finds that they get more done and still meet as often as actually needed, commit. If the change leads to unforeseen problems, modify the policy based on what you've learned and try again. Continue until the suggestion is either validated or conclusively ruled out.

PICK LESS, TEST MORE

Winnowing can be done, but an ideal innovation environment wouldn't involve any winnowing at all. There is no question that experimentation trumps picking every time. No matter how good your track record for spotting winners might be, you can't beat the learning you get from real-world tests. It may sound tedious or just impossible to test everything, but once you learn the quick and effective experiment techniques in the next two chapters, you'll find that running useful tests—and ruling out vast swaths of ideas at a time—is faster and easier than you think. Then you'll *really* need to amp up ideaflow.

Our friend Nicholas Thorne is one of the original partners at Prehype, an exceptionally innovative venture development firm. Prehype launches its own ventures and invests in other start-ups, so the team is constantly evaluating new ideas and putting money behind the most promising ones. In the beginning, Nicholas and his partner Henrik Werdelin, the disciplined documenter we met in chapter 2, tried the usual venture capital approach of picking winners. It didn't work very well.

"We've learned that we have terrible intuition about which of our countless ideas are good ones," he told us. Instead, Prehype began to rely more and more on experimentation. As they learned to trust test results over opinions and hypothetical projections, the company's hit ratio drastically improved. Today, they hope to dispense with picking entirely. "We're trying to get ourselves out of the 'Is this a good idea?' thought process altogether," Thorne said.

Prehype tests ideas using a process they call "signal mining." At one time, the team might be weighing investments in a gut biome suppository, a co-working company, and a van-commuting app. To glimpse the future, they advertise these not-yet-existent offerings to millions of people through social media. Then they track how many people click through. The data generated by each experiment leads to another, more refined version of the pitch until the demand is undeniable. In this way, Prehype rapidly vets possibilities in the marketplace, reducing the uncertainty involved in any single investment.

Thanks to this elaborate validation system, Prehype explores many more directions at once than any of its competitors can. Now having racked up multiple billion-dollar exits, Thorne carries great credibility when he advocates against any picking whatsoever. He knows enough to know that he doesn't know.

As a venture capitalist, Thorne can benefit from a diverse portfolio of businesses, taking multiple bets at once and hedging his risks. Founders have no such luxury. VCs abhor dilettantes. They invest in entrepreneurs who pursue a single business idea obsessively. You can't have multiple half-finished projects and prototypes underway at once if you expect serious investors to commit to your idea. The real risk for an entrepreneur, Thorne told us, isn't failing to build a successful business but succeeding in building a good-enough one. Clear failure is great because it means you can pick up stakes and move on to something more promising. But what if the idea doesn't fail unambiguously? What if it *kind of* works? How do you know whether it's successful enough to justify your commitment? Entrepreneurs aren't the only ones who struggle with this question.

Consider the opportunity cost of launching any business. It takes years to get the typical start-up off the ground. The only way to be sure you're getting the best possible return on that investment of time and energy is to think up many different business possibilities, test each one, and refine based on what you learn, just as with any other kind of idea. In Thorne's experience, however, very few entrepreneurs go to the effort of considering *any* alternatives before committing to the first good one they have. If they manage to become profitable, they consider it a success, never realizing that their second or third idea might have achieved far greater heights with less effort.

Just because something turns a profit doesn't mean it's the best possible use of your time. "You have to ask: What other ideas are out there?" Thorne said. "Is this the best idea for me?" Again, the only way for an aspiring entrepreneur to know for sure is to fill the funnel with lots of business ideas and then test them. This calls for patience that most entrepreneurs don't possess. "The trick as a VC," Thorne said, "is holding entrepreneurs in the blocks a little longer to evaluate their options."

Even with the signal mining Prehype offers entrepreneurs, many still resist exploration. "Testing is exhausting," Thorne explained. "It's easier to say, 'This is a pretty good idea.' It takes discipline to hold yourself back, to try more than one thing, to ask, 'Can I approach this differently?'" Of course, the payoff lies in the difference between a nicely profitable little business and a billion-dollar exit. Counterintuitive as it sounds, there really is no distinguishing between the two at the start. "We've seen our wackiest ideas become big businesses," Thorne said. "Selling a monthly box of dog treats and toys is now worth $2.5 billion. BARK has performed much better than businesses that were objectively better in terms of market analyses and research. We've learned viscerally that trivial ideas can be huge. So trying to be a good picker feels wrong. I'd rather play probabilities."

~

Now that we've established the value of experimentation, the question remains, how do you actually *do* it? How do you build the kind of fast and effective experimental pipeline that makes a company like Prehype so extraordinarily effective at validating ideas? When we talk about testing, your mind may go straight to heavy-duty, high-risk investments of time, money, and overall bandwidth. Let go of that mentality. You'll be surprised by how much you can learn by something as simple as walking down the street and asking a stranger, "Wanna buy this?" A rough prototype or a few simple questions can eliminate 80 percent of the possibilities on your list with 20 percent of the investment involved in a formal, bureaucratic testing process. Always seek to maximize experimental efficiency. A well-designed experiment delivers a big payload of actionable information in return for a tiny amount of time, energy, and money. You invest more effort only when the results warrant it.

"You can't help but recognize traction," Thorne told us. "Things that aren't working are always 'Maybe this is working, and maybe it's not.' Good ideas are abundantly clear. Everything becomes a lot easier. Exponentially easier." Promising numbers deserve a closer look, but when the results are unambiguously great, when everything gets much easier, move on to the next stage of development.

5.

Put Your Ideas to the Test

I n 2014, a global real estate company with over a hundred shopping centers and tens of billions of dollars in assets under management faced a small but serious problem. For some time, rents had been plummeting on the fourth floor of its luxury mall in a major urban center. Hoping to lure affluent office workers to shop and eat at the new mall, the company had spared no expense, and the mosaic-lined, dome-topped fourth floor was the pièce de résistance. Hop an elevator and you could enjoy panoramic views of the entire city.

Unfortunately, few people ever did that. It was a ghost town on four, and fourth-floor tenants struggled and succumbed one after the other. No matter what the company tried, it simply couldn't drive enough foot traffic to four to keep those stores viable. To address this problem, management held a brainstorming session. There, about ten minutes in, someone dropped a big old anchor that would steer all the subsequent discussion.

"Let's build a beer garden."

What a great idea! After all, what paired better with a beautiful view than a frosty lager? After a long day at work, local employees could sample organic microbrews while surveying the streets like Greek gods slurping ambrosia from the heights of Mount Olympus. The brainstorming continued, but the gravitational pull of that anchor was irresistible. Every subsequent suggestion showed its influence:

"Forget the beer garden for a sec. What about . . . a *wine* garden?"

Charming as the notion of a beer garden seemed in that conference room, the company wasn't going to invest more money in a failing endeavor without confirming *desirability*. Would shoppers even want to drink beer on the fourth floor of a mall? Would a beer garden convince more people to brave the elevators—and, more important, do a little shopping while they were up there? For a business, the question of desirability *must* precede feasibility. It doesn't matter whether you *can* offer a product or service if nobody wants it. But how do you confirm desire for something that doesn't yet exist?

The company started by asking the customers what they thought of the idea. A team led by the general manager brought clipboards to the food court. Approaching one diner after another, they asked the same question: "If we put a beer garden on four, would you check it out?" Of the thousand or so customers they asked, 85 percent replied in the affirmative. Just like the execs in the conference room, the food-court diners had no trouble envisioning how nice a beer garden with city views might be.

With a clear majority of customers in favor of the project, the company invested hundreds of thousands of dollars in building out a beer garden. The new facility featured premium brews on draft, an array of gourmet bites, and luxurious seating. Signage on the lower floors and a social media campaign directed shoppers to enjoy the new offering. All the company had to do now was wait for that inevitable flood of customers. The fourth floor was as good as saved.

A month later, the general manager checked in for a progress report and discovered that the flood had yet to arrive. In fact, the new beer garden had drawn fewer than a dozen customers a night. Impossible! Over eight hundred shoppers had promised they'd come! It isn't possible that they all *lied* to us, is it?

This is what would have happened at most companies, anyway. Luckily, the general manager and her colleagues had reached out to us before tackling this problem. Having embraced the experimentation techniques you'll learn over the next few chapters, they were fully prepared when those food-court customers earnestly proclaimed their interest in a fourth-floor beer garden. The company already understood there's a difference between what people *say* they'll do and what they actually *will*. Behavior proves desirability, not surveys. To know whether you have something of value to others, you must dangle it in front of them and see if they bite (or sip). The question isn't "Do we have the capacity to do this?" but rather "Would anyone want it if we did?" Not "Can we build it?" but "Should we?" As Charles Eames once said, "The first question of design is not how it should look, but if it should even be."

With the survey results in hand, the general manager and her team designed a quick, cheap experiment. With printed table tents in the food court and posts on the mall's social media channels, they directed customers to the fourth floor for a selection of free wine and beer. No fancy seating, no bar, just a folding table, wine and beer by the bottle, and a single person to take IDs and pour. Every Saturday over the course of a month, the company ran the same incredibly cheap test, and each time they drew fewer than a dozen customers to the fourth floor.

"If we couldn't get people to come upstairs with free wine and beer," the general manager told us, "we realized we needed to rethink the whole beer garden from the ground up." That's something they still had runway to do, because instead of sinking hundreds of thousands of dollars into what seemed like a very promising idea, the company had disproved its desirability for a few hundred bucks *total*.

To test your ideas, you must make them real, but only real enough to prove behavior, whether the sought-for action is a purchase or something completely non-transactional, like replying to an email or following a new internal procedure. The purpose of an experiment is to prove a hypothesis: "If I do X, person Y will respond by doing Z." As any scientist will tell you, the work lies in *disproving* hypotheses. Design experiments not to confirm your existing beliefs but to challenge them. That's where the most valuable creative inputs are hiding: the gap between what you imagine to be true about the situation and the situation as it really is.

As we'll see, it's OK to offer something that exists as a prototype, as at the shopping mall, or even something you haven't made yet at all—there are ways to mitigate those risks and keep customers happy, as we'll see. To ensure success, you must give yourself as many at-bats as possible. That means maximizing experimental efficiency. In this chapter, we will show you how to put even your biggest ideas to the test.

OVERCOME RESISTANCE

You may already be thinking, *That could never work at my company.* If you lead the charge for experimentation at your organization, you can count on various forms of opposition. When a creative culture hasn't yet been established, people resist testing for various reasons, each of which needs to be addressed strategically if you hope to prevail.

A software engineer we know at a premium audio technology brand conceived of an innovative way to record high-fidelity live performances in one take using several smartphones. Each phone records audio and video for a single performer in a group. During the performance, the software automatically determines which one's performance is most prominent and seamlessly switches the video feed. When the singer sings, it automatically cuts to the close-up. Ditto for the lead guitarist. When everyone's playing together again, back to a wide shot. The resulting video looks like it's been professionally produced by a multi-person crew, but a teenage garage band could pull it off without help. To the company's software engineer, this idea seemed tailor-made for musicians making videos for TikTok and other online video platforms. Offering it might serve to introduce the company's premium audio technology to a new generation of content creators.

With software, the most obvious test for desirability is a downloadable beta version. While a free download isn't as definitive a proof as an actual purchase, the data can still be valuable in honing the value proposition. When the engineer suggested this approach, however, the company's leaders categorically refused to let him incorporate the brand name in the app. "One of our products available for *free*?" they scoffed. "We're a professional brand. No way."

In the engineer's view, the company's branding was essential to the experiment. How else could they determine whether production professionals would trust the software in a real-world scenario? To win a core audience of experts and tailor the software to their needs, the experiment needed the brand. But the notion was a nonstarter at the company based on the implicit belief that "anything we make is going to be huge," a common assumption at large companies and one that is nearly always wrong. In fact, no one will notice most of your failed experiments. (That's a good thing.)

Like the software engineer, you will run into many objections when you first propose experiments within your organization. Some will blindside you. To anticipate and work around objections, try a tool we call a retroactive. Project yourself into the future and look back at your pitch as though it has already been rejected. From that perspective, list every objection that your most paranoid self can imagine.

It sounds simple, but a retroactive will quickly reveal holes in your argument. By mentally positioning yourself after a future failure, it becomes much easier to see flaws and potential missteps that didn't register in your consciousness beforehand. Thanks to your cognitive biases, committing yourself to an idea makes the downsides harder to notice even as they remain obvious to others. That's why objections catch us flat-footed when we propose an experiment to key stakeholders. We didn't *want* to see them. Flip the frame with a retroactive and the problems in your plan will be visible once more.

The audio engineer could have used a retroactive to overcome internal objections to his experiment. If he'd spent even ten minutes with his notebook imagining a scenario where leaders categorically refused to allow the beta to proceed, concerns about the trademark would almost certainly have made the list.

Once you've created your list of potential objections, strategize a response to each one. In most cases, resistance to experimentation boils down to misperceived risk. If leaders see an experiment as a big investment of time and money that's likely to fail, they aren't going to go for it. After all, a successful test isn't a final product being sold to customers. It's just a chance to run even more tests.

To circumvent this mindset, design experiments so cheap and quick that the risk doesn't even register. Choose something you can do tomorrow, however imperfectly—even better if you can do it without any buy-in from above. Your first few tests at an organization shouldn't tie in to major initiatives, either. Start close to home by running an experiment that relates mostly to your own work and doesn't touch on the live wire of a major profit center or time-sensitive process. Even if the experiment isn't enormously significant, follow through and document the process. Then show your work. A few intriguing results will overcome internal resistance to testing better than any argument. Once you show how even a little testing can indicate desirability and therefore reduce risk, leaders will be more likely to approve more ambitious efforts. Start small. Start today.

Resistance to testing can be frustrating, but remember that it isn't a matter of intelligence or business acumen. Conventional business education runs directly counter to the innovation mindset. In fact, the more experienced and competent your colleagues and managers, the *more* likely they are to be wary of experimentation. A study of over a hundred start-ups by our Stanford colleagues Michael Leatherbee and Riitta Katila found that MBAs in particular resist the testing demanded by lean start-up methodology. Once you're comfortable making plans and then following through on them, it requires a major shift in attitude to use real-world tests to validate your assumptions instead.

Tom Wujec is a fellow at Autodesk, the maker of AutoCAD and other software for creative professionals. Over the years, Wujec has conducted design workshops around the country with people of all ages and all walks of life. At each workshop, he tasks participants with the Marshmallow Challenge: Given twenty sticks of dry spaghetti, tape, string, and a marshmallow, you have eighteen minutes to construct the tallest possible tower. According to Wujec, the crux of the challenge is the marshmallow itself. It's heavier relative to the spaghetti than people assume and requires a sturdy foundation.

Aside from engineers—who are playing with a loaded deck—the most effective tower-builders in Wujec's workshops are the kindergartners. The least effective? Recent MBAs. Not by a small margin, either. On average, kindergartners successfully build towers over twenty inches tall. Business school grads build ten-inch towers on average. Why the gap? *The kindergartners know that they don't know.* So they try things. Since they have no preconceived notions about, for example, the tensile strength of dried pasta, they will add the marshmallow to the tower early on. When the structure collapses, they have time to try a better approach. The MBAs, in contrast, arrive at the table as fully accredited spaghetti engineers, carefully building an elaborate structure based on false assumptions.

"Business students are trained to find the single right plan," Wujec explained in a TED talk. "And then they execute on it. And then what happens is, when they put the marshmallow on the top, they run out of time and what happens? It's a crisis." Learn-by-doing versus learn-by-thinking.

We observe the same thing in Stanford MBA students in our Launchpad program. With only so much time to launch a business, they will always try to devote the lion's share to drafting the business plan. But what good is a plan without data to demonstrate product-market fit? It takes sustained effort on our part to convince these students to let data shape their assumptions.

All of this is why you should anticipate stiff resistance to testing from otherwise intelligent and experienced business leaders. When you've been taught over and over that failing to plan is planning to fail, trying things out to see what happens seems like sacrilege. You'll have to show them otherwise.

Doing a retroactive based on what you know about your company and its business will reveal numerous potential objections to your experiment, from fears about tarnishing the company's reputation, as we saw at the premium audio technology brand, to squeamishness about the very idea of advertising products or services that don't yet exist to your customers. In each case, use that potential objection to refine your pitch. To do so, seek out concrete examples of successful experiments in similar arenas. These reveal both how much learning can be delivered by a few quick tests as well as how little risk such tests actually pose. If our friend the engineer had walked into the meeting prepared with successful examples of beta apps launched transparently by other technology brands, he might have won the approval he sought.

It won't always be so difficult to make your case. Over time, experimentation proves its value. Organizations that adopt an experimental mindset soon see how tests reduce uncertainty and save time, money, and effort. They start looking to offload their decision-making to data wherever possible. Until your organization is over the hump, however, gather successful examples of experimentation wherever you find them. Some tests are light, fast, and easy. Others, especially at companies with deeply embedded creative cultures, can be more elaborate and still be considered enormous bargains relative to simply pulling the trigger. You don't have to build a full-scale customer innovation lab overnight. Start where you are and build from there.

MAXIMIZE EXPERIMENTAL EFFICIENCY

Ideas become a reality not through planning but by doing. You need an action-oriented, experiment-driven process for the development, refinement, and implementation of your ideas. To maximize the odds of success, thought experiments must give way to *actual* experiments, even for something as simple as the font used on a website. Real-world tests outperform discussion, gut instincts, even formal market research. The dose of reality that an experiment provides punctures overconfidence and sidesteps the subconscious desire to avoid hearing no at any cost.

To make all this testing feasible, we're going to have to get scrappy by designing simple, cheap, and imperfect experiments that deliver just enough information to design better, higher-fidelity experiments down the road. The answers from each test help you ask better questions next time. That's how you get from inspiration to conviction.

Your goal when testing ideas is to maximize experimental efficiency. As you see some scrappy experiments in action below, you'll get ideas for increasing the efficiency of your own tests. Testing is easier than ever. Today's technology makes it possible to test assumptions and validate possibilities in ways undreamed-of by entrepreneurs of the past. You can easily offer an array of products or services to large numbers of people and find out who will pay for each one. Online tools like Wix, Squarespace, Canva, and Figma make it easy for non-designers to whip up posters, online advertisements, simple websites, even software interfaces, to prototype ideas. The results may not be perfect, but they'll be polished enough to test desirability with real customers. A winning idea will overcome mediocre graphic design. Even physical prototypes are within reach for novices. User-friendly software and affordable 3D printers make it possible to create nearly any shape for an experiment. While nothing will replace the work of designers, engineers, and other skilled artisans when it comes to the final product, prototyping tools offer a way to cheaply and rapidly vet different approaches in parallel. Why test one tagline, color scheme, or product shape when you can test ten at once? The more quickly and cheaply you can rule out directions, the longer you can keep trying new ones until you land on a winner.

The most creative companies test *everything*. For example, while you can attribute the success of Marvel's superhero movies to luck, or the zeitgeist, it's no coincidence that the company now previsualizes every film in its Cinematic Universe. Unlike standard storyboarding, where a key moment of each scene is sketched out prior to principal photography, "previs" involves digitally animating a scene in its entirety during the development process. Sophisticated animation tools make it possible to iron out all the camera movements, stunts, and special effects before a single actor arrives on set. In the beginning, Marvel's filmmakers used previs only for the most complicated, effects-heavy scenes in a film to get a sense of what all the real and digital elements would look like when brought together. As the tools got faster and smarter, however, Marvel expanded its use of previs to the entire running time of each film.

Why leave any aspect of your story to the day of the shoot, even a one-on-one conversation at a table? Now a director can work out the smallest kinks of pacing, story, or set design on a laptop before setting foot in the studio. As these tools become cheaper and easier to use, what makes sense for a $300 million blockbuster today will soon be standard practice for $30,000 independent films. Likewise, tests that once made sense only for global corporations are now common at two-person start-ups. With the right tools and a little effort, nearly any aspect of your idea can be prototyped and tested in the real world with reasonable fidelity.

The key to effective innovation is velocity. More tests in a given amount of time. You can't fiddle with any idea forever. Getting your experiments done quickly, ideally in parallel as part of a portfolio, means you can improve them and zero in on the most viable approach long before hitting the end of your runway.

More than any other factor, the key to this is cost. Expensive tests maximize red tape. The cheaper the experiment, the easier it is to win approval, and the more frequently you'll be able to try variations before throwing in the towel. What makes organizational innovation so difficult is the bureaucracy that keeps most ideas from getting off the ground in the first place. Complicated approval processes and other procedures—helpful and even necessary protections during day-to-day business operations—are impediments to rapid learning. Drive the cost of an experiment down and you will inevitably lower the roadblocks as well.

We brought our methods to a large and venerable industrial company. Several leaders who worked with us were each tasked with advancing a different idea. We asked the one working on a new service platform to tell us how much funding he'd need to test it with their customers.

"Thirty million, give or take."

At the risk of stating the obvious, there aren't many organizations that can afford to run a portfolio of $30 million experiments in parallel. That's why we pushed this leader to cut costs. After eliminating unnecessary features of the experiment and focusing only on immediate next steps, he came back to us with a revised estimate of $200,000. Not a bad savings! Still, we wanted him to think smaller, faster, cheaper. Looking closely at the assumptions driving his estimate, we saw that he planned to hire three full-time customer service agents to field support calls.

"Who said anything about hiring folks on annual salaries for an experiment?" we said. "*You* can be the customer service department!" In his two decades of service at the company, this leader had never hired anyone for less than a yearlong increment or at less than a full-time salary. After a little pushback at the prospect of answering calls in the middle of the night—at the d.school, founders do this routinely—he agreed that an existing team in another time zone could easily handle any calls that might come at night. Without the need for a full-time customer support staff, the cost of the experiment dropped to fifteen grand, a pittance in comparison to the usual corporate R&D investment.

Make your experiments cheaper to run and watch the obstacles fall away. Sometimes this involves cutting-edge technology, but more often it simply requires that you reexamine your assumptions. Question those, and you, too, might save $29.8 million in a single week.

GROWTH THROUGH CONTINUAL INNOVATION

You never just come up with a bunch of ideas in "idea mode" and then put them out into the world in "action mode." Forget modes. Ideation and action should feed into each in a continual cycle. Examine a rapidly growing business and you will see a feedback loop driving it. Testing, feedback, iteration. When growth is off the charts, it's because doing and learning are linked. Likewise, a stagnating business inevitably operates without sufficient feedback, or there's an institutional lack of willingness to act on the feedback it gathers. Implementing ideas without tapping into outcomes is like running with your eyes closed. You can charge forward as swiftly and confidently as you like—you're still going to eat concrete.

The two most powerful brands in athletic footwear are Nike and Adidas. Both companies were built by obsessive tinkerers who worked closely with athletes to refine products in real-world conditions. These innovators understood that changing a shoe's design is pointless if you have no way to test that iteration and compare its effectiveness with what you had before. Add all the stripes and swooshes you like—you can't judge the speed of a shoe from its appearance.

The German shoemaker Adi Dassler loved competing in track and field and got his start in athletic footwear by refining the spiked shoes used for these events. At first, he tested his creations himself to see how they performed in the field, but he eventually decided that world-class shoes required world-class athletes to test them. Pioneering the idea of athletic sponsorships, Dassler convinced star athletes like Lina Radke and Jesse Owens to wear his shoes in Olympic competitions. The media coverage helped the business grow. More important, Dassler could now observe great athletes using his shoes in real-world competitions. This was a huge improvement over lacing up in his backyard.

When the head coach of Germany's Olympic track and field team reached out to Dassler, this opened up another, even more direct source of feedback for the creative cobbler. All of Germany's young track-and-field athletes began wearing Dassler's designs and reporting on the results. This ongoing flow of feedback proved essential to what became Adidas.

Decades later and five thousand miles away, University of Oregon track-and-field coach Bill Bowerman wanted to improve sneaker performance not to sell a product but to help his players win competitions. Unlike Dassler, Bowerman didn't know the first thing about making shoes but, as we've seen, you don't always need specialized skills to run quick and cheap experiments that test your assumptions. Once you've validated a direction, you can always bring in experts to execute on it properly. Instead of spending years learning a new craft and making his ideal shoes himself, Bowerman tested his ideas by modifying the sneakers his athletes were already wearing.

"He was constantly sneaking into our lockers and stealing our footwear," Phil Knight, a member of the track team at the time, later wrote. "He'd spend days tearing them apart, stitching them back up, then hand them back with some minor modification, which made us either run like deer or bleed." As coach of the team, Bowerman had a laboratory and its mice. The ultimate goal of all this prototyping was lightness. "One ounce sliced off a pair of shoes, [Bowerman] said, is equivalent to 55 pounds over one mile," Knight wrote. Reducing weight required trying out a vast range of alternative materials, from kangaroo leather to cod skin, and tracking the effect on athletes' run times.

Years later, Knight convinced Bowerman to partner with him on importing Onitsuka running shoes from Japan. Again, Bowerman tinkered, using his athletes to test each variation: "[Every] race had two results for Bowerman," Knight wrote. "There was the performance of his runners, and there was the performance of their shoes." The difference was, Bowerman could now send his ideas to Japan to be realized by Onitsuka's professional designers. Once the product came close enough to Bowerman's vision, Bowerman and Knight decided to launch their own company to achieve the shortest possible feedback loop. Nike was born.

Close the circuit. You won't supercharge innovation at your organization until you've established a short, direct feedback loop for all your ideas. It's time to stop running in the dark.

THE WELL-DESIGNED EXPERIMENT

When Reed Hastings and Marc Randolph first came up with the idea of sending movies through the mail, they discovered that VHS tapes were too bulky to ship in a cost-effective way. With no alternate delivery mechanism available, they shelved the notion until learning about the new DVD video format available in Japan. A five-inch plastic disc would be cheap enough to mail, so that was one obstacle out of the way. What else would need to be true for this Netflix idea to work? For one, you'd have to be able to mail one of these DVDs to someone without the post office breaking it. Since the new format wasn't available in the United States yet, Hastings and Randolph tested this assumption by mailing a music CD to themselves. When the collection of Patsy Cline's greatest hits arrived intact, they knew they'd taken another step toward validating their business model. Today, Netflix is worth hundreds of billions of dollars, but the experiment that started it cost under twenty bucks.

Experimental validation is an incremental process. Once Hastings and Randolph knew they could mail DVDs to customers, they took the next step forward by building a simple website. E-commerce was still in its infancy in the late nineties, so pretty much every assumption about online selling required thorough testing. They would meticulously build out a version of a movie's web page to see how different combinations of images and copy and links translated into disc sales. (They started renting movies later.) After two weeks of painstaking development, they would run a test and, more often than not, it would fail.

"We'd look at each other and say, 'We just wasted two weeks,'" Randolph recalled in an interview. "And we'd say, 'Okay, faster.' And we'd cut some corners and do a test a week. And it would fail. And then we'd cut some more corners and we'd begin to do a test every other day. And then pretty soon a test every day. And soon we were doing four and five tests in the same day." There was nothing painstaking or meticulous about the development process by that point. They were slapping test pages together in hours instead of weeks. But Randolph and Hastings realized they could still get usable data with these cheap, fast, and imperfect experiments. Designing the wrong page perfectly wouldn't win them any awards, whereas a successful test would ring bells with customers despite all the spelling errors and broken links. Progress wasn't a matter of having good ideas but rather "building this system and this process and this culture for testing lots of bad ideas."

Never put what you *can* do (feasibility) ahead of what the market *wants* (desirability). Once we pinpoint desire with an experiment, we can nearly always find a feasible way of satisfying that desire. The first few cycles of experimentation should always focus on desirability. Do people want this? If not, what about this instead? Wherever possible, prototype in parallel.

Which option do people prefer more than all the others combined? Once you see a huge spike of desire for an idea, you'll be amazed by how quickly feasibility gets figured out.

Validate a single assumption with each experiment. Does the website visitor click? Does the customer make the call? Does the colleague show up to the meeting? The first few experiments should always be faster and cheaper than instinct suggests. See what you can accomplish in under two hours. If the test you want to run will take a day or longer, reexamine your assumptions. Drill down to a small question with a big payoff. You're just entering the maze. You have no idea where it will lead. Are you going to turn left? Or right?

Above all, never build anything that someone hasn't already requested. For example, if you conceive of an app that does X, don't build the app just to gauge the demand. Instead, *be* the app. In the tech world, this is sometimes called "turking," in reference to the famous Mechanical Turk, an eighteenth-century chess-playing automaton that turned out to be an elaborate hoax. (A human chess player was hidden inside the "machine.") The concept was further popularized when Amazon named its crowdsourcing engine after the automaton. When in doubt, turk it. Before you buy a single chair, put up some signs and see who comes to the fourth floor for a beer. Surveys are useless. Judge desire by people's actions, not their words. Incorporate a transaction into every test. For the experiment to succeed, people must go, click, buy, join, sign. There must be a commitment. Whatever the offering, find a way to simulate it and watch how people respond. When the demand is there, the data will be unambiguous.

What follows is a simple but fully functional experimentation process that can be adapted to your needs. Consider it a starting template and let your experiences guide you in refining an experimental approach that works best for your organization.

Design the test

An effective way to put an experiment or a series of experiments into motion within an organization is to schedule a postmortem to review what you will have discovered. Decide in advance the results you plan to discuss at that meeting. Then, work backward from that fixed point on everyone's calendar to figure out what each person will need to do and by when to ensure that the meeting happens on schedule.

Remember, if an experiment will take more than a couple hours of effort, especially early on, come up with a simpler one. Think direct, informal, personal. There is always another, more *obvious* way to measure desire, and it usually involves elbow grease and shoe leather, not VC funding. What can you do with a stack of paper, a Sharpie, and some tape? What about a webpage, brochure, poster, or wireframe hacked together using user-friendly design software like Canva or Adobe Spark?

What if you simply walked outside with your product and offered it to a real person? Henrik Werdelin and Nicholas Thorne started BARK by showing a prototype box of dog treats and toys to their canine-loving acquaintances. "Oh, that's awesome," their friends would say. "I'll sign up when you're ready."

"We have Square on our phones," they'd reply. "We can take your money right now." Werdelin and Thorne signed up dozens of customers this way, swiping credit cards using their phones when the company was nothing but "a WordPress site that didn't really work." Note that, unlike the mall shoppers at the beginning of the chapter who simply affirmed their willingness to patronize a beer garden, these dog owners were actually completing transactions—that's the kind of data you want.

Seek momentum, not perfection. Each cheap, fast, and imperfect experiment provides data that will lead you to a better one that delivers more accurate and relevant answers. Thought experiments just lead to more thinking.

The specific tactic you use will depend on your context:

- Add a button to the website.

- Distribute a poll internally.

- Design and distribute brochures, signs, or door hangers with a URL call to action or QR code that you can track.

- Send emails with different subject lines or offers and compare open rates, clicks, or replies.

- Make a post or send a message to targeted users on social media and track responses.

- Build two possible slides to cap off a presentation and test them with colleagues.

- Give meeting participants the ability to vote between options.

- Add offers to customer service calls and track responses.

Don't worry if a test seems *too* simple. Do it and keep going. You can always raise the bar next time. Start as simple and small as you can.

If you have a mailing list, don't email everyone at once. Use a small segment of the list first to make sure you're on the right track before expanding to a larger one. If you don't already have a mailing list or a customer base to work with, you'll need to find participants another way, but don't rely too much on close friends and family. Their incentive will be to support you, not prove you wrong. Also, they may not be representative of your target market. Reach out to the people your solution is intended to help. Are people complaining about this problem on Twitter or Facebook?

Reach out to them there. Are they congregating somewhere on Reddit or Twitch or Discord instead? Ditto. Go where the people with the problem are and make them the offer directly. Do they want it or not?

When you make your offer, remove any conditional language. Don't be tentative or people will doubt you from the start. Forget "We're thinking of doing X" or "Would you be interested in Y?" Werdelin and Thorne showed up at dog runs with their Square credit card readers in hand. Bring that level of commitment to every test no matter what the scale. Otherwise, you won't be able to trust in the results.

Establish your hypothesis

Establishing a hypothesis is a crucial and often overlooked step in informal experiments. Decide in advance exactly what you're setting out to prove. What variable will you change, and what do you expect to happen when you do? Which metrics will you track? Be specific, get it down *in writing*, and make sure all the stakeholders sign off. If you are vague about what you're hoping to discover, everyone will be tempted to revise the hypothesis to match the results.

To determine the most desirable color for a new product, it isn't enough to see which hue generates the most clicks. Decide in advance how many clicks you'll need at a minimum to proceed. If you fail to drive sufficient traffic to the page, you'll need to run the experiment differently next time. Four clicks on blue and two on yellow don't count as decisive evidence, as tempting as that may be when time is short. Lay out your goals, including the volume of data you hope to gather, and tweak your experiment until it meets the bar instead of tweaking your bar to meet the experiment.

Establishing your hypothesis first forces you to be clear about the single behavior or decision you're hoping to drive. If you're going to measure the impact of increasing X, don't simultaneously fiddle with Y and Z. That will only muddy the results. The goal is to compare apples to apples as closely as possible.

Gather data

Establish a baseline *before* changing anything. If you're testing the effect of a new sign on foot traffic into your store, measure the existing traffic first. Take daily and seasonal variations into account, too. If you set a baseline for retail traffic in July and run an experiment in December, that will skew your results.

Work with what you've got. Most large companies keep careful track of their key metrics, but there are plenty of organizations that aren't fastidious. Don't let the lack of perfect data stand in your way. A start-up, for example, probably doesn't have a baseline, and that's OK. Run an A/B test, changing a single key variable between the two, and compare results. For example, you can split incoming web traffic between two landing pages, compare the effectiveness of promotional signage between two store locations, give different welcome scripts to two customer greeters, or send different subject lines to two segments of a mailing list.

In other words, establish a baseline if you can, but don't let the whole year go by just so you can get a complete picture of seasonal demand before moving forward. Speed matters. When it comes to ideas, now beats never.

Close the loop

After each test, compare your results to the baseline, or to one another. When you experiment all the time, it's surprisingly easy to forget that you're experimenting. To offer a personal example, Jeremy and his wife were talking about how her energy flagged at the same time each day under the new homeschooling schedule. Discussing the problem, she suddenly remembered that she had changed the schedule a few weeks prior to see if it would increase the kids' engagement, only to forget her intention. Remembering the hypothesis she'd set out to test, she could mindfully review the results of the change and decide how to proceed.

You might think a team at a large organization would be less likely to lose the thread of an experiment than an overworked parent, but this happens all the time at companies. It's easy to change something and call it an "experiment." If you don't sit down for a postmortem, however, you'll never analyze the data, let alone act on it. In fact, this is where we see most experiments at organizations fail. The new way might work better, or it might not. You'll never know for sure if you don't evaluate the results against your hypothesis. How was the efficiency of the experiment—was there a good ratio of effort to learning? Did you get a clear answer, even if it wasn't the one you'd hoped for, or were the results inconclusive? What can you do differently next time to deliver more significant and actionable data?

Experimentation lowers the bar for trying things, but if you lower the bar so much that your efforts lack rigor, you're not learning. You're turning the steering wheel, but you've still got a blindfold on. If, as in the example above, you didn't see more than a handful of clicks on any of your color options, figure out how to boost overall traffic to the site. Inconclusive data is often a sign that the experiment itself needs work. Fix the test before you change the offering (more on this in the next chapter). Any idea looks lousy in the light of a poorly designed experiment. You shouldn't move forward with or abandon a possibility until you've either proved its worth or revealed a more promising avenue of exploration. Most early efforts at experimentation should be followed by better experiments—true failure takes much more work than that.

If you're still struggling, ask a colleague outside the project to cross-examine you on your approach. It's easier to spot someone else's errors in judgment. Get someone with a very different perspective—different department, even a different industry—to look at your hypothesis, methods, and results. Let them tear it all apart without mercy. Which of your assumptions aren't merited? The idea isn't on trial here. That's the experiment's job. It's the experiment itself that needs work. Is it giving you good data, or only obscuring the truth?

The best way to ensure that you close the loop on an experiment is to book the postmortem at the start of the process. Carve out a time that works for everyone before the experiment even begins. That'll give everyone a deadline and ensure proper follow-through. Otherwise, your exploratory efforts will get sidelined by more urgent, though ultimately less important, demands.

Revise, repeat, and, when necessary, pivot

In most cases, a well-designed experiment gives you the data you need to design a better one, a more refined test that answers more specific questions and gets you even closer to the right idea. Experiment for direction, not destination.

A definitive yes is terrific, of course. When you achieve the winning combination—product-market fit, for example—you know it. The right idea doesn't work just a little better than the alternatives. It delivers dramatically superior results. You should see a big gap between option A and options B through Z. This can be hard to spot if you're testing only one variation at a time, however. The advantage of running multiple tests in parallel is that you can quickly see a range of possible outcomes.

For example, if you mention a potential baby name to a friend, they will express enthusiasm for it no matter what. If you mention ten potential names, one will probably delight them relative to all the rest. When an idea works, it blows the lid off.

As fun as it can be to succeed, don't underestimate the value of an unambiguous failure. It means you gave the idea a fair shot and now you know for certain: it's a dud.

As the head of Michelin's Customer Innovation Labs, Philippe Barreaud has learned to prize a definitive no. Organizations are naturally biased toward the successful completion of projects, lending undeserved momentum to ideas without proven desirability. Rather than accept failure and change course, leaders pour more money and effort into realizing ideas that nobody wants. Low-risk experimentation frees you from the incentive-driven push to succeed at all costs. "Half of the value we bring to the organization is in killing stuff," Barreaud told us. "The more ideas you kill, the more resources you free up for other things that have a chance of going all the way. The stuff that will resonate with customers."

To ensure you're always making better mistakes instead of repeating the same ones in different forms, keep track of everything you test, *especially* the failures. As we saw with Netflix and VHS tapes, a failed idea can find second life thanks to a change in technology or shift in the marketplace. Rather than go back to square one, you can return to your data to get a jump start.

There is no ideal experiment that will answer all your questions and resolve all stakeholder concerns. Be patient, not perfectionistic, and don't get too attached. Innovation is fishing, not hunting.

"Don't get hung up on the prototype as a solution," Barreaud tells Michelin's leaders, "but as something we do so we can learn. It will give us an opportunity to readjust at a later stage. Know that you will still have time to narrow it down. Early stage, you're still diverging." Experiments are how we unearth hidden opportunities. You're listening for the buzz of interest and attention. Sometimes you can even pick out an idea that's adjacent to the one you're trying to validate. Chasing the wrong idea can lead you to the right one if you're willing to pivot. Barreaud emphasizes the importance of putting ideas into the world to learn what's *worth* putting into the world.

At Michelin, a team developed a tool for managing tire pressure, an ongoing concern for drivers in the off-roading community. When they showed the prototype to customers, however, the response was tepid. This was something off-road enthusiasts already knew how to handle. The added convenience of high-tech tire pressure sensors didn't offer enough added value to capture their interest. What they really wanted to know more about, the team discovered, were the off-road trails themselves. These drivers were always hungry for tips on familiar trails and searching for new ones to explore. Pivoting, Michelin prototyped an app enabling off-road drivers to share location-based tips with one another. In contrast to the tire-pressure sensor idea, this one caught fire right away. Off-road advice was not a direction the team would have considered while sitting at their desks. Putting the "wrong" idea in the hands of real users yielded a valuable insight. It often does.

In the next chapter, we'll look at effective experimentation in action across business contexts. As you'll see, it's not about designing the "perfect" experiment as much as about learning quickly. This requires the flexibility the rubber experts at Michelin displayed when their idea went flat. Ask yourself: Are you willing to deviate from the "plan"? Can you let go of your first idea to grab hold of a better one? As Barreaud told us, "Most of the time, the *problem* is the problem." If you're not willing to reframe the problem to explore a more productive avenue, you'll end up spinning your tires.

6.

Make the World Your Lab

Inspiration suggests the combination of an
active principle—hard-earned expertise—with
a passive principle—unencumbered and
trustful receptivity.

—ROBERT GRUDIN, *THE GRACE OF*
GREAT THINGS: CREATIVITY
AND INNOVATION

You now have a step-by-step process for testing assumptions and validating solutions. To go from following a rote process to adopting a mindset, it will help to see experiment-driven innovation in action across different contexts. Real-world examples should inspire insights into the experimental approach best suited to your needs.

At Eisai, the Tokyo-based pharmaceutical company, Bill Gibson is a senior leader in the group tackling Alzheimer's disease, the most common form of dementia. According to the Alzheimer's Association, 6.2 million people over the age of sixty-five have this form of dementia in the United

States alone, and by 2050 that number is projected to reach 12.7 million. The pressure to find new therapies is enormous, but moving forward based on untested assumptions can be risky. To respond as effectively as possible to the challenge of Alzheimer's, the industry must rigorously test its assumptions, whether inside or outside the lab. It's too risky to do otherwise.

After completing a leadership program at the d.school, Gibson wanted to work with us to help bring an experimental mindset to Eisai. Despite endless, rigorous pharmaceutical testing in the company's vast laboratories, the "think, then decide" binary approach to idea generation and selection remained entrenched elsewhere. To drive continual improvement and make a real impact on Alzheimer's, Eisai would need to get in the habit of testing *all* its assumptions, pharmaceutical and otherwise. This was especially true due to the extraordinary pressure to accelerate. "Before we jump to an answer, we must identify assumptions and alternatives," Gibson told us. "If we discipline ourselves to first identify and then really question the assumptions we're operating under, we will naturally begin to develop alternatives that could be game-changing."

We spend our working lives making decisions based on what we think the results will be. The practice of regularly conducting real-world experiments teaches us just how wrong we can be in even our most basic assumptions about how our business works. To make experimentation an ingrained habit, begin by seizing even the smallest opportunity to let data inform your decision-making. For Gibson, this meant running tests on day-to-day activities. In fact, he realized he could run a test on something as simple as an internal email.

To encourage serendipity and collaboration among the various teams in the Alzheimer's group, Gibson established a monthly forum for people to share informal updates and toss out new ideas. To maximize attendance, he ran A/B tests with his email invite subject lines. This was a bit of a shift at a company that routinely tests ten thousand pharmaceutical compounds in its labs. Could an informal little test involving dozens of recipients and no control group accomplish anything useful? As it turns out, Bill's experiment taught him valuable lessons about the power of specificity. Today, all his call-to-action emails announce their subject, desired action, and timing right at the top, and that bit of learning is spreading throughout the organization. Beyond that single lesson, Gibson's timely injection of experimental thinking has opened Eisai up to quick, cheap, informal testing that complements the scrupulous approach its scientists use to develop new medicines.

"We're finding ways to do quick-hit learning exercises," Gibson told us. "For example, I wanted to explore the question of how patients start a conversation with their primary care doctor around cognitive impairment." Rather than plan and execute a formal market research campaign over the course of weeks or months, Gibson polled other Eisai employees: Would you rather use a self-administered test or visit your doctor for an evaluation? "We're all people for whom this could be a reality," Gibson explained. "And we found that people were more comfortable talking to a general practitioner even though at-home screening might be more convenient." Simply polling people around the building gave Gibson a useful direction to explore. "Now, we're trying to help more primary-care physicians spot the signs of Alzheimer's and encourage routine screening."

As you read through more examples of experimentation in this chapter, pay less attention to the specifics than to the underlying curiosity. Imagine how a similar approach might demolish false assumptions undermining your own efforts or validate an idea before it becomes a wild goose.

And if you read one of these stories and think, *I'd never have made that silly assumption in the first place,* remember that other people's blind spots are easy to see. Yours are a different story.

SELL IT BEFORE YOU MAKE IT: MAN CRATES

There's a reason for the old joke about dad getting the same tie for Father's Day every year. Buying gifts for guys is a notoriously difficult task, even for other guys. Jon Beekman was a Stanford MBA student who joined our Launchpad program to solve this problem. He'd already been told by others that gifts for men was a terrible business category. Beekman doubted that assumption. On top of the usual occasions—Valentine's Day, Father's Day, birthdays, graduations—people needed gifts for male friends, colleagues, and associates for all kinds of reasons throughout the year. Since they didn't know what to get, how might a company make the process of guy-gifting quick, easy, even fun?

Beekman had noticed curated gift box businesses springing up left and right. These boxes, most clearly intended for female recipients, featured themed assortments of items at various price points. Think a physical manifestation of a *Cosmopolitan* gift guide: A beach read. A lipstick. A tube of scented moisturizer. Despite the popularity of the concept, no one had attempted a gift box for readers of *GQ* or *Esquire,* male-oriented magazines that publish more than their share of gift guides. To Beekman, this seemed like a potential solution to the guy-gifting problem.

Research into gift boxes revealed that measuring demand is a challenge. You have an array of different products to keep in stock, some of which are perishable. Without an effective way to measure the desirability of each gift box, you either underbuy and miss out on revenue or overbuy and end up with a warehouse full of random items, some of which will spoil. Beekman's business idea promised to be a logistical headache even if the concept appealed to customers.

In our accelerator program, Beekman realized that instead of trusting surveys, he could gauge the desirability of each box with an experiment. To run his test, he got a rugged pine crate (with matching crowbar) to serve as a prototype. Then he came up with six box concepts, three of which were eliminated after he realized it would be prohibitively difficult to ship alcohol. The remaining three boxes featured snacks and candy he could pick up at a big-box retailer. Beekman figured that if the crate, opening experience, and brand were strong enough to work with off-the-shelf basics, it would be even more successful with premium gifts that weren't readily available. In the meantime, he didn't want to lose momentum on his idea. If he waited until every aspect of the product was perfect before launching it, it would mean he'd waited too long.

Once Beekman generated his box concepts, he purchased one of each item and, over the course of a single-day photo shoot, arranged all three sets of items in front of the same prototype crate. He didn't have a warehouse, a supplier, a distributor—or even a backup crate!—but thanks to the photo shoot he had his first catalog. Roughing up a bare-bones website for what he dubbed "Man Crates," Beekman uploaded the product photos and assigned each crate a price that would deliver a viable profit margin. Then he ran Facebook ads to drive traffic to the site.

Visitors began to trickle in. Whenever someone bought a nonexistent crate, Beekman would immediately void the transaction. Then he'd call the customer, explain that the whole company was just a scrappy one-person start-up, and ask them for their thoughts on the product, site, and buying process. Despite the frustration they must have experienced initially, the people Beekman called were uniformly delighted by this unusual experience. Most had never been involved with a tech start-up, and all were happy to share feedback that might end up being significant. At the end of each call, Beekman gave them a 50 percent discount on a future purchase.

You may find yourself wondering why Beekman gathered feedback at this stage if surveys aren't an effective way to gauge demand. In this case, he had legitimately validated the individual's intention to purchase a Man

Crate. They had clicked the buy button and entered their credit card information. At that point, their input became highly relevant. These people were, in a very real sense, Beekman's first customers.

Offering a product that customers can't buy yet—disappointing them—strikes most leaders as too risky to attempt. It isn't. Tracking those first "disappointed" visitors in his database years later, Beekman found that many went on to become loyal customers. In the meantime, the prototype site gave him an ideal laboratory to validate his assumptions before filling a warehouse with assorted tchotchkes that might or might not sell.

"You're obviously looking for the things that work," Beekman told us, "but discovering mostly the things that don't. Learning what works is more valuable, but even learning what doesn't work helps shape your judgment and gut on what to try next."

Beekman iterated on various marketing messages to see which one resonated best, eventually zeroing in on the tagline "No bows, no ribbons, no fluff." It wouldn't have been the winner in his own mind, but there was no arguing with the data. Day after day, he kept tweaking the copy and the pricing until he felt confident about every aspect of his offering. Beekman let the market tell him what it wanted instead of deciding that he knew best. To his surprise, an experiment showed that poking fun at the competition worked really well. For the company's take on "get well" baskets, the most effective landing page tagline was: "Don't send him a gift basket. He's already hurt."

Since Beekman launched the business knowing just how many crates he could sell and at what price points, stocking inventory was simple arithmetic. But why stop there? Beekman still occasionally launches new products as "ghost crates." Any time a customer tries to put one in their shopping cart, they are compensated with a discount for their inconvenience. (There is no longer any need to allow the transaction to go through and then void it. Beekman has experimentally validated that putting a crate in the cart correlates closely enough with a purchase for the data to count, which isn't the case with every business.) Ongoing experimentation ensures that Man Crates rarely misses the mark in its merchandising decisions.

Man Crates grew rapidly using its customer-centric approach to learning, landing at spot number 51 on the Inc. 500 list of Fastest-Growing Companies in 2016. Beekman is currently launching a new start-up in another space, and you can probably guess how he's starting there, too.

BEGGING FORGIVENESS OVER
ASKING PERMISSION: CYBEX

Safety is a major concern in the fitness industry. It's ironic that a practice intended to extend life and improve health so often leads to injuries. A morning run can result in anything from a blister to a heart attack. Add weights and complex machinery into the mix and the perils multiply. In 2021, Peloton, then on a stratospheric growth trajectory, was forced to recall a new treadmill after its unusual design was alleged to have led to the death of a child and dozens of injuries. Fitness equipment is one area where frequent, iterative experimentation is even more crucial to the safe development of new ideas. There's no predicting what people will do when they climb onto an unfamiliar machine, and you can't expect them to read the manual every time.

Bill Pacheco had just been named senior director of product design at Cybex when he was given a new mandate. By the end of the year, the CEO wanted to go from number six in the treadmill category to number one. Since treadmills are the most ubiquitous type of fitness equipment, moving even three rungs up the ladder would have a dramatic effect on Cybex's bottom line. Pacheco wondered what design change could possibly have such an enormous effect on demand. Time to apply what he'd learned at the d.school.

In the typical gym, an unsupervised adult, often older, often out of shape, and with no prior experience on that particular brand of machine, charges forward on the treadmill's fast-moving conveyor belt. It's a recipe for disaster, and the internet is filled with videos of people face-planting or otherwise hurting themselves while running on a treadmill. All it takes to lose your balance is a glance to the side, especially at high speed. (Good thing gyms put all those TVs everywhere.) Meanwhile, any change to the treadmill's design raises the very real risk of introducing unexpected new dangers, as Peloton's problems illustrate. People often use unfamiliar exercise equipment without asking for help or following instructions. The first question when changing any piece of equipment is "What's the worst that could happen if someone were to misuse this without proper supervision?"

Pacheco knew the dangers that treadmills posed. In fact, many potential users avoided treadmills because of that perceived risk. For every clueless newbie who misuses one and ends up injured, there are many more too intimidated to even try one. How might Cybex make a treadmill welcoming to hesitant gym-goers? Answering that question might spur the demand the CEO sought.

Noodling on this prompt, Pacheco observed people on Cybex treadmills in a variety of gym settings. If he didn't empathize so deeply with these struggling weekday warriors, he would have found the sight humorous. Though people tried to project confidence, most ended up clinging to the console for dear life. The console wasn't designed for continual support while exercising but as a place for controls and storing personal items. The assumption at Cybex was that you were supposed to run exactly the way you would on pavement, arms swinging freely. Empathetic observation revealed, however, that people feared losing their balance. Despite the awkward angle and the way it impeded their workout, runners clamped down and held on for dear life.

If you see most of your customers using a product in an unintended way, it's a sign to rethink your intentions. Pacheco wondered whether prominent stability handles might give people the security they craved. If handlebars were placed right in front, close enough to reach but canted away so as not to impede their stride, people could hold on throughout an entire workout without strain or stress. Not only would this be safer than clinging precariously to the console, the change might also attract new users too cautious to hop on a regular treadmill.

When Pacheco brought the idea of dedicated handlebars back to Cybex, it fell flat. Margins were slim enough without adding forty dollars or more to the manufacturing cost. Plus, handlebars would look weird. Cybex's model would stand apart from every other treadmill on the market. "I don't like anything in this entire presentation," the head of R&D told Pacheco. "Come up with something else."

Pacheco saw no point in arguing over subjective impressions of customers' subjective impressions. Instead, he decided to apply the scrappy approach he'd learned at the d.school. An experiment would prove the desirability of his concept more effectively than any PowerPoint slide. Pacheco went to a nearby hotel gym and requested permission to install prototype handles on a couple of Cybex treadmills in the gym. The hotel's manager understood the potential immediately. Who cared if the handles were ugly if they helped avoid a lawsuit? Given the go-ahead, Pacheco jury-rigged handles on two of the hotel's ten treadmills and sat back to observe.

Morning after morning, guests voted with their feet. If the prototype treadmills were available, eight out of ten chose to run on them over the eight without handlebars. When Pacheco asked people why, the answer was unequivocal: "It looked and felt safer." Data in hand, Pacheco convinced Cybex to make the change. By the end of the year, stability handles on its treadmills had grown Cybex's treadmill business by 20 percent for two consecutive years.

CYCLE THROUGH EXPERIMENTS QUICKLY: WESTPAC NEW ZEALAND

For a business, a beta offering serves a useful purpose beyond gathering customer feedback: forced learning. Projects have a way of getting swept under the rug and forgotten when they don't succeed immediately. You don't learn that way. Releasing something as a public beta offering pushes the company to stick with an idea through difficult turning points. To do anything less would betray the early users who offered feedback and tolerated hiccups. By opening up the development process, a beta keeps steady pressure on the organization to keep improving.

Not every idea is intended for the public, of course. Many valuable ideas are internal, but a beta period can still serve the same vital purpose.

A few years ago, Westpac New Zealand's IT team decided to revamp an integral piece of software relied on by its thousands of branch managers. Since the software played a key role in every manager's day-to-day work, even a small improvement would constitute a significant efficiency boost for the company.

Enterprise software development is a magnet for failed innovation efforts. This has less to do with talent or skill than faulty systems and incentives. When software is created for internal use by a large organization, the users have little input into the development process. Key decisions get made by people in another department or simply further up the org chart. The product is then handed down from above with an explanatory Power-Point presentation. This top-down approach short-circuits the crucial feedback loop that drives improvement. Since unhappy users can't switch to a competing product—other than by quitting their jobs—there isn't much incentive to address the parts that fall short. As a result, enterprise software gets the job done without being easy to learn or pleasant to use. Dealing with it becomes a resented chore, something people do out of necessity alone.

Westpac wanted to do better. Its leaders sincerely wanted to incorporate the feedback of its branch managers. Unfortunately, good intentions don't solve problems. When progress on the project stalled, the bank asked us to run a boot camp with its IT department. Examining the process together, we discovered no fewer than *seven* layers of bureaucracy between the branch managers and the IT department. Seven! If a user wanted to report a bug or suggest a feature, it would have to pass through all seven layers before arriving at someone who could act on it. Successful iteration requires a direct feedback loop to function—real change will never happen through seven layers of bureaucracy. It's a game of telephone.

The first idea out of the boot camp was to "graft" an IT department onto a branch by putting a developer in the room with a branch manager to work on solutions together. For the branch manager in question, this was a great setup—at first. They were free to ask the developer for help at the first sign of a problem with the software. It became clear, however, that managing a busy branch didn't leave much time for offering software feedback throughout the day. Developers ended up twiddling their thumbs instead of coding, a waste of a valuable resource.

Having tried something ambitious and failed, many businesses would have slunk away to address other, more pliable problems. By sharing about the innovation boot camp over the company's discussion forum, however, Westpac had made a visible commitment to this process. Branch managers across the organization were watching things unfold in what was essentially a public beta. By operating transparently, the bank had left itself no way to get out and save face. This was forced learning at its best. They'd simply have to figure this out, iteration by iteration.

For its next experiment, the team assigned a product manager to act as an intermediary between IT and all the branch managers. But suggestions were soon getting delayed or misinterpreted once again. They'd reintroduced bureaucracy.

The fastest path to learning often involves a walk around the building or down the block. *When in doubt, just go out.* Talk to another human being. We're shocked by how often this simple tactic works to jump-start creativity. In our postmortem discussion with Westpac's IT department, we suggested a quick chat with an actual Westpac branch manager. Why not? There was a branch right on the corner.

In the branch, we soon discovered that its manager, Rachel Compton, had tons of ideas for improving workflow and clearing away all the little frustrations costing the bank millions in lost productivity. Since raising these suggestions through official channels had never resulted in meaningful changes, she'd assumed that no one in corporate considered them worthwhile. As it turns out, those seven layers of bureaucracy meant IT had never gotten the memo. After talking to Compton, the team decided to try a new approach. Instead of grafting IT into the branch, they'd graft the branch into IT. Compton came to the corporate office to work directly on the product with them.

This worked so much better than the other way around. Given time in her schedule specifically for this purpose, Compton was able to get right to work with the developers on addressing the specific problems that had plagued her. Before long, the team rolled out the first result of this collaboration. Imprecise language in the software had led to countless time-wasting calls to IT for tech support. Long aware of the problem, Compton had finally been given the opportunity to fix it by clarifying the process for users, saving the company time and money as well as making her own work easier. To cap off this successful innovation effort, Rachel evangelized the solution—and the way it had happened—over the company's internal discussion forum. She even included a photo of herself, a nontechnical employee, pushing the code live. The fact that one of their own had championed the change boosted morale and engagement among Westpac's thousands of other branch managers.

When running experiments within an organization, keep things as transparent as possible. To force learning and maintain momentum, leave yourselves no room for retreat. Connect the people with the problem and the people designing solutions directly and let everyone else observe what happens.

In addition, if busting a logjam means leaving your chair and chatting with another person, especially someone you don't know well, don't be shy. Face-to-face interactions like this are one of our richest sources of creative input.

FAKE IT TILL YOU MAKE IT: BRIDGESTONE

Erica Walsh and her innovation team at the Japanese tire manufacturer Bridgestone brought us in to help them find ways to leverage the rise of ride-sharing services. From the research, they knew that Uber and Lyft drivers' cars encountered mechanical problems at a rate well above the average. Compounding the problem, these drivers were even less likely to bring their vehicles in for routine maintenance, since a trip to the mechanic translated directly into lost revenue. As a result, minor problems went undetected for so long that they culminated in outright mechanical failures, often with a customer in the car. For a ride-share driver, a breakdown like this means not only lost income but also damage to their rating on the app.

If getting to the mechanic regularly wasn't feasible, how might we help these drivers conduct routine diagnostics in their own garage? They might be willing to bring their cars in to fix a specific problem spotted by a diagnostic test. Self-diagnosis might prevent the failures that were costing these drivers money and damaging their online reputations.

According to Bridgestone's engineers, a mat fitted with sensors might be able to detect certain problems early. Software could even schedule a trip to the mechanic automatically using the driver's online calendar. This might be a boon for busy drivers—and for Bridgestone, which would sell tires every time a mat detected excess tread wear.

Walsh and the other Bridgestone execs loved the idea. It seemed like a logical extension of the brand, as well as a neat way to grow demand. Meanwhile, the engineering team salivated over the technological possibilities. Forget angels on the heads of pins—how many automotive sensors could one squeeze into a plastic mat?

With all this internal enthusiasm, the typical R&D approach would have been to spend six months and a bundle of money on the development of a fully functional prototype. The question of whether ride-share drivers *wanted* a pancake-thin diagnostics suite could wait. Not this time, however. Walsh decided that rather than spend a fortune flattening and reinforcing a diagnostic supercomputer, the team could quickly and cheaply determine the desirability of the product. How? Fake it till you make it.

They bought a stack of vinyl bath mats and deployed them in a garage used by ride-share drivers. Then they told the drivers that each mat contained cutting-edge sensors. At night, a team from Bridgestone would manually inspect each car and create a detailed diagnostic report by the morning. What would have cost Bridgestone hundreds of thousands or even millions of dollars to prototype ended up costing about eighteen bucks to simulate.

As Walsh and her team at Bridgestone understood, you should never move forward with an idea until you're confident that people want it. The bath-mat test revealed that ride-share drivers had no desire for complicated reports projecting the possible need for replacement of some obscure part. A car nut might appreciate the diagnostic detail, but these customers had little interest in their vehicles beyond their capacity to earn. For ride-share drivers, all that mattered was whether the car would function reliably or not.

Failure isn't frustrating once you reframe it as a source of learning. It feeds right back into the innovation cycle. For Walsh and her team at Bridgestone, the bath-mat "failure" sparked a new line of thought. What if a failed diagnostic report didn't go to the driver at all? Instead, what if it signaled a service that retrieved the car, brought it to a mechanic for repair, and returned it, all during the driver's off-hours? If a repair would take too long, the service might even replace the car with a loaner vehicle so that drivers wouldn't lose out on any business.

Bridgestone didn't offer a maintenance valet service. Nor did it have a fleet of loaner cars. If experiments proved sufficient demand, however, it could confidently invest in developing these offerings, or partner with companies that do.

Time for more tests.

BIG IDEA, TINY TEST: LENDLEASE

Resist the logic that says big projects at big companies demand big experiments to match. The largest tree can grow from the smallest seed. At the start of the innovation process, it should never require a huge investment to deliver useful answers and get to the next step. Even ambitious ideas at large organizations can be vetted with quick, cheap, and imperfect experiments. At the Australian real estate giant Lendlease, for example, a multibillion-dollar development started life as a fifty-dollar Facebook ad.

Natalie Slessor is a social psychologist specializing in the workplace environment. As a senior leader at Lendlease, Slessor works with companies to understand their evolving needs to shape Lendlease's response to changing trends. Slessor brought an idea about one of those trends to our innovation accelerator.

Every weekday morning, Slessor and hundreds of thousands of other workers would commute an hour or more from the suburbs surrounding Sydney to offices in the city. As an expert in the future of work,

Slessor knew that flexible work arrangements were increasingly popular. Since Sydney's army of knowledge workers was doing most of its work on laptops, it made little sense for them to spend hours shuttling back and forth every single day of the week. Financially, environmentally, and practically, a solution allowing Sydney's corporate commuters to occasionally skip the trip would deliver value to all stakeholders, including the public.

Slessor saw a potential solution to the problem in Barangaroo, Lendlease's successful city center development. Barangaroo features high-end retail shops, restaurants, and cafés along with luxurious shared workspaces. Workers could enjoy spacious and elegant surroundings, with ready access to fancy coffee, organic salads, and yoga classes. Barangaroo flourishes because it offers workers the same amenities they enjoy in their upscale suburban neighborhoods. If Barangaroo succeeded by bringing neighborhood comforts to the office, Slessor wondered, could Lendlease flip that and bring the office to the neighborhood?

A shared workspace could be set up in any suburb with clusters of corporate employees, one that met stringent corporate security standards and offered a place close to home without the distractions of home. Employees could then spend their time doing something more valuable than playing games on their phones on a long train ride. The offering might make financial sense for big companies if even a fraction of their employees used the space for only a few days each week. Based on her research, Slessor could make a strong case that the added flexibility would increase productivity, employee satisfaction, and talent retention, all key issues for Lendlease's corporate tenants.

An idea on this scale would normally gestate through an elaborate and expensive multistage development process before a single tenant was approached with the offer. Lendlease would visit sites, conduct research, and price everything out to the nearest penny, all without signing up a single paying customer. At the time we ran the accelerator program, Slessor and her team had already been speculating about this ecosystem of satellite workspaces for two years, struggling to build the internal momentum needed to drive such an effort. When we learned about the idea, we told Slessor to stop speculating and start running ads for the new workspaces immediately. It wouldn't take much money or time to vet desirability. Thanks to the power and sophistication of ad targeting, small-scale tests can deliver highly relevant results quickly.

Lendlease was reluctant to advertise a product that didn't yet exist. A company serving a small set of large corporate customers will be more sensitive to the possibility of annoying or frustrating those customers than a web-based start-up like Man Crates. To address this concern, Slessor targeted Facebook ads at commuters living in nearby suburbs without mentioning Lendlease at all. Anyone who clicked on an ad promising "Barangaroo near you" could put themselves on a wait list to learn more by indicating which company they worked for. These sign-ups revealed substantial demand and even indicated the degree of demand at each Sydney-based company. Now, instead of filling a pitch meeting with hypotheticals, Lendlease could go to its customers and say, "Five hundred of your employees in Manly alone have signed up to learn more. How many seats will you rent?"

The pilot project, dubbed The Local Office, opened a year later to great fanfare and no small amount of local media attention. Demand from day one exceeded Slessor's initial data. "We couldn't keep people away," Slessor reported. Lendlease tested different commercial models before settling on one that worked well: bundling the cost of the satellite space into the rent paid by these companies for their main Sydney offices. Feedback from users about the space itself also proved invaluable during the pilot. Based on that feedback, Lendlease added improvements like reserved quiet rooms and free coffee delivery. Though COVID-19 eventually forced the shuttering of the pilot, Lendlease has its proof of concept and is now partnering on an entire network of near-home workspaces like The Local Office.

Slessor, for her part, found the process of rapid learning exhilarating: "I don't know why I haven't worked this way all my life," she told us. "The accelerator program helped me shake off the 'ask for permission' mindset and get into the 'show them your data and validation' mindset." Slessor's experience has changed her approach to validating all her ideas. "A big business like ours gets really confused about the difference between risk and uncertainty," she told us. "It's high uncertainty, but not high risk, to do something like those Facebook ads. The real risk is missing out on insights."

DEFER PERFECTION: MANiME AND RAVEL LAW

Don't let perfectionism get in the way of rapid learning. Releasing a low-fidelity version of an idea into the world can be especially painful for a company with a commitment to quality. It's genuinely uncomfortable for established organizations to relax their standards to move—and thus learn—more quickly. In fact, that's what gives entrepreneurs their competitive advantage. Start-ups have no standards to meet because they haven't set the bar yet. There are no customer expectations to satisfy when there are no customers. That's why new companies drive so much innovation. They have nowhere to go but up. If large organizations want to innovate like Silicon Valley start-ups, they must learn how and when to loosen up.

Jooyeon Song and David Miró Llopis came to our Launchpad accelerator program with an idea: custom-fit press-on nails. Song loved the look of manicured nails but abhorred the two-hour routine at the salon. "I dreamed that changing my nail style could be as simple as changing my shoes," she told us. Press-on nails couldn't be more convenient, but the results are often disappointing. Since the nail bed of every finger is a little different, there are unsightly gaps.

Song and her cofounder believed that custom-fit nails would solve this problem for many customers. If you could buy press-on nails that fit each of your nail beds perfectly, why spend hours at the manicurist? The product would not only save time, it would also open up a world of expressive possibilities. Customers could buy press-ons in an array of styles and change them at a whim. Instagram had made stars of a new generation of manicure artists. Unless you happened to live within driving distance of an influencer's salon, however, the best you could do if you liked their work was show it to your own manicurist and hope for the best. With custom press-ons, creative manicurists could contribute their designs to an online marketplace where fans around the world could get them delivered to their doorsteps.

There was only one problem with the concept. Neither founder had the necessary technical skills to implement it. While it seemed feasible to create custom press-ons using a photo of the customer's real nails, even a prototype offering would require specialized expertise in image processing and 3D printing.

Maybe, maybe not, we told the two founders. Either way, the question of technical feasibility could wait until after they'd established desirability. Would people buy this product if it did exist? To find out, Song and Miró Llopis roughed up a simple website, wrote some copy, and ran Facebook ads. When the orders started coming in, they got creative, cutting press-on nails out by hand based on customer photos. These were little more than glorified stickers, but they still fit better than store-bought nails. It was enough to get to the next step.

Having proved desirability, Song and Miró Llopis won a spot in a hardware-focused accelerator run by Black & Decker. The founders now had access to world-class tools and advanced technical training. As a result, their execution of the concept rapidly improved. Before long, they were collaborating with top nail artists to stock their online marketplace with trendy designs. This step would have been a challenge for any new company with no big names attached and almost no revenue. Despite their eagerness to close deals with influencers, however, the founders decided from the start to tell nothing but the truth. Being open and honest with potential partners would be essential not only to establishing collaborations but also to maintaining their company's reputation as it grew.

"We came to the negotiation table transparently," Song told us. "'This is where ManiMe, the business, is today,' we said. 'This is as much as we can promise at this stage. And this is the vision of where we want to go. Working with you is a crucial milestone along the way.'" The first designer they approached was so impressed by the founders' willingness to share costs and revenue that she overlooked its small scale. "That's why we were able to close the deal," Song recalled.

This is yet another example of how little you really need to get an idea off the ground. You don't have to wear a turtleneck and inflate your results, as Elizabeth Holmes did at Theranos. If you bring your collaborators, clients, and customers into the creative process and make them your coconspirators, you will be surprised at how willing many are to share the risks. As Theranos lies in ruins, ManiMe's robust sales are climbing.

If Song and Miró Llopis had waited until the technical execution was perfect before testing desirability, they'd still be waiting. Instead, they moved forward under the assumption that custom-fit press-on nails were feasible, and that the details could be sorted out if the demand was there. The technology existed, after all. Rather than waste valuable time mastering it, they trimmed the nails themselves—cheap, fast, imperfect—to prove there was sufficient demand to justify the investment of time, money, and energy required to get the technical aspects sorted out.

As laborious as cutting nails by hand sounds, ManiMe's early struggles pale in comparison to those at Ravel Law. Daniel Lewis and Nik Reed were Stanford law students when they came to Launchpad. Coming from a family of lawyers, Lewis had grown up with an awareness of the painful and outdated technology tools available to lawyers, something that Reed encountered for the first time in law school. The antiquated legal research platforms lawyers used made preparing for a case in court or drafting an opinion truly laborious. To find relevant case law and understand judicial precedent was a daunting task when performed with books. One would think digital technology and the internet would have made the task much easier, but the leader in legal research, LexisNexis, had seemingly stopped innovating. It offered basic search tools only, and as the amount of available data ballooned, those tools simply weren't evolving to keep up.

Lewis and Reed believed that data visualization and machine learning could make the process far more efficient. For example, instead of presenting search results as an endless list of links, why not map the cases visually to reveal useful connections? Or allow the user to jump to the most recent precedent? Or, taking it a step further, what if the search engine could spot every time a judge granted or denied a certain kind of motion, or identify the most persuasive precedents or legal language for a certain judge? Ravel's founders envisioned many ways you could use digital technology to swiftly zero in on the exact document or argument that might help you win. They also imagined ways to replace mind-numbing rows of text with colorful and compelling diagrams to orient lawyers within the search results and help them navigate.

As with ManiMe, neither founder had the technical know-how to execute their ambitious vision. They could still test its desirability, however, by simulating their imagined software with paper mock-ups to pitch the concept to customers. As law firms signed up for the service, the founders used what they learned from customers to guide the developers who were creating the software. Once the software could deliver on the vision, the company soared. Only five years after founding Ravel Law, Lewis and Reed sold it . . . to LexisNexis.

At both ManiMe and Ravel Law, ambitious founders put desirability ahead of feasibility. Through sheer manual effort, they simulated their ideas with just enough fidelity to run useful tests. If either team had tried to achieve anything like the final product before starting, they would have run out of time and money long before building a viable business.

Your organization may balk at releasing an offering to customers before it's fully realized. This hesitance may feel safer in the short term, but it stifles the innovation necessary to survive, as LexisNexis discovered when it started losing major customers to two young entrepreneurs turking away without functioning software. If fidelity is a concern, know that there are many ways to communicate the unfinished nature of a new offering in a way that inspires curiosity and loyalty in customers rather than frustration and disappointment. The key is setting expectations with early users and acting rapidly and transparently on what you learn from them. If you don't get something right, address it quickly and keep them in the loop.

Experimentation is a liberating concept in the polished world of large organizations. As one leader told us, "It gives my team permission to try something new. When you say 'experiment,' you know it doesn't have to succeed and it doesn't have to be perfect. You know you're doing it to learn something you don't already know."

LEARNING HOW TO LEARN: BJ'S RESTAURANTS

A significant portion of the delivery business for most restaurants now comes through apps like DoorDash and Uber Eats. These intermediaries control the customer relationship entirely. This arrangement put upscale casual dining chain BJ's Restaurants in a tough spot. When customers had problems with an order, they didn't know whom to contact. If they called the app, support would blame the restaurant and give the customer a refund. BJ's wanted to try helping customers with their order problems directly by, for example, rushing out that missing dipping sauce. But how could they even try that approach if they never got the call in the first place?

BJ's asked us to help them improve the delivery experience. They'd already tried adding a note to each bag: "Hi, I'm Hannah and I packed your food. This is my personal number. If there's a problem with your order, contact me and I'll make it right immediately." To test this idea, they'd stuffed the notes into all the lunch orders going out of a single BJ's location. Twenty-three orders had gone out, but nobody had called or texted. What now? Were notes a "bad" idea?

Maybe. But it had definitely been a bad experiment, and that took precedence. As we pointed out to the leaders at BJ's, the employees preparing these orders had known about the notes inside. Consciously or unconsciously, they'd paid careful attention to getting each order right. Mistakes were rare enough, but this made any problems even more unlikely. An appetizer might go missing once a day at the average BJ's location. They would need to put notes in every order for months and months to gather a meaningful amount of data.

That's when the VP of marketing suggested something brilliant: "Let's mess up some orders on purpose." There were shocked looks around the room.

"No way," someone said. "We can't do that to our own customers."

Ask yourself and your team: How committed are we to learning? Do we care enough about improvement to do the equivalent of sending out an incorrect delivery order on purpose? The fact is, fail to learn and you will fail your customers anyway, just *invisibly*. For example, it's possible BJ's was messing up more than an order a day at each location. How would its leaders know for sure when customer complaints for over half its orders were being intercepted by other companies?

In a single day, the restaurant could conclusively validate its idea *and* open up a new channel of communication with those customers who relied on third-party apps. Sure, a few people might have been annoyed about a missing order of dipping sauce, but that frustration could have been addressed in the experiment's design. As we saw with Man Crates, simply explaining the experiment to customers can flip their perception of it. It's rare to see an established business actively working to improve your experience. A discount on a future order would have been another way to take the sting out.

Experiments can be crafted thoughtfully to deliver crucial learning and even *enhance* the customer relationship. As you adopt an experimental mindset and begin to see the benefits of real-world testing, you will become more comfortable with taking small risks now that forestall bigger ones down the road.

When the results of a test are inconclusive or otherwise counterintuitive, consider your methods before consigning the idea to oblivion. By reviewing not only the outcome but the design of their experiment, BJ's spotted a flaw in the test before abandoning the idea itself. This shift away from testing as a binary, yes-or-no process transformed the company's approach to learning.

~

Once you've validated the desirability of your idea, keep going. Hone what you've built with more experiments. Perhaps you can raise your profits—try raising the price incrementally until people stop adding the product to their shopping carts. Be deliberate and methodical. Now that you know people want what you've got, can something extraneous about the offering be pared away? Can the process of fulfillment be simplified? Measure the time and effort involved in doing some aspect and streamline it. Above all, keep questioning your assumptions. Is this solution sustainable? Will it be resilient under different conditions? This is the stuff you want to figure out *before* you go into full production mode.

Turking with vinyl bath mats and manual nail cutting will get you only so far. Once you've proven that an idea is both desirable and viable, make it real. This is the stage to rope in more people and resources. Ramping up is much easier once you've built a convincing case based on real-world data. You've tested your assumptions and addressed many of the questions that stakeholders will present. You're ready to elevate your approach.

Part Two

Elevate

7.

Mine for Perspectives

Many ideas grow better when transplanted into
another mind than in the one where they
sprang up.

—OLIVER WENDELL HOLMES

I n the first part of this book, you learned how the most effective creators and problem solvers move along the path from inspiration to
conviction. With what we've shown you so far, you could build and
run an innovation laboratory. (If that feels a little ambitious to start, get
the ball rolling with the corkboard R&D department described in chapter 4.) Either way, you've learned the fundamentals of the innovation
mindset and you know the basics required to implement an innovation
pipeline within an organization.

In this second part of the book, we address the central question: How
do you get breakthrough ideas? As we first mentioned in chapter 2, ideas
aren't something you can just grab on demand like picking up a bunch of
broccoli at the supermarket. You must *cultivate* ideas, steadily feeding

your brain a rich diet of divergent inputs. In these chapters, we will teach you the fine art of idea cultivation, beginning here with the best creative input of all: other people.

~

Consider the ancient parable of the three blind men and the elephant. The first man feels the elephant's trunk and decides it's a snake. The second touches the leg—hey, that first guy's wrong! This is obviously a tree. The third encounters the tusk. Clearly, both the other guys are mistaken, and not all that bright to boot. It's patently obvious that this thing is a spear. How could they miss something so obvious? "I should update my LinkedIn," each man thinks. "My colleagues are dimwits."

In some versions of the tale, the three start throwing elbows over which interpretation is the "right" one. It's tragic, don't you think? If only they could share their observations in a safe atmosphere, they might arrive at a novel solution: *pachyderm*. Ideally, they'd listen to one another's viewpoints with open minds and even express gratitude to one another for contributing valuable perspectives on a very perplexing problem. In a way, the three men are lucky to have touched different parts of the same animal. Together, they might just piece the answer together. Unfortunately, that isn't what happens in the story, nor in most teams.

This book argues that the *quality* of your creative output—successful solutions to novel problems—is largely determined by its *quantity*. More ideas equals better ideas. However, it's entirely possible to generate a whole host of "ideas" that are simply variations on a theme: long trunk, short trunk, thick trunk, thin trunk. *Divergent* thinking is crucial to explore the full space of possibilities before converging on the most promising direction.

The diversity of ideas you generate is driven by the diversity of your creative inputs. Volume *and* variety of inputs are both critical to healthy ideaflow. From colleagues and collaborators to customers and clients, there is no substitute for gathering an array of unique perspectives on a problem. Creative collisions provoke fresh thinking. Hotbeds of corporate innovation like Xerox PARC and Bell Labs flourished because their leaders assembled experts from very different disciplines and refused to put them in silos. In fact, they did everything they could to encourage intersection.

Prolific innovators cultivate a constellation of peers and collaborators, investing in a long-term portfolio of perspectives that will pay dividends throughout their careers. If you haven't put much time and energy into building your own portfolio, start now. The results will surprise you. Nothing elevates creativity like the serendipitous meeting of different minds. Logitech CEO Bracken Darrell prioritizes the outside perspectives like few leaders we've met, eating breakfast at the same restaurant every single day and inviting two or three start-up founders to join him and talk shop. Although "90 percent of these meetings are a waste of time, probably the most inefficient thing in the world," he told us, the other 10 percent are so valuable they more than make up for it. Founders show Darrell where the "edge of things" is in the industry. Despite regularly devoting substantial amounts of time to these and other "inefficient" input-gathering practices, Darrell has led Logitech on an extraordinary growth trajectory during his tenure, increasing its valuation eightfold over the past five years alone.

Psychologist Heidi Grant and leadership expert David Rock make the argument that "nonhomogeneous teams are simply smarter," marshaling convincing evidence for the positive effect of ethnic, racial, and gender diversity on business outcomes. Diverse teams perform better and make fewer mistakes even as they innovate more effectively. Our experience working with organizations and teaching at Stanford's d.school bear these findings out. Mashing diverse perspectives together unquestionably drives innovation.

When seeking to build a diverse portfolio—among contributors, on a team, across an organization—you can go beyond an arbitrary demographic checklist. A pizza chain exec is a pizza chain exec regardless of their gender or heritage. A dozen pizza chain execs in a room will still give you the same three perspectives: small, large, and extra cheese. Think different walks of life. Think different ways of thinking and solving problems. Think, who's the *last* person I'd ever ask about this? There are no shortcuts and no prescriptive checklists when it comes to assembling divergent perspectives—it's about having the courage to go wide, starting a conversation with someone very different from you.

Even if you aren't consciously aware of the bias toward the familiar in yourself, assume it's there and work against it. While it takes time and energy to assemble a richer, deeper, and broader portfolio of perspectives on a problem, it's worth every bit of effort required. We're asking you to open a dialogue with someone you suspect will disagree with you. That takes guts. Lean into it. *Eagerly* seek out those people likely not only to see the flaws in your thinking but to offer up alternatives way out of left field. This never means you must do as they say, of course, but striking sparks leads to creative conflagrations.

Homogeneous teams perform straightforward tasks efficiently. The Rangers could probably learn a lot from talking to LeBron—but they wouldn't win the Stanley Cup by recruiting him to the team. But cookie-cutter teams are terrible at generating novel solutions. People with different expertise and experience interpret one another's observations in surprising ways. They build on one another's ideas along unexpected lines. A team who can draw on a broader range of analogies reaches uncharted territory much faster. Certainly, intersections between different personalities with different worldviews can take the form of conflict. As a leader, it's your job to ensure these conflicts remain creative, not destructive. Direct the energy at the problem, not at one another.

On your own, maximize your odds of running into people unlike yourself and cultivate the necessary patience and tolerance to do so. Assembling a diverse portfolio of perspectives isn't about catching mistakes before they happen. You don't bring in other people to have half the team police the perspectives of the other half. The goal is to gather inputs you couldn't have gotten any other way.

Mining for perspectives is how the most interesting treasures are found.

BEING COLD ISN'T THE SAME AS NOTICING YOU'RE COLD

In chapter 1, Perry related the story of how post–9/11 worries about customer demand stymied the flow of ideas at Patagonia. By the time he realized his error, Perry needed new products, and he needed them fast. Patagonia's leadership team decided to pursue growth by entering the surfwear market.

At the time, innovative, youth-friendly brands like Quiksilver and Billabong dominated the category. How would Patagonia stand apart? To consider as many directions as possible before plunging in, the company assembled a diverse group to study the problem on a surfing trip in Mexico. Many leaders, including Perry, already loved to surf, so they had domain expertise to draw on. However, this also meant they would all see the problem through a certain lens. Expertise is obviously crucial, but it can leave you blind to things that newcomers would notice immediately. To diversify this portfolio of perspectives, they would leverage "inexperienced experience": Who knew enough about Patagonia's business to be helpful but didn't know the first thing about surfing?

For this crucial beginner's perspective, the company selected Tetsuya Ohara, a junior employee who managed raw material sourcing for the company. Ohara had never gone surfing before. In fact, this would be his first time in a wet suit. What would a complete newcomer notice about surfing and surfwear that the rest of the group took for granted?

There is no substitute for a genuinely fresh perspective—a novice can't help but see everything about a new experience in vivid detail. Take full advantage of that.

Ohara noticed something important about surfing right away: *this water is really cold.* Perry and the rest of the team took the bracing discomfort for granted—if anything, the cold water was a familiar aspect of an experience they loved. Not so for the novice. The whole point of a wet suit, as Ohara had understood it, was to keep you relatively warm in the water. The discrepancy between his expectations and the frigid reality lay in the word "relatively." Tetsuya was freezing his butt off while Perry and the rest of the team, inured to the cold through long experience, happily surfed the waves.

To take his mind off the temperature, Ohara ruminated on the technical problem from the perspective of his expertise with textiles. Neoprene, the typical fabric for a wet suit, had many good attributes but it clearly didn't keep you all that warm. Nor did it dry quickly, fit comfortably, or even smell very nice. In fact, it smelled like a new tire. Surely, there was a better solution to this problem.

Also, as Patagonia's raw material manager Ohara knew that petroleum-based fabrics are environmentally destructive. Even if neoprene was perfect in every other way, it had no business being used by Patagonia, one of the most environmentally conscious manufacturers in the world.

In light of all this, Ohara devised a frame to spur ideas: How might we make surfwear that keeps people comfortable in cold water using natural materials alone? Noodling on that question, Ohara considered parallels in nature. Many warm-blooded mammals stand outside in cold and wet conditions all day without getting cold. Sheep, for example. Ohara imagined a flock of sheep milling about the Welsh countryside, blithely enduring the chilly and damp winter weather thanks to their thick wool. Even better, wool doesn't smell as unpleasant as neoprene does when wet. If you started with wool and added a natural rubber lining, you'd have a wet suit with impeccable environmental bona fides that would perform better in every way than neoprene, from heat retention to odor to fit.

Before long, Patagonia had developed a wet suit that met the conditions of Ohara's framing question. Other surfwear products followed as the company slowly captured a toehold in the category. Years later, Patagonia would replace the wool in its wet suits with recycled polyester to further minimize waste, but this iterative development was made possible only by Ohara's initial contributions. Ohara himself eventually became Patagonia's head of research before moving on to other opportunities. After an illustrious corporate career including a stint as head of the Gap's supply chain, he now consults with companies on ecological innovation.

At the time of the Mexican expedition, someone in Ohara's position at most manufacturers would have been added to the product development process only after the team had decided on the approach, too late to make a contribution like this. By bringing the surfing novice in for his perspective, however, Patagonia cultivated a game-changing idea.

While experienced surfers might have purchased neoprene wet suits from Patagonia, how likely would they have been to switch brands in the first place, especially to a brand that was new to the category? Novice surfers were the key to gaining traction, so anything that stuck out to Ohara would probably stick out to another surfing newbie. Perry and the other leaders were simply too familiar with the existing solution to see its flaws clearly. They were limited by their knowledge. Thanks to inexperienced experience, one of seven tools for leveraging perspectives introduced in this chapter, they got their breakthrough.

DIVERSIFY YOUR PORTFOLIO OF PERSPECTIVES

Each of the following seven tools will help you feed ideaflow with other people's perspectives. Don't expect any of them to work perfectly out of the box, however. Mining for perspectives takes practice. While people are a great source of input, they can also be opinionated, insistent, sometimes irritable. You know, people.

As for the tools themselves, you may already rely on one or two. Several at least, however, are likely new to you and your organization. Keep using what works, but consider adopting a couple of new ones to broaden your horizon. Each of these has been vetted in organizations of every size and across industries. They work. Think of them as levers you can pull when ideaflow falters. Over time, you'll develop a sense of which lever is most appropriate for the problem at hand.

Remember the advice of our friend Dan Klein, head of the Stanford improvisers, from chapter 3: Never *try* to be creative. Dare to be obvious instead. In a diverse group, what is obvious to one person will be unexpected, provocative, and interesting to the rest. Call on contributors to bring their thoughts to the table as clearly and directly as possible. No one should strain to impress anyone or reach for "originality." The more each person sticks to their own opinions, reactions, and first impressions—and welcomes these authentic contributions from others—the more thrilling the resulting intersections will be. As the Nobel-Prize-winning economist Thomas Schelling once wrote, "One thing a person cannot do, no matter how rigorous his analysis or heroic his imagination, is to draw up a list of things that would never occur to him!" The magic of ideaflow is that a group of people brave enough to be obvious together can collectively imagine things that would never occur to any one member individually.

Learning circles

Unlike tactics tied to a specific role, project, or enterprise, establishing a Learning Circle—a group that connects regularly to share and discuss ideas—will provide a lifetime of divergent inputs for you. That's why we offer this tool first. The effort to establish and maintain your own Learning Circle will pay dividends throughout your career.

Beyond his many accomplishments as a diplomat and statesman, Benjamin Franklin invented bifocals, the lightning rod, and, of course, the stove that bears his name. Every time you borrow a book from the public library—including this one, perhaps—you have this Founding Father to thank. The list of his creative contributions goes on and on. Clearly, extraordinary creative output like this required an equally robust set of inputs. Franklin deliberately gathered these inputs from the beginning of his career.

As a young printer in Philadelphia, Franklin corralled a group of acquaintances to attend regular structured meetings devoted to mutual improvement. Though the group and its operation evolved over the years, the founding purpose of Franklin's "Junto" was the exchange of knowledge, whether through intellectual debate or the sharing of expertise. The members of the Junto held different professional roles, but they shared an interest in personal development as well as in the city's growth as a center of commerce and enterprise. These were busy people, with businesses of their own and families at home, yet they made time to meet each week because of the abundant value delivered by the Junto. The original group, also known as the Leather Apron Club, lasted nearly four decades, and one branch persists today as the American Philosophical Society.

Considering eighteenth-century social mores, Franklin assembled an incredibly divergent mix for the time: rich and poor, young and old, clerk and merchant alike. These were all white men, of course, but for his time, Franklin was breaking down barriers. Every Friday evening, the Junto would congregate to share the essays its members had written on subjects of personal interest. A debate on ethics or natural philosophy, aka scientific inquiry, might follow. To ensure civility, the group levied small fines for direct criticism or personal attacks. Many of these men had no higher education, but they were curious, intellectually intrepid, and, of course, avid readers. Franklin made sure of that in selecting them.

Franklin's Learning Circle proved useful both to his creative output and his business, sometimes simultaneously. For example, when there was a drive to print more paper money to facilitate trade in the colony, the Junto debated the issue. These debates inspired Franklin to publish an anonymous pamphlet in favor of the idea. Divergent input, creative output. After the pamphlet helped get the motion passed, there was a need to print more currency. You'll never guess which young Philadelphia printer scored the lucrative gig.

Artisans, artists, scientists, and entrepreneurs have always formed groups to drive learning and innovation. What made the Junto so effective was the diverse mix of its membership, a factor driven by Franklin's intrepid curiosity and the relatively egalitarian society of colonial America. In the centuries since, others have sought to replicate the Junto's success. Today's corporate leaders, for example, assemble brain trusts as a way of breaking out of the company mindset and regaining an outsider's perspective. When Mark Parker was CEO of Nike, he held dinners on a regular basis for a group of artists and other creative acquaintances to discuss product ideas and brainstorm potential collaborations. Parker started his career as a designer and still craved inspiration: "I like the eccentricity, to be surprised," he said. These dinners kept Parker wired into urban culture—sneakerheads and hip-hop, skaters and graffiti art—even as he spent much of his time cloistered at Nike's headquarters in Portland.

Learning Circles take different forms, but they share key characteristics: First and foremost, a Circle exists outside any one organization. Since the goal of a Learning Circle is to bring divergent perspectives and experiences together, the more far-flung its membership, the better. Plus, a cadre of members from a single company would inevitably form a clique within the larger Circle, stifling open discussion. Second, a Circle meets at a regular cadence, so that trust and familiarity can grow, and topics can be discussed across multiple meetings. Third, a Circle establishes basic guidelines to keep each meeting on the rails, as with the Junto's rule against personal attacks. Finally, a Circle meets in real time, not through asynchronous communication like Slack, whether the meetings happen in person or virtually.

Beyond these core elements, the structure and focus of a Learning Circle should serve the personal and professional goals of its members. A group might coalesce around a certain industry (electronics, shipping, education), a target market (Millennials, Gen Z), or another focal point altogether. For Franklin's Junto, that focus was on advancing the cultural and commercial ambitions of Philadelphia and the colony as a whole. Your Learning Circle should develop its own focus to spark discussion and sharing, open-ended enough to allow for serendipitous discovery but with enough structure to prevent meetings from becoming mixers.

Pen pals

Charles Darwin made good use of the postal service in his scientific work, corresponding regularly with hundreds of collaborators across more than a dozen fields of inquiry. In the decades between his voyage aboard the HMS *Beagle* and the seminal publication of *On the Origin of Species,* Darwin developed the theory of evolution in large part through the mail, clipping pieces of his nascent work into letters and sending them to experts in other areas for their perspectives. In this way, Darwin made one of the most imaginative intellectual leaps in history while serving as a valuable hub of information within the larger scientific community. His habit of correspondence lent vitality to his own work while connecting people and ideas that otherwise might never have intersected.

Today, we correspond constantly—via email, social media, and increasingly through online video and audio—yet most of what we share with others is redundant. Rather than contribute meaningfully, we affirm the beliefs and interests of our peers. The Pen Pals tool is about shaking up that tendency by engaging in deliberate correspondence. Contribute constructively to others' work and invite their contributions to your own. Considering the interests and pursuits of current and former colleagues, fellow experts in your field, and mentors and mentees, ask yourself: What can I add to the discussion? What new light can I shed on the topic at hand? Instead of echoing what is being said by others, make a habit of propagating fresh thinking that has yet to receive wider notice, either your own or what you discover along the way.

As regularly as possible, send contributions directly to the people who will benefit from them rather than broadcasting every thought to everyone you can reach in your network. Take the effort to maximize your signal-to-noise ratio. The people you know will appreciate your selectiveness and weigh your words more heavily as a result.

In search of insights, our d.school colleague Leticia Britos Cavagnaro routinely shares unfinished works in progress with colleagues in other academic departments. When she stumbles on something relevant to the research efforts of peers and students, she sends it along. If the podcast she's listening to includes an anecdote or piece of information that might be of interest, she'll stop jogging mid-stride and fire off a quick email. It's a hassle, but Leticia's generosity has instilled a culture of serendipitous sharing and reciprocity that echoes far beyond the d.school.

By sharing both selectively and generously with the Pen Pal tool, you will boost your own creative inputs. The more you contribute, the more input you'll receive in return. That said, worry more about what you can give than what you might get. Being a Pen Pal requires cultivating an awareness of the ongoing efforts and interests of friends, peers, and colleagues. This means making a commitment to not only share but to listen as well.

What are the people in your network working on? What thorny dilemmas are they struggling to resolve? In a way, their problems can become frames to more effectively sift the information you consume anyway. The habit of regular correspondence becomes a tool for focusing your own attention on what is truly valuable, whether to you or others. Over time, being an active Pen Pal will sharpen your perception and accelerate your learning, all while creating a virtuous cycle of constructive sharing across your network.

Customer council

Understanding the needs of the customer is the most important function of any business. "People don't want to buy a quarter-inch drill," Harvard Business School marketing professor Theodore Levitt would say. "They want a quarter-inch hole!" Once you understand this, much else falls into place. At the d.school, we emphasize empathy above all leadership traits.

Two Stanford MBAs who went through our program, Miri Buckland and Ellie Buckingham, took this lesson to heart when they founded Landing, "a digital space for visual curation." The site offers tools for designing mood boards and sharing anything from favorite products to life goals. To better empathize with their customers, Buckland and Buckingham formed a council of forty "super-users." Members of the Landing's Customer Council get to see and offer feedback on early iterations of the company's initiatives. They're even given access to the company Slack and invited into internal discussions. This kind of customer collaboration, for all its potential risks, delivers value to the company by shortening its feedback loop. Who better to vet a potential change to the product than the people who use it the most? When better to welcome that feedback than the moment of an idea's inception?

As both a mother herself and the founder of Xplorealms, an award-winning ed-tech start-up in the UK, Reedah El-Saie understood the need for high-quality and immersive educational apps. But she also knew that she was not the end user. "I had not grown up on games, nor did I play them," El-Saie told us. "I knew that the concept had to be co-designed with our user group: children." After conducting dozens of user interviews with kids, parents, and educators, she saw how valuable this input could be throughout the product's development. "I decided to set up an advisory board of children rather than adults," she said. "We called it the Board of Brilliant Brains, or BBB." The BBB now has over a hundred participants. It serves as both a source of user insight as well as a roster of brand ambassadors. "All the children are on a WhatsApp group for safety purposes along with their parents," El-Saie explained. "They give feedback on aesthetics, game-play ideas, and curriculum content. Since they are located in different regions, this has also helped to launch the app in different countries very quickly."

Bringing the customer in as a collaborator is about sharing products and services with the people you hope will use them before it's too late to make substantial changes. Among other things, it can help you avoid a misfire before it's too late to correct your aim. The earlier this collaboration occurs, the more valuable it can be. Over time, a company's Customer Council becomes a "perpetual stew" of input that delivers valuable insights on every move the company contemplates.

Note, however, that this isn't something to jump into before doing the hard work of establishing psychological safety within the organization. Your best customers will have strong opinions. The team should feel comfortable with one another's honest feedback before opening the floodgates this way.

Leaders make various excuses when we suggest this tool. "We can't do that," they tell us. "We need to patent things!" What use is a patent on a failed product? As the nineteenth-century German military strategist Moltke the Elder once wrote, "No plan of operations extends with any certainty beyond the first contact with the main hostile force." The fact is, no idea survives its encounter with your customers intact. Something as transparent as the Landing's design council may not be feasible for your business, but there are always options for collaborating more closely with your customers. Their thoughts are too valuable a source of input to leave for after the launch.

Cross-pollinate

As important as your ties with collaborators and colleagues are, putting *all* your energy into your close working relationships can stifle innovative thought.

According to Duke University sociologist Martin Ruef, embedding yourself in a network of strong ties exclusively can insulate you from divergent inputs and pressure you to conform to the group's way of thinking. Seeking out serendipitous encounters with people outside your normal circuit, even professionals in very different industries, balances this out, leading to valuable discoveries and insights. These weak ties between acquaintances in separate networks opens the flow of what Ruef calls "nonredundant" information. In short, networks outside our own are rich with the divergent inputs we need to drive abundant creative output.

In a study of over seven hundred entrepreneurial teams trying to start new businesses, Ruef found that groups with social networks that mixed strong and weak ties innovated at almost three times the rate of more isolated networks consisting only of strong ties. In short, a mixed network is a healthy one. It allows members to simultaneously "access diverse sources of information" and "avoid pressures for conformity."

Don't forgo close relationships in favor of onetime encounters with random strangers. Instead of becoming a social butterfly, strike a balance between strong and weak ties. The Cross-pollinate tool is about injecting the optimum dose of serendipitous social mixing into your schedule.

Try forging a new habit—meals are a great place to start. At Princeton, Richard Feynman sat with his fellow physicists in the dining hall until he decided to mix things up: "After a bit I thought: It would be nice to see what the rest of the world is doing," he later wrote, "so I'll sit for a week or two in each of the other groups." These encounters sparked Feynman's curiosity. After sitting with the philosophers, he joined their weekly seminar; the biologists convinced him to do a graduate course in biology. Feynman's interdisciplinary explorations fed his imagination and broadened his worldview—James Watson even invited him to deliver a lecture to Harvard's biology department. Would the legendary thinker have gained anything like this intellectual nourishment by talking shop with his fellow physicists for an additional hour each day?

Likewise, Bill Baker, head of the research division of Bell Labs, made a practice of sitting with the first person he saw in the cafeteria, "whether he was a glassblower from the vacuum tube shop or a metallurgist from the semiconductor lab." Baker would then "gently interview the employee about his work and personal life and ideas." Baker had an extraordinary memory for these details and could highlight important connections between disparate areas of research that might otherwise have gone unnoticed. This simple habit broke down silos and closed circuits on electrifying new ideas.

If you don't have a convenient cafeteria, schedule meetups. Amy Yin, founder and CEO of the software start-up Office Together, encourages cross-pollination at group dinners she holds regularly as a way of "intentionally bringing [her] most talented friends together." Encouraging participants to share what's top of mind with their businesses, Yin unearths "amazing synergies," connecting people with jobs, investors, and other opportunities: "I introduced one of my portfolio companies to three of their first five customers." If you're at a large organization, reach out to colleagues in other departments and invite them to coffee on a regular basis. After going through one of our programs, Brad van Dam, CEO of Marich Confectionery, started walking around the building and soliciting ideas from random employees. People weren't sure what to make of this behavior, but when a maintenance technician's suggestion became a new product, the contributions started rolling in. Employees saw that van Dam wasn't just making a show of asking. He was listening.

Look for nodes. Reach out to someone whose work straddles interdepartmental borders. It's at the junctions between silos where you're most likely to make useful discoveries. Likewise, do your best to position yourself as a node. Volunteer for interdepartmental projects. Join committees. Go out for the company baseball team. Take any opportunity you can to interface with people outside your usual trajectory. You never know when a different perspective might shed light on new possibilities.

As efficient as strong ties are at getting things done, it's through weak ties that we stumble onto our most exciting discoveries.

Inexperienced experience

For a fresh perspective, invite an expert in another area. Developing a skill set in one context gives you a unique set of metaphors, heuristics, and other useful mental tools for solving problems. Placed in an unfamiliar context, an expert can often apply this toolbox to new problems with interesting results. They may not know the "right" way to approach a certain problem, but in trying to solve it *their* way, they may reveal fascinating avenues for exploration. Translating expertise from one domain to another can be incredibly fertile, as we saw with Tetsuya Ohara at Patagonia. If a problem doesn't respond to the usual expertise, call in a different kind of expert altogether.

You can leverage inexperienced experience by hiring someone who is good at what they do but has never done it in this particular way before. Marvel routinely hires filmmakers with experience in other genres—comedies (Taika Waititi, *Thor: Ragnarok*, Peyton Reed, *Ant-Man*), dramas (Ryan Coogler, *Black Panther*), thrillers (Jon Watts, *Spider-Man: Homecoming*)—to direct their first superhero movie. Marvel has deep expertise in making special-effects-driven action movies. Why double down?

Another way to tap into unexpected insights is to shuffle experts between departments. IBM developed the revolutionary System/360 series of computers in the 1960s by, in the words of CEO Thomas J. Watson Jr., "forcing people to swap sides." At a time when the small- and large-computer divisions of the company were in a state of fierce rivalry, the head of product development put a leader from one division in charge of the other. To the teams, this move "made about as much sense as electing Khrushchev president," according to Watson. But the gambit worked. Coming to the large-computer side from the small-computer side, Bob Evans immediately realized how valuable it would be to transition *all* of IBM's computing products to a single compatible system. Not only would that save effort across the organization, it would also allow customers to transition from smaller computers to larger ones as their needs grew without having to rewrite all their software. By integrating the company's efforts, the small-computer expert made the mainframe division far more competitive, and IBM went on to dominate business computing for decades.

Notice Novices

Most of the time, the keepers of conventional wisdom should be trusted. They're nearly always right. Occasionally, however, the weight of experience anchors the thinking of experts. Distinguishing revolutionary ideas from absurd ones can be much harder for the pro. To avoid this trap, give newcomers in your organization the space to ask questions and suggest ideas, even if the questions reveal ignorance and the ideas seem ridiculous. It's because newbies don't know any better that their contributions can be so valuable. If "Notice Novices" aren't given any leash to explore, the organization can't expect to discover opportunities outside its known horizons.

Meghan Doyle was in a junior-level role as a cataloger at Christie's New York, the legendary British auction house, when she first heard about non-fungible tokens, or NFTs. Based on the same blockchain foundation as Bitcoin and other digital currencies, NFTs make it possible to sell a unique piece of digital art like a JPEG or other digital asset. In a sense, anyway.

Technological novelty aside, would it be possible to convince clients of the value represented by an NFT? To those with years of experience in the auction world, the instinctive answer was no. Doyle, being relatively new to the art business, didn't know enough to know what wouldn't work. When the quiet inclusion of an NFT with a physical artwork led to a bigger-than-expected sale for Christie's toward the end of 2020, leaders received sufficient outreach to compel further investigation. But who would be the right person to chase down the lead? Doyle fit the bill. For one thing, she had more bandwidth than senior members of the department. For another, she was genuinely curious about NFTs. A newcomer brings energy and enthusiasm to risky explorations that more experienced practitioners might be too jaded or busy to pursue.

More than happy to invest time and energy talking about digital artists with blockchain and NFT platform experts, Doyle embraced the project with enthusiasm. Mistakes don't weigh as heavily on a novice. Expectations are low. The sky is the limit.

After talking to a platform experimenting with NFTs and embarking on a "crash course in crypto," Doyle proposed a simple test to her superiors: selling a digital-only artwork without the physical component present in that 2020 sale. If there was no physical component to the artwork whatsoever, would the digital token be sufficient to drive a sale? At first, the idea was met with resistance. There were too many physical artworks already slated for the catalog. With the enthusiasm of a novice, however, Doyle persisted, addressing practical concerns and building enthusiasm across internal departments.

"We can always bury it in the back of the sale and hide it if it doesn't get any interest," she pointed out. Christie's took a leap of faith and ended up in a video chat with Mike Winkelmann, aka Beeple, a digital artist whose star was on the rise in the NFT world. With burgeoning support across the business, Winkelmann's work *EVERYDAYS: The First 5000 Days* became an event in itself, offered in a single-lot online sale in early 2021. In another sign of Doyle's success evangelizing crypto, the company decided to accept digital currency for the first time. The bidding for *EVERYDAYS* started at $100. It was still an experiment, after all. When $100 became $1 million in the first eight minutes, however, Christie's realized that Doyle had contributed a far more valuable perspective than anyone could have guessed. When the piece sold for $69 million, the art world changed forever.

At Lockheed Martin's Skunk Works division, a young mathematician named Denys Overholser unearthed a formula in a decade-old technical paper written by a Russian scientist that suggested a way to design aircraft that could evade radar detection. Unfortunately, designing a plane along these lines would run counter to conventional aerodynamics. Lockheed's engineers scoffed at Overholser's idea and suggested—jokingly?—burning him at the stake as a heretic. Yet Ben Rich, the newly appointed director of the program, approved the project.

"Most of our veterans used slide rules that were older than Denys Overholser," Rich recalled, "and they wondered why in the hell this young whippersnapper was suddenly perched on a throne as my guru, seemingly calling the shots on the first major project under my new and untested administration. I tried to explain that stealth technology was in an embryonic state and barely understood until Denys unearthed the theory for us; they remained unconvinced." The final design ended up registering a truly minuscule radar signature, winning Lockheed Martin lucrative defense contracts and cementing the division's place in the annals of aerospace history. Overholser's novice intuition led directly to the Lockheed F-117A Nighthawk, the first operational stealth aircraft. The F-117A would go on to play a crucial role in the Gulf War and other conflicts.

There's something to be said for plain old lack of experience. Fresh blood. Whenever she works on a new book, for example, Harvard Business School professor Linda Hill includes a recent college graduate on her team. While writing one book, Hill's twenty-four-year-old collaborator suggested an octopus as a metaphor to illustrate a theory of organizational learning. The idea proved useful, and the octopus sketch is now framed on Hill's desk as a reminder of the value of a novice's perspective.

"If I write book after book," Hill told us, "it becomes rote. A novice makes it messy again. They provoke me to stop and see things differently because they're grappling with questions for the first time and making me challenge long-held assumptions. It's frustrating, but it drives quality."

One last personal example of the power of a Notice Novice: Jeremy's father, an attorney, briefed a case in front of the U.S. Supreme Court on behalf of GEICO and a number of its affiliates. The winning argument came from an attorney with eighteen months of experience. He walked into Jay Utley's office to ask a "stupid question" and Jeremy's dad decided to hear the young attorney out. It *was* a stupid question in the sense that a more experienced attorney would have dismissed it. However, it sparked a fruitful line of inquiry. In being willing to ask it, the young attorney helped win the case. Today, Jeremy's dad is building a new law firm staffed almost entirely with new attorneys. He's got the expertise and experience—what he needs are fresh perspectives.

Complementary collaborators

The histories of art, science, and invention reveal the surprising power in pairs: John Lennon and Paul McCartney. Steve Jobs and Steve Wozniak. Susan B. Anthony and Elizabeth Cady Stanton. Why is collaboration between two very different people such a common factor in world-class achievement? It isn't just about the moral support.

The value of what psychology professor Kevin Dunbar calls "distributed reasoning"—creative collaboration—lies in the way another person helps us see into our own blind spots. No matter how good you are at what you do or how much experience you might possess, you will always be limited by your singular perspective. The beauty of collaboration is that we each have *different* blind spots.

According to Dunbar's research, collaboration spurs innovation because what's hidden from us is often obvious to someone else. (Remember Dan Klein's dictum: "Dare to be obvious.") Two heads beat one because each person can look at the same picture and come to a very different conclusion. Reconciling these conclusions—think the three blind men and the elephant—leads to dramatic discoveries. In his research, Dunbar found that scientists in one lab made more progress than those in other labs doing the same kind of research by taking turns proposing alternative explanations for the same data. Each induction from one scientist sparked a divergent one from another, creating a chain reaction of ideas that accelerated creative output.

John Bardeen and Walter Brattain worked in tandem at Bell Labs to develop the solid-state transistor. Bardeen, the theoretical physicist, would write equations on the blackboard while Brattain, the experimental physicist, prototyped those ideas at the breadboard. What Brattain saw fed back to Bardeen, who incorporated these findings into more refined equations. Back and forth, blackboard to breadboard, theoretical physicist and experimental physicist accomplished a world-changing feat of technological innovation.

As a duo ourselves, we're partial to this strategy. This book wouldn't exist without it. Nor are we alone in placing such importance on partnership. If you look closely, you will see two very different individuals at the inception of nearly every significant human endeavor—book, business, or building. As a creator, you simply can't see very far from your own perspective alone. We all make reasoning errors. We all have blind spots. Our quirks will either stymie our solo efforts or serve as a rich source of creative input for a collaborator.

As with many other creative strategies, the key lies in leveraging differences. To find a good partner, seek someone as far apart on an axis—any axis—as possible. Whether you come from very different backgrounds, possess very different personalities, or take very different approaches to solving the same problems, the disparity will help you complement each other. Friction is essential to productive collaboration. We don't know what we don't know: "Individual subjects have great difficulties in generating alternate inductions from data," Dunbar wrote, "and also have great difficulties in either limiting or expanding inductions." Without a collaborator, anyone will be limited in what they can achieve.

Even within the structure of a traditional organization, it's possible to connect with a Complementary Collaborator, whether formally or informally. As head of an internal start-up at Procter & Gamble, Claudia Kotchka needed someone to balance out her bold vision. So, for a regular dose of pragmatism, she turned to her finance director.

"Claudia," he'd often tell her, "we can't change strategies every day." Sometimes, of course, she could and would pivot to seize an opportunity. As her counterpart, however, the finance director provided invaluable input precisely because he saw the same picture in a very different way than she ever could.

Space for candor

After we conducted a pilot training program for Hyatt at its Santa Clara location, CEO Mark Hoplamazian convened staff members for a debrief. Our mandate had been to bring human-centered design to Hyatt's operations. Before we rolled the training program out to the entire organization, however, we wanted to ensure we'd tuned our approach to Hyatt's specific needs. Hoplamazian put the question to a room of thirty employees: How'd the program go?

"Awesome," one person remarked. Another added: "We loved it."

Then, after a pause, a hand went up.

"I have to admit, this whole thing wasn't my cup of tea," she said, standing up to address the room. "In fact, I was uncomfortable throughout the entire process." Hoplamazian nodded encouragingly. "Quite frankly," she added, "I don't even want to continue." Having said her piece, the woman sat back down again.

Boy, did that take guts. It's all too easy to align with the crowd. As we saw earlier in the book, psychological studies confirm a strong, subconscious bias in all of us to join the consensus. Once the other employees indicated their approval, it became that much more difficult to express a diverging opinion. Again, this isn't just because of peer pressure. The consensus subconsciously shifts your actual perspective. You can easily find yourself nodding along when you had previously felt otherwise.

Since our goal is to generate the widest possible array of perspectives, it's crucial to actively inhibit this instinct. The most important tool for doing so is Space for Candor. As a leader, you must explicitly establish psychological safety by supporting and empowering every member of the team to express their authentic viewpoint no matter where it lands on the spectrum. If disagreement is in any way discouraged, let alone punished, the consensus will steer every decision.

At the Santa Clara Regency Hyatt, the thirty participants in our pilot had that sense of safety thanks to Mark Hoplamazian's efforts to establish it. He had his senior leadership team record videos encouraging unorthodox and countercultural behaviors during the program. In one, the CFO held a sign that read, "Don't be afraid to break things!" Hoplamazian even sent each innovator-in-training a "Get out of jail free!" card to assuage any remaining fears that trying something new might harm their career. That's why, at the crucial moment, the dissenting participant felt safe raining on everyone's parade.

It's a good thing she did, too. None of us had even considered the need for an opt-out for the program. Her contribution sparked a valuable discussion. In theory, any Hyatt employee could request not to participate in the human-centered design program, but would they feel comfortable doing so without an explicit process for doing so? Probably not. There would inevitably be concern about professional repercussions. This gave us a new frame: How might we make it socially and emotionally acceptable for unwilling participants to bow out? Whatever their reasons might be, their half-hearted participation would only hold everyone else back. As we've seen, the process of innovation demands a sense of playful experimentation—the one guy grinding his teeth in the back of the room would only spoil the fun. That single dissenting voice in Santa Clara inspired a way for employees to bow out without fear of repercussion, greatly increasing the ratio of willing and receptive participants.

"Thank you," Hoplamazian told the employee at the end of the discussion. "That's awesome you spoke up."

Candor is crucial to ideaflow. Where there is space for it, people feel safe both to give *and* receive critical feedback. In the ideation process, every perspective is valuable. In fact, two, five, or ten people agreeing on an idea doesn't get you one step closer to correct when it comes to new ideas. The value of each additional perspective during idea generation lies in where it falls on the graph relative to the consensus. Votes shouldn't winnow ideas; that's the job of experiments.

Popular wisdom suggests that criticism has no place in the creative process. If everyone feels like they share the same goal and are in it together, they can build on, tear down, and diverge from one another's ideas vigorously without ever attacking one another. It's all about increasing ideaflow.

When he senses the need to reinforce a shared purpose among employees, Jesper Kløve, CEO of the pharmaceutical engineering company NNE, takes his people into the field. Not the field as in the marketplace but as in the woods. "We once built a ten-meter-long pine raft and lived on it for several days," he told us. The raft was so big that Kløve's team of engineers had to work together to paddle it down the river. After several days struggling to overcome natural obstacles while sharing their life's experiences, the team dynamic had shifted. "By the end, all of us, including myself, were crying," Kløve recalled. This may sound woo-woo, but NNE's CEO gets results that prove the efficacy of this approach. The raft was a metaphor for getting people to paddle together. If a team can tackle a river without drowning, it can conduct a candid brainstorming session without bruising egos. "Trust is the only thing in this world you can't buy," Kløve told us. "You have to earn it."

To create space for candor, walk the walk. Even if you can't take your team into nature, build psychological safety in other ways. Encourage them to share unfinished work. Solicit critiques of ideas, beginning with your own. Only through steady reinforcement of these behaviors—by, for example, welcoming dissent as Mark Hoplamazian did—will you normalize candor and make it a part of your culture.

Rituals help. Pixar holds regular dailies meetings where film directors can review their works in progress with others in the organization. The purpose of each meeting is to solicit "constructive midstream feedback." The trick, according to cofounder Ed Catmull, lies in how the feedback gets handled: "Participants have learned to check their egos at the door—they are about to show incomplete work to their director and colleagues. This requires engagement at all levels, and it's our directors' job to foster and create a safe place for that." The capacity to share unfinished, imperfect work with our colleagues, receive unvarnished feedback on it, and take what is useful while leaving the rest doesn't come naturally. Pixar actively encourages this behavior with new hires accustomed to playing defense in more adversarial environments. "When the embarrassment goes away," Catmull wrote, "people become more creative. By making the struggles to solve the problem safe to discuss, everyone learns from—and inspires—one another." Making this happen requires empathy, patience, and, above all, the willingness to be vulnerable yourself.

Encouraging and welcoming dissent is not the same thing as changing your mind to suit whatever feedback you receive. In the case of Hyatt, dissent sparked a valuable discussion and led to action. Often, however, the single dissenter is alone in their dissent for a reason, and the divergent perspective can be safely dismissed. To get to that point, however, you must listen to dissent dispassionately and judge the contribution on its merits. If no one feels safe to offer a contrasting viewpoint, you'll never know whether there was an alternative worth considering in the first place. Can you afford to ignore that possibility?

~

Take this opportunity to review your current approach to mining perspectives and see where one of these tactics might make a useful addition. Focus on one area by, for example, corresponding about an idea with an industry peer. Or bringing an unexpected contributor into an existing project. Or establishing a regular candor ritual like Pixar's dailies meeting for your team. One way or another, bring a new perspective into one of your most pressing problems and see what happens.

Whatever you choose to try, don't keep it a one-off. If you take the effort to introduce a strategy and find it helpful, make it a routine practice. These tactics each require effort and consistency to reap their full rewards.

Even if you're not the leader of a team or organization, we hope this chapter will spur you to look at your network as a creative resource. Whether through Learning Circles, Pen Pals, or another tool, you can mine your collaborators, peers, clients, and customers for valuable perspectives and insights that will take your ideaflow to another level. In a world transitioning further into hybrid and fully virtual work for many, we can no longer count on chance encounters at the watercooler or in the cafeteria to spur fresh thinking. A deliberate approach to connecting and creating with other people is more valuable than ever.

8.

Shake Up Your Perspective

It is only afterward that a new idea seems
reasonable. To begin with, it usually seems
unreasonable. It seems the height of unreason
to suppose the earth was round instead of flat,
or that it moved instead of the sun, or that
objects required a force to stop them when in
motion, instead of a force to keep them moving.

—ISAAC ASIMOV

To succeed, we're told to "hunt" for opportunities as though they're hiding out there somewhere, waiting to be discovered by the most diligent and perceptive inventors and entrepreneurs. Far more often, opportunity is staring us right in the face. So wrapped up in what we expect to see, we miss it entirely.

Perry learned this lesson the hard way at Patagonia. In fact, the lesson was so painful, it's haunted him ever since. He shares the story here in the hope that you can avoid his fate. In this chapter, we will show you how to see all the opportunities that are right there in front of you, waiting for you to notice them.

~

Chances are you've got at least one polar fleece vest, jacket, or pullover in your closet. Fleece is an amazing textile. Members of the business elite have even taken to wearing fleece vests under their suit jackets during the winter in lieu of an overcoat. (The rich ain't like the rest of us.)

As you may realize—but have probably never considered too closely—there is no actual wool in a polar fleece garment. No sheep are involved whatsoever, in fact. Polar fleece got its start as so many innovations do, with a question.

Wouldn't it be great if . . .

In 1906, Hungarian immigrant Henry Feuerstein founded a textile mill in Malden, Massachusetts. Wool from Feuerstein's flocks ended up not only in Malden Mills sweaters and jackets but even in bathing suits. Before the rise of synthetic fibers, wool was your best option for staying warm while working in and around the water, or simply working up a sweat. Unlike other natural fibers, wool doesn't break down when wet. It can even wick away moisture. That said, wool is heavy and itchy. *Wouldn't it be great if wool was soft and light?* the company wondered. They might have tried breeding sheep with softer, lighter wool, but there was another avenue to explore first: synthetic fibers.

In 1884, the French scientist Hilaire de Chardonnet used cellulose from trees to make the first synthetic fiber, viscose. Later, the American chemical company DuPont developed a petroleum-based version: nylon. Elastic and strong, DuPont's textile soon appeared in everything from toothbrush bristles to stockings to, during World War II, parachutes.

Over the years, more synthetic fibers were developed, but it wasn't until 1979 that Malden Mills developed the first viable alternative to wool. Malden took polyester fibers and brushed them until they developed piles resembling those of natural wool. Soft, light, and water resistant, Malden's new material, originally known as Synchilla—synthetic chinchilla—insulated twice as well as wool. Like wool, it didn't smell when wet or absorb body odors. To clean it, you just tossed it in the laundry. These convenient characteristics made Malden's fleece ideal for rugged outdoor use, which is why Patagonia started making clothes with it. Patagonia's fleece pullovers may have been ugly—let's be honest, they *were* ugly—but they were a big hit with hikers, skiers, and others working up a sweat in cold conditions. The pullovers soon became iconic, and the partnership between Malden and Patagonia thrived.

Over the years, the two companies collaborated on incrementally improving polar fleece, making it lighter, softer, warmer, more water resistant. Windproof and resilient polar fleece started cropping up in all kinds of products beyond the outdoor category, from beanbag covers to Christmas stockings to the iconic Snuggie blanket. Patagonia started using Malden fleece for thermal underwear using the trade name Capilene. Capilene base layers became the de facto choice for outdoor activities from rock climbing to skiing. By the time Perry became a VP at Patagonia, Capilene was a reliable profit center for the company. That's when a much larger opportunity came and banged on Patagonia's front door. Would anybody answer?

A Malden factory manager came to Perry with a hot tip. A new manufacturer was buying up larger and larger quantities of Malden's polar fleece. Was this a dangerous new competitor entering the outdoor market? If so, Perry would need to address the competitive threat. No, as it turned out. The upstart actually made workout gear. Whew. Since this "Under Armour" wasn't horning in on Patagonia's territory, Perry dismissed the new, fleece-hungry brand and turned his attention back to his work.

Examine this fateful decision closely. From where Perry was sitting, Patagonia's market was one thing and Under Armour's was something completely different. Sure, UA was enjoying extraordinary growth by selling clothes that keep you warm and dry outdoors using the same technology and the same vendor as Patagonia, but it was a *sports* brand. Even as more people started wearing Under Armour outside the gym and off the field, Patagonia continued to ignore it because sports brands weren't the competition. This associative barrier prevented Perry and the company's other leaders from spotting an opportunity exponentially larger than Patagonia's entire business. Remember, there was no obvious problem, no squeaky wheel, to trigger a response. Patagonia's Capilene underwear kept selling nicely. Meanwhile, one Malden production line after another was dedicated to Under Armour.

You may be familiar with a famous psychology experiment. Participants were asked to count the number of times a ball is passed back and forth between a group of people in a video. At the end of the video, the participants share their estimates. Then they were asked a simple question: Did you notice the gorilla? As the participants discovered on rewatching the video, a man in a gorilla suit walks right into the middle of the frame halfway through, bangs his chest, and walks off-screen. Caught up in the task of counting ball passes, most participants failed to notice.

This may sound implausible, but we fail to notice the obvious all the time. In Perry's case, a gorilla known as Under Armour was banging its chest right in Patagonia's face, but they were too busy selling long underwear to notice. Yes, Under Armour was a sports brand, but what are rock climbing, skiing, snowboarding, and hiking but outdoor sports? If Perry and Patagonia had been looking closely, they would have realized that consumers weren't sweating the distinction. The outdoor market had long been trending toward sportier looks. The funky, hippie vibe of classic, 1980s-era Patagonia pullovers, with their jarring patterns and color combinations, were no longer trendy. Customers were ready for a sleek, modern look and Under Armour's growing market share reflected that pent-up demand.

It wouldn't have taken much effort for Patagonia to develop a small line of garments targeting that adjacent market to test demand. Instead, the company blithely ignored its supplier's warnings. Today, Under Armour has grown to a large multiple of Patagonia's entire business. Could Patagonia have captured all that value itself? Perhaps not, but clearly this was an epic miss. If Perry and Patagonia's other leaders could have found a way to see what was right in front of them, the company might have broken into a parallel market and grown far beyond its current size.

~

Companies make the same mistake every day. Part of the lesson in the story of Under Armour's meteoric rise is strategic: Don't let another company build a business in your backyard. The more fundamental lesson, however, is simple and universal: Listen. Look. Notice. Ideaflow depends on inputs reaching a receptive mind. It isn't enough to expose yourself to lots and lots of information. If that was all it took, scrolling through social media for hours would be a productive use of your time. It's the easiest thing in the world to look without seeing and hear without listening. There is a discipline to effective observation. It takes effort and skill. The payoff, however, is immense. In this chapter, we will show you how to observe the world around you in a way that nurtures and enriches your creative output.

It often comes as a shock to learn how different our individual perceptions can be. Heated online arguments years ago over the color of "The Dress" or the sound of "Laurel" versus "Yanni" revealed surprising idiosyncrasies in the ways people perceive the same sensory inputs. These quirky variations in how large numbers of people interpret certain sense impressions are only the beginning of the story. As artists and meditators have long understood, there is the world "out there" and then there is the 360-degree sensory and imaginative theater in your head. Just as what you perceive can shift your perspective, changing your perspective can change what you perceive.

Why is seeing what's right in front of you so hard to do? Blame the brain for being so efficient. When we hear a word or see an image, it triggers a series of associated images, facts, and ideas inside our heads. The brain forms these associations when we first encounter anything unfamiliar, chaining the unknown together with the known in an ever-expanding network of thought. In the future, it can fall back on these fixed patterns of related people, places, things, and concepts whenever it needs to decide quickly. This saves time and energy compared with developing a fresh response to each situation. What do you get at the movie theater? Popcorn. Your own association may be different, but that you *have* a default association is certain. To see the unexpected and unimagined hiding in plain sight, you must lower these associative barriers.

In this chapter, we offer methods for shaking up your perspective so you can finally see the opportunities right in front of you. Only by short-circuiting your usual modes of perception will you ever notice the extraordinary possibilities hiding right in front of you.

FIND BETTER PROBLEMS

You first learned about Henrik Werdelin, founding partner of the prolific New York venture development firm Prehype, in chapter 2. An investor, founder, and adviser, Werdelin pays attention for a living. For him, noticing the right problem is the first step in generating any business idea. He considers himself problem- rather than idea-centric. A good idea may not be viable, but a good problem will usually lead somewhere.

In his ongoing search for better problems to solve, Werdelin forages the digital world. He doesn't just mindlessly scour social media, however. Instead, he methodically seeks out rich new veins to mine, usually in the form of new tools and technologies. By positioning himself at the cutting edge, he becomes aware of problems most people have yet to encounter, but inevitably will.

"You can't come up with NFT [non-fungible token] ideas without having bought an NFT," he says. "You have to walk in the shoes. I install dozens of apps a week. Every time I try a new tool, I build something with it, tinker with it." Werdelin is so effective at observation because his parameters are clear and consistent. His brain knows why it's looking, even if it doesn't know exactly what it's looking for. "Just build stuff," Werdelin advises. "You have to do that to generate ideas. If I don't build stuff, I dry out very fast."

The brain, intent on its objectives, tends to work around problems, compensating for them without even letting them register consciously. You'll trip over the same uneven paving stone outside your front door a dozen times before it occurs to you to get it fixed. This habitual filtering of life's annoyances means that juicy problems are hard to see. There are probably two or more viable businesses within reach of where you're reading this book. An entrepreneur like Werdelin takes a systematic approach to observing the world as it is, noticing the parts that need work and attacking those problems with ideas.

As we saw in chapter 2, central to Werdelin's process is the discipline of documentation. Writing things down is a way of forcing yourself to observe. It also ensures that you learn from your experiments. Werdelin provokes his own curiosity with three simple words: "It sucks that . . ." This crucial phrase appears on stacks of custom Post-it notes around the Prehype offices. Every new business the company incubates starts out as something that sucks, a problem in need of solutions. Not just any problem will do, however. Something that can be resolved swiftly and easily is boring. Thirsty? Buy a bottle of water. For Werdelin, an interesting problem runs deeper. It sparks a dialogue with customers and creates a stronger connection with them. "Netflix and Peloton are relationship-capital companies," Werdelin told us. "They seek to understand their customers better in order to make products that help them understand their customers even better than that." The better your grasp of the kind of problems you want to solve, the better you'll be at finding them.

Prehype's most successful venture is the dog subscription box service BARK. As that company's founding partner, Werdelin is always seeking canine-centric problems, filtering them based on whether they have the capacity to deepen the company's relationship with its customers. "It sucks that my dog has bad breath," in Werdelin's view, doesn't facilitate a dialogue. Brush the dog's teeth or give it a minty biscuit. In fact, the company now offers a dental product line—but that's the end of the story. On the other hand, "It sucks that I have to go to work and leave my dog alone all day" leads in all kinds of interesting directions. It's weighted with emotion and ripe with possibilities. The right solution might lead to an ongoing relationship with BARK. A problem like that sparks many possibilities to test and might spawn more than one successful business line. Good problems suggest multiple avenues of exploration. That's important because you always want to be testing and learning until something clicks.

BARK got its big break in retail thanks to a failed experiment. The problem there was "It sucks that dogs can't do their own shopping." Talk about something that sparks a dialogue with dog owners. "We set up an experience to let dogs choose their own toys," Werdelin recalled, "but owners would never buy the toys the dogs selected. They always bought the ones they thought were funny." Doggie shopping was a nice idea, but it wasn't viable, so the experiment failed. Technically. "Today, BARK products are in 26,000 stores," Werdelin continued, "and I will almost guarantee we wouldn't be in a single one if we hadn't run that experiment. Target saw what we did, decided we knew something about reinventing retail, and put us in all their stores."

This is the essence of ideaflow. You can't think your way through problems. There is no way BARK could have planned its way into Target's stores along this circuitous path. Instead, problems spark ideas, ideas suggest tests, tests generate forward momentum. "The path to the right thing isn't linear," Werdelin told us. "You just have to try things. Shots on goal."

Today, Werdelin feeds possible solutions into a spreadsheet and scores them against factors like the size of the potential market and how well they play into existing assets. No matter how efficient the experimentation process gets, he can't test every single idea, so he does whatever he can to increase the odds that the next one will pay off. At this stage, Werdelin is less interested in brainstorming a bunch of ideas to solve a single problem than in building an algorithm that can find many more problems. Until we have an ideaflow AI, however, it's on all of us to rewire our perceptions to see more of the world in front of us.

REVERSE YOUR ASSUMPTIONS

After the 2008 stock market crash, many Millennials became hesitant to invest in the stock market. Fidelity Investments came to us for some fresh thinking on how to reach these younger customers.

Naturally, our first stop was Urban Outfitters.

OK, maybe this doesn't seem that natural. But the store suited our purposes perfectly. At the time, Urban was popular with the very same Millennials that Fidelity wanted to woo. Even better, there was a shop right down the road from the corporate office. Cheap, fast, imperfect.

Inside the store, Fidelity execs observed a young woman digging through a pile of clothing strewn under a table. Talk about shoddy merchandising! This was the very opposite of the clean, orderly, and welcoming customer experience Fidelity always sought to deliver. Eyes rolled.

Once the snickering subsided, we asked the scornful Fidelity execs to assume that Urban knew what it was doing. One way to notice what you're missing is to consciously identify your assumptions and then deliberately flip them upside down, a tool we call the Assumption Reversal. What if digging through clothes on your hands and knees was a delightful and rewarding experience *for that customer*? What if there was nothing accidental about that sloppy pile of clothes seemingly forgotten under the table? This woman was in the exact demographic Fidelity hoped to attract. Instead of trading stocks on Fidelity's clean and easy-to-use app or talking to an adviser in one of its spacious and well-lit retail locations, she was kneeling on a linoleum floor and digging through wrinkled blouses. Let's assume this was part of the plan. What was Urban up to?

That's when it clicked. The customer in front of us wasn't just shopping. She was on a *treasure hunt.* Excited by the possibility of finding something special, something the "average" customer would never have spotted, she was searching a pile of clothing a staff member must have neglected to tidy up. Since no ordinary retailer leaves piles of clothing under a table, she considered it a happy accident. After all, at most trendy fashion retailers, the most desirable items sell out quickly. It stood to reason that the best way to find something exclusive or special would be to look somewhere unexpected. Like under a table.

Examining the store with their assumptions reversed, the Fidelity team realized that the "hidden" clothing was part of a deliberate merchandising strategy. Urban was mimicking the shopping experience of a hip used-clothing boutique, the kind of place where an eye for fashion gives you a leg up on the other shoppers. Millennials didn't want to feel like they were being herded toward the same cookie-cutter looks. Instead, they wanted something that felt unique, even though the artful piles and their hidden treasures were the same in every Urban Outfitters across the country.

Assumption Reversal freed Fidelity from the confines of their own experience. The insights they generated at Urban Outfitters sparked a slew of creative possibilities that helped them reinvent the customer experience to appeal more directly to Millennials.

When we met with TaylorMade Golf to look at their consumer experience for young golfers, we asked ourselves, "Who delivers a great shopping experience for younger people?" Among other chains, we visited Claire's Accessories. No, TaylorMade wasn't aiming to woo tweens to golf, but sometimes going all the way along a spectrum can highlight useful distinctions.

Like their counterparts at Fidelity, the TaylorMade execs were skeptical about studying a business so obviously unrelated to their own. What could a store that offers free piercing with every set of earrings teach a high-end golf brand? Once we coaxed them into the bright and colorful location, their skepticism deepened. How disorganized! A TaylorMade distributor would never merchandise a store so chaotically. The company took great pride in its product presentation, whether online or in-store. Everything in its place, according to function: drivers with drivers, putters with putters, wedges with . . . you get the idea. This sense of pride stood in the way of true understanding. It was time to do an Assumption Reversal.

"What if Claire's knows exactly what it's doing?" we asked them. "What if its customers find this arrangement delightful?" If nothing else, the sport of golf teaches patience. Once we'd stood there long enough, the execs stopped looking and started seeing. Claire's organizes its stores not by function but by context. These accessories were appropriate for school, these for a party, and these for a weekend away. Suddenly, the "chaos" revealed its own elegant harmonies. A tween might come to Claire's before her very first date with no clear idea of what was fashionable among her peer group, nor what was specifically appropriate for a night at the movies. Through organization alone, Claire's steered these nervous customers toward a coordinated, appealing, and trendy set of accessories.

Likewise, a young golfer might be overwhelmed by the neat rows of irons, woods, and putters in a store and yet unwilling to admit ignorance or ask an employee for help. If clothing, gear, and accessories were arranged according to experience level—for example, laying out a complete kit appropriate for a novice golfer in one spot—these customers could find everything they needed without owning up to their amateur status.

It might have taken a full eighteen rounds of effort to get TaylorMade in the door at Claire's, but once they'd seen the benefits of reversing their assumptions, the team wanted to visit every tween-oriented store in town. There was only so much they could learn from studying competitors who also spent all their time thinking about golf. Claire's spends its time thinking about youth, and that perspective proved invaluable.

Conducting an Assumption Reversal is about identifying what you're taking for granted about a situation and deliberately assuming its opposite is true. To apply this tool to your company's customer experience, go where the customers you're trying to reach already are. Then, rather than judge the experience through your usual lens, reverse your assumptions. These customers must be there for a reason. It can't be all bad no matter how discordant it feels. In fact, pay close attention to any elements that challenge your definitions of a quality experience. Customers find something about this appealing. Your job is to figure out what. Don't stop at one guess, either. We've condensed our experiences at these retailers. The Fidelity and TaylorMade execs generated a ton of possible explanations for what they saw and then verified them with actual customers. Go into an Assumption Reversal with a quota to meet. Keep asking why. Every member of the team should generate several explanations to explain what they're seeing. Once you've met the quota, test each possibility with customers. Do they agree?

You can use this tool to spur fresh thinking around anything from the design of a product to the structure of an online sales funnel. Find a successful example of what you're trying to create but in a very different context. Assume everything about its design is intentional, even if none of it makes sense or looks "right" to you. Then, set a quota and start coming up with plausible explanations for its success. Finally, verify your guesses in the real world.

Fidelity used what they learned at Urban Outfitters to craft an investment experience for Millennials that felt like a treasure hunt. TaylorMade used what it learned at Claire's Accessories to imagine how a store's organization might answer questions a self-conscious new player wouldn't want to ask. When you're no longer blinded by your own assumptions, new vistas appear.

INTERVIEW WITH EMPATHY

To gather unexpected insights from your users or customers, you must explore their thinking with an open mind. Doing that is difficult when they're talking about a subject you know well: your product, your service, your area of expertise. We can't help but interpret everything that gets said through our own filters. To really understand the behavior of others and finally grasp what they *mean* with the words they use, shake up your perceptions using the Empathetic Interviews tool. This will help short-circuit your preconceived notions to reveal the genuine feelings, beliefs, and preferences of others. It's the difference between hearing and listening.

As the largest dental insurance company in the United States, Delta Dental provides benefits to over 39 million Americans. Delta and the thousands of providers in its network often find patient behavior inexplicable. The average dentist spends their entire career repairing the kind of damage that could easily have been avoided with a little daily maintenance, and these repairs are often costly and painful. People figure it out eventually, if a little late. Ask a dozen elderly people about their biggest regrets in life and half or more will mention their teeth. By middle age, the calendar of the average American is riddled with remedial visits to the dentist. Poor brushing habits don't just lead to fillings, crowns, and root canals, however. They also play a significant role in overall health. Another way of looking at this, of course, is that a little effort when you're younger delivers a huge payoff down the road for your entire body.

As part of its mission to care for American mouths, Delta had mounted one campaign after another to encourage oral care. Unfortunately, most of these attempts did not make a significant impact. No matter how much the company persevered—through emails, posters, social media—it failed to make a dent in the public health crisis. They couldn't convince more young people to brush and floss consistently. When the company came to us for help improving oral care for the 114 million Americans without dental health benefits of any kind, they were out of ideas. The scare tactics fell flat. *That guy in the ad with all the crowns might regret his choices now, but he's old. That's way off in the future for me—I'll start flossing as soon as life slows down a bit.*

Two of the senior leaders at Delta grappling with this, Casey Harlin and Liz Black, had attended the d.school's executive education program. They welcomed the opportunity to have two of our grad students, Andre and Andy, help Delta innovate on the problem under our guidance. Before generating ideas, however, we clearly needed to understand the terrain better. While the company had data on the attitudes and beliefs of its generally older and more affluent customers, it knew relatively little about the young, uninsured people it most wanted to reach. This struck us as an ideal use case for Empathetic Interviews.

When you talk to a user or customer with this tool, your goal is to understand their experience on an emotional level. Contrary to what abstract words like "empathy" and "emotions" might suggest, specificity is everything. You never ask, "What do you think of our product?" Instead, you ground each question in a discrete experience: "Tell me about the last time you returned an item to our store."

"Well, I usually . . . ," a customer will almost always say, but "usually" is useless. "Please be specific," you respond. Don't let the discussion devolve into generalities. "Tell me about the very last time you returned something." Or ask about the best return experience they've ever had. Or the worst. One way or the other, lead the interviewee to call up a specific instance from memory. Then, follow that journey with them while charting its emotional ups and downs. If you're not specific, you'll get a blur of impressions assembled from multiple experiences. Once the interviewee brings a particular instance to mind, walk through it step by step, always bringing it back to where their emotions were at each moment. When the user does something in the story, ask them why. Then, ask them how it felt.

What you're seeking here are surprises, things that contradict your current understanding. Since it's your product or service, you think you know what the experience is like. Your lack of new ideas reflects that false certainty. Empathetic Interviews puncture that confidence. Follow up on anything unexpected: "Tell me more about that." Ask why, and when they tell you, ask why about that, too. As part of the Toyota Production System, engineer Taiichi Ohno famously advocated asking why five times when diagnosing a problem to get as close as possible to the true cause. Repeated whys went on to become standard in subsequent management systems like Six Sigma. Does the exact number make a difference? No. What's important to understand is that one why isn't enough. The first explanation is nearly always insufficient and even misleading. In your search for clues, go beneath the obvious answers to the truths that lie beneath.

Talking to a friend or family member, it feels good to reciprocate: "Oh man, I know exactly what you mean." When conducting an Empathetic Interview, rigorously resist this bias toward reciprocity. It cuts off the flow of learning. You're telling the other person that you understand what they're saying. But you don't. That's the point. The gap between your assumptions and their reality is where you'll find your insights. Never stem the tide of learning by affirming the interviewee's experience in any way. Instead, question everything.

This even applies to word choice. People often use common terms differently than you do. In casual conversation, these little differences work themselves out. In an Empathetic Interview, however, it's easy to miss something crucial by taking definitions for granted. If a word feels pivotal, ask the user to define it, or to put the same thought another way. "You said that was 'challenging'—what do you mean by that exactly?" In your mind, challenging might carry a negative charge while the interviewee sees it as a benefit, the way a puzzle can be an enjoyable challenge, for example. Let them tell you. Painstakingly withhold judgment.

Stories also help make abstract ideas concrete. If the customer says that "relief" is a part of their experience, say, "You've been mentioning 'relief.' Can you tell us another time in your life when you felt that kind of relief? It doesn't have to relate to this." Though it feels unnatural to resist the normal flow of conversation in these ways, keep questioning your own assumptions and probing for more and you'll be surprised by how deep the learning goes.

Once you've completed an Empathetic Interview, diagram the user's journey. Draw a line from left to right representing the start and end of the experience in question, whether it's the first time they used your website or the last time they purchased something at your store. Then, map out each event in the journey, placing it on the vertical axis to indicate the emotional charge. For example, in the journey of a product return, searching for the tossed receipt in the wastebasket near the start of the experience would be a stressful dip near the left side of the board. Getting the full refund with no fuss would be a positive bump near the right.

If you can, conduct Empathetic Interviews with "extreme" users: youngest, oldest, tallest, shortest, most frequent, most critical. Talking with users at the end of the spectrum—any spectrum—reveals avenues for exploration that might remain hidden with average users. For example, leaders at Levi's interviewed one customer who happened to be pregnant. When she mentioned buying new jeans every few weeks to keep up with her expanding waistline, a light bulb went off. One leader suggested a subscription service for jeans, something with potential appeal not only to pregnant customers but to customers concerned about the environmental impact of denim production, those who change their look frequently, dieters, and so on. To be clear, you don't seek out extreme users to develop niche products for them. You do it to spur new thinking with implications across the board. Randy Hetrick, a former Navy Seal, designed the TRX suspension training system for professional athletes but soon saw its benefits for average users. As Hetrick told us, "From the pros to the Joes."

What the Empathetic Interviews Delta conducted made clear was that oral health simply wasn't on the radar for the people they were trying to reach. When we asked a question to evoke a discrete experience—"Tell me about the last time you thought about your teeth?"—the answers related to physical appearance alone. While young, uninsured people were concerned with their teeth, that concern went only as far as their smiles. Would teeth whitening improve their appearance on Instagram or Tinder? How hard was it to straighten teeth—have you heard about clear aligners? And so on. Root canals were off in the distant future, but talk about smiles and you had their undivided attention in the present.

We'll discuss what Delta did with the results of its Empathetic Interviews in the next chapter.

OBSERVE FOR LONGER

Scientists rely on patient, careful observation to make discoveries. Some have taken this principle to extremes, however. The biologist David Haskell once spent an entire year observing a Tennessee forest. In his Pulitzer-nominated book, *The Forest Unseen,* he documented some of the extraordinary lessons he learned about the intricate web of relationships spanning the forest ecosystem, the twist being that he limited his observation to a single square meter of soil.

If a biologist can write an entire book about the epic drama among flora and fauna that takes place on a single patch of soil, you can spend a few more minutes observing customers navigate your online form. You don't have to watch every day for a year. But that little voice in your head insisting you've seen enough for now is not to be trusted. The rewards of observation usually lie on the other side of boredom. When in doubt, look a little longer.

It takes dedicated effort to force yourself to really look at something. Most of our sensory perceptions drift in below the level of conscious attention. We look without seeing all the time, ruminating on the past or worrying about the future while on automatic pilot through the present.

By the time we're adults, we read so fluidly that the meaning of what we're reading enters our minds without much conscious awareness of the words themselves. Read the same word over and over, however, and its shape will become meaningless, the letters a row of squiggly abstractions. Psychologists call this phenomenon semantic satiation. You can try it now with any of the words on this page. Semantic satiation exposes us to the concrete reality of those specific shapes in that specific order, short-circuiting the fluid reading process.

This is the simplest and most direct way to short-circuit the brain's filter. With enough patience, you'll be able to look at a situation long enough to finally see it. As the seconds tick by, new details will emerge, and this will keep happening long past the point you feel certain you've seen everything there is to see. When you're absolutely convinced there's nothing left to notice, wait another minute. There it is: one last, crucial detail that unlocks a flurry of possibilities. And another detail after that.

In chapter 3, we saw how the brain tries to convince us that we're "out of ideas" when brainstorming and how, if we hold ourselves to a fixed idea quota, new ideas will keep arriving well past that "creative cliff." A similar phenomenon is at work here. Set a timer. When observing a situation— whether it's a customer entering a store or a user fiddling with a new product—decide in advance how long you'll continue to watch. Make it uncomfortable. If watching something happen for five minutes feels weird, set a timer for ten. Then, settle in.

As you observe, your brain will almost immediately tell you that you've done enough looking for now. Everything worth seeing here is plainly visible on the surface, it will argue. Take that impulse as a sign of encouragement and keep returning your attention to present. Before you know it, the brain will insist more urgently. *Nothing to see here. Move along.* Respect the timer, however, and you will eventually exhaust the brain's capacity to filter out the unknown and unexpected. Insights will begin to emerge as you surrender to the moment. As your awareness deepens, write down your interpretations. Again, the key question is *why*. Why is the customer doing this? Why am I not seeing what I'd expected to see? As with an idea quota, write down as many possible interpretations of your observations as you possibly can. Doing so will not only create valuable fodder for ideas but also keep you engaged in the process of observation.

Drawing is another way to immerse yourself in what you see. This is true even if you really can't draw. Bringing pencil to paper, even in a rudimentary way, forces you to notice instead of simply look. At Pixar, even nonartists are taught basic drawing skills—it's considered fundamental training in the crucial capacity to observe. As Pixar's president and co-founder Ed Catmull explained, "[It] is possible, with practice, to teach your brain to observe something clearly without letting your preconceptions kick in."

Jennifer L. Roberts, a professor of the history of art and architecture at Harvard University, requires all her art history students to write a research paper on a work of art of their choosing. "And the first thing I ask them to do in the research process," she explained, "is to spend a painfully long time looking at that object." Three full hours, in fact. Many students resist the task, arguing that there simply can't be that much to see in any single painting or sculpture. Routinely, however, they are amazed by what they discover. "Just because something is available instantly to vision does not mean that it is available instantly to consciousness," Roberts explained. This principle isn't just about fine art, either.

Our mentor David Kelley, the founder of the design firm IDEO, once spent several hours observing a soda vending machine. At first, all he saw was what he expected to see: one person after another depositing coins and then retrieving their cans from the dispenser. After a while, however, something clicked, and Kelley could finally see what he'd been looking at. People were stooping to retrieve their soda. *Stooping.* Why? Because the dispenser tray had been placed at knee height. Why was the dispenser so low that people had to stoop for it? Probably, Kelley surmised, because the first, pre-electric vending machines let gravity do the work of moving the cans. Why hadn't the design of soda vending machines evolved with the invention of electricity? Why hadn't someone designed a machine that brought your soda to a convenient height? *Good questions.*

Here was a big, expensive piece of equipment found in nearly every office building, sports arena, train station, academic facility, and hotel in the world. Yet all it took was a little patience to innovate a significant improvement to its fundamental design. Electricity had been around for a century, so it wasn't a matter of technological progress. It was simply that people, even—or especially—people working at vending machine companies, didn't see the actual device anymore. They just saw what their brain expected to see. They might update the signage or tweak the machinery to cut down on jamming, but that was about it. Most of us, most of the time, optimize for efficiency. We get better at doing what we've already been doing. True innovation requires rethinking the fundamentals and, to do that, you must *see* them.

~

Developing your power of observation isn't always a matter of brute force. Curiosity can pull you where discipline and willpower would otherwise have to push. Most of us aren't in the habit of cultivating our own curiosity, however. Instead, we usually let it guide us where it will. If you've ever spiraled down an internet rabbit hole, you know how powerful—and pointless—this undirected, undisciplined curiosity can be.

Managed deliberately and strategically, curiosity can be an extraordinarily powerful force for innovation, both as a part of your own creative toolbox as well as for inspiring and directing the efforts of others. Curiosity is a way of getting people to observe more closely, think more deeply, and imagine more vigorously.

In the next chapter, we will explain how to spur curiosity and then leverage its magnetic pull toward great feats of innovation.

9.

Stoke Curiosity

It is a familiar and significant saying that a problem well put is half-solved.

—JOHN DEWEY

Having completed the Empathetic Interview process discussed in the previous chapter, Delta Dental needed a provocative prompt to spark the idea-generation process discussed in chapter 3. Something that would really pique everyone's curiosity. The interviews inspired a killer one:

How might we convince people who care about their appearance to care about their oral health, too?

Eyes lit up around the room. Vanity as a Trojan Horse? *Very* interesting! A flood of ideas quickly followed, and Delta soon had a portfolio of ideas to test, such as a smile diagnosis app that sent selfies to dentists for feedback. With a single good frame to provoke discussion, Delta escaped its creative dead end—scare tactics—and unlocked a world of possibilities they'd never previously considered.

Within six weeks, Delta had launched a prototype retail concept through our Launchpad program dubbed the Dazzle Bar. Conceived as a premier beauty service, the first Dazzle Bars were pop-up stores featuring comfy and casual decor far from the sterile, intimidating atmosphere of a typical dentist's office. Dazzle Bars offered fast, convenient, and affordable cleaning, whitening, and breath-freshening services. Once customers were in the chair for these cosmetic procedures, they could be given a little basic dentistry as part of the package, along with referrals to dentists for more serious problems. The prototype confirmed that appealing to vanity really did lead to healthier dental outcomes overall. Customer feedback confirmed the success of this strategy. Remarks like "pleasant, quick, and simple" and "fun and relaxing" are rarely made after a trip to the dentist. The prototype Dazzle Bar pop-ups were so successful they inspired other innovation prototypes and teams at Delta. One leader told us that the Dazzle Bar was the company's first radical idea in its sixty-year history.

When the answers run dry, ask a better question.

CURIOSITY DRIVES INNOVATION

To steer the brain's efforts in useful directions, you need the right frame. Leveraging the brain's extraordinary capacity to pan for gold comes down to asking it questions that attract its interest and activate its attention.

A good question is specific. For instance, think of white things. What comes to mind, and how swiftly? Now, think of white things you find in the typical refrigerator. Do you notice the difference? With the first question, possibilities sputter to the surface: Snow. Uh. Polar bear. Paper? With the second, the possibilities *flow*: Milk, cheese, yogurt, cottage cheese, take-out containers, eggs, does white bread count? And so on. The more specific the frame, the stronger the flow of ideas it will inspire. A good frame stokes curiosity. Once your interest is piqued, your brain gets to work on solving the problem in earnest. Ideaflow increases. A juicy question can make it difficult to *stop* thinking of new possibilities. A dull one, on the other hand, leads nowhere. You simply can't fake curiosity. If you aren't genuinely interested in a problem, don't expect much in the way of creative solutions.

Sometimes a frame is literal. The legendary artist and educator Corita Kent had her students create what she called a "finder" to "take things out of context." A finder is simply a frame made of cardboard. It "allows us to see for the sake of seeing, and enhances our quick-looking and decision-making skills." You can use your phone's camera as a finder or even something as specialized as a cinematographer's viewfinder. But a square made of cardboard will do. Try looking at your problem—the product, the store, some aspect of a physical experience—through a finder and watch how a frame can make the hidden visible.

Even if you start with a provocative question, there's only so much you can do by looking at a problem from one angle. When ideaflow ebbs, move your frame. As discussed in chapter 3, when the popcorn stops popping, switch things up. Steady ideaflow means crafting lots of good questions and cycling through them as you generate ideas. When a different question reveals a new facet to the problem you're trying to solve, interest reawakens. Don't wait for things to fizzle out before thinking about other questions. Instead, generate lots of frames systematically at the start. When ideaflow wanes, nimbly change frames to keep the energy up. By generating the questions (frames) before the answers (ideas), you will dramatically grow the funnel of possibilities to test.

In this chapter, we will show you how to design questions that stoke curiosity to spur a flood of ideas. This isn't just about getting people in a room to generate a million possibilities in one go. Group sessions as discussed in chapter 3 are helpful from time to time, but develop a habit of framing interesting problems for yourself and keeping them in the back of your mind to fuel your Idea Quota. Think about the bug list and corkboard R&D department suggested in chapter 4. Collect compelling, specific questions and review them frequently. If you keep interesting things simmering, your brain will always be at work for you in the background, searching for inputs to power world-class creative output.

GENERATE A PORTFOLIO OF FRAMES

Ask yourself an interesting enough question
and your attempt to find a tailor-made
solution to that question will push you to a
place where, pretty soon, you'll find yourself
all by your lonesome—which I think is a more
interesting place to be.

—CHUCK CLOSE

Nearly every good frame begins the same way: How might we . . . ? A good HMW question allows for plenty of exploration while leaving enough structure to keep the discussion focused. A question like "How might we create an ice cream cone that doesn't drip?" doesn't leave room for the unexpected. It directs your attention toward a very specific and narrow engineering issue. A laser-focused question generates laser-focused fixes. A prompt can also be too broad: "How might we reinvent dessert for a new generation?" For the owner of an ice cream store, this isn't going to lead anywhere useful. You need constraints. The brain doesn't know how to "reinvent dessert"—that's clearly too abstract. Yet companies try to "reinvent communication" or "reimagine urban transportation" and wonder why nothing happens.

The goal is a large portfolio of different frames. You're never looking for one perfect question—a single frame limits your thinking no matter how well it's designed. Each prompt opens a different set of possibilities to explore. Introducing a good question spurs curiosity even when everyone at the table is certain they've thought through all the possibilities around a given problem. The more questions you have lined up, the longer you'll be able to sustain ideaflow. Always prepare a hefty stack *before* beginning the ideation process.

There are several ways to craft useful HMWs around a problem or insight. For example, as an ice cream store owner struggling to reinvent dessert, you might notice a customer lick their friend's cone. You're struck by how intimate and tender it is to taste someone else's ice cream, and a little light goes on. Something about the social aspect of eating ice cream together, a factor that isn't present with sandwiches or steaks. Likewise, eating ice cream alone conveys loneliness. Why? What can you do with this seed of an idea? Once immersion in a problem leads you to an insight like this, use the following set of "dials" to craft powerful HMW questions.

> Scale. Play with the zoom knob. In their classic short film *Powers of Ten,* Charles and Ray Eames show a man and woman enjoying a lakeside picnic before zooming out at an exponential rate, revealing the surrounding park, then the city of Chicago, then the Earth, the solar system, and so on. Once the magnitude of the entire universe is revealed, the camera zooms back in, down to the planet, the city, and the couple, before continuing the zoom into the man's hand, reaching the scale of skin cells, molecules, and atoms.
>
> Scale changes everything. There is always both a bigger picture and a smaller one. Each degree of magnitude reveals something unique that can't be seen at any other level of magnification. What happens to your problem if you narrow in on one small aspect? What happens if you widen your frame to include more surrounding context? Play with scale and watch more ideas flow.

o   How might we celebrate the dripping of an ice cream cone?

o   How might we make every single bite an experience of its own?

o   How might we create an experience that can be unlocked only by more than twenty people at a time?

o   How might we get thousands of people to post an ice cream cone on social media?

Quality. Take a positive aspect of your starting insight and double down on it. Or, explore questions that suggest cheaper, faster, more imperfect approaches to the problem. Deliberately seeking "bad" ideas relaxes perfectionistic tendencies. Aerosmith, one of the best-selling American hard rock bands of all time, holds weekly "dare to suck" meetings where every member of the band brings ideas they consider terrible. Often, the results really are terrible, but now and then they get a hit like "Dude (Looks Like a Lady)." If it wasn't worthwhile, would they still be doing it after all these years?

Likewise, Second City, Chicago's legendary improvisational comedy theater, devotes one day a month to ideas they would normally never do. On "Taboo Day," improvisers are encouraged to propose outrageous, expensive, and impractical ideas that would normally be (not) laughed off the stage. Kelly Leonard, a leader at the storied organization, told us that a deliberate effort to suggest the "wrong" thing nearly always generates rich and useful material.

So turn the quality knob all the way up and all the way

down. Either way, relax your sense of "should" and allow for silly, weird, surprising, or outrageous instead. What's the worst that could happen?

o How might we make a "tandem" ice cream cone?

o How might we make the melting of ice cream a feature, not a bug?

o How might we make a cone that prevents you from eating the ice cream?

o How might we design an ice cream parlor as the perfect first-date venue?

o How might we make a visit to the ice cream parlor the best experience of a customer's day?

Emotion. What emotions does your insight inspire, and where might those lead? Consider the full spectrum here, not just positive emotions like happiness and joy but also sadness, loneliness, even fear. Whatever emotions you assume are appropriate to the situation, dial the knob the other way. It's surprising how often this simple flip unlocks new directions.

o How might we help a father show *love* to his child with ice cream?

o How might we design an ice cream cone that says goodbye?

o How might we create the "I'm sorry" ice cream experience?

o How might ice cream make you laugh?

Stakes. Try both raising and lowering the stakes of the situation to shake up your perspective. Sometimes, seemingly trivial aspects hide something profoundly meaningful. On the other hand, levity and lightness can be found in some of the most serious contexts.

o   How might we design an ice cream experience around mourning?

o   How might we integrate ice cream into a wedding ceremony?

o   How might we make ice cream the go-to destination for breakup meals? For proposals?

o   How might ice cream save your marriage?

o   How might ice cream provoke a thoughtful conversation?

o   How might ice cream seal a promotion? Or crown a tough negotiation?

Expectations. What are you taking for granted about the problem? For this dial, it can be helpful to make a list of all the assumptions you're making about how the product should work or how the solution should otherwise function. Then swap each assumption with its opposite.

o   How might we share ice cream without a cone or a cup?

o   How might we make ice cream hot?

o   How might we make ice cream the appetizer rather than the dessert?

o   How might we eliminate the post-ice-cream
    sugar crash?

o   How might ice cream be NSFW?

Similarity. Analogy is one of the most powerful creative tools. We'll dig deeper into the power of analogy in the next chapter. Here, consider parallel contexts at one end of the dial and completely unrelated ones at the other. To think of good analogies to try, start with the intended outcome. Want to make ice cream faster? "Who or what is built for speed?" Want to delight your customers? "Who or what delights people?" The brain solves new problems in this way, using its understanding of a familiar topic to grapple with one that appears very different on the surface.

You might apply the lessons of high school football to your first job managing a team, or transplant one of Napoleon's battlefield strategies to a product launch. Consciously or unconsciously, we distill principles from observations and then see where else they might fit.

o   How might we make ice cream like a therapy
    session?

o   How might an Olympic sprinter serve up an ice
    cream cone?

o   How might Apple design a container for ice
    cream sprinkles?

o   How might eating ice cream feel like a roller
    coaster? Like a magic show? Like a horror
    movie?

HMW questions can be silly or serious. The important thing is to seek a middle path between too specific to generate divergent possibilities and too broad to generate any.

Generating HMWs should happen separately from generating the solutions themselves. Resist the impulse to start ideating. If a compelling solution does come to mind as you're generating questions, it can easily anchor you, cutting off the flow of good problems. To return to a divergent mindset, spell out the problem implicitly being solved by your existing idea as a new HMW. Ask yourself, "What would it actually *do*—for the user, customer, company—if we made this idea a reality?" Then ask yourself, "What are other ways we achieve the same thing?"

Say you come up with the idea of introducing a subscription model for your ice cream parlor. Now, instead of generating more interesting frames, you're working out the mechanics of subscriptions. How much would customers pay and on what schedule? Will they need membership cards or should we use an app? Is this for unlimited ice cream or a certain number of cones each month?

Before you know it, you're deep in the weeds. When you find your thinking converging this way, look at the problem being solved. What would an ice cream subscription accomplish? "Well, it would give customers a regular touchpoint with us." That's one *why*. How else might you accomplish that *why*? Now you've got a useful frame: "How might we establish a regular touchpoint with our customers?"

Ideas start flowing again: You might offer a refer-a-friend bonus. You might give out a coupon for a free topping if they come back the following week. You might send a monthly newsletter announcing new flavors. Keep generating different ways to achieve the same impact as the original idea. Narrow things too quickly and risk leaving your best ideas on the table.

HMW questions keep your energy up and spur divergent thinking during the idea-generation process. Make a habit of establishing, exploring, and discarding frames to keep ideaflow steady. Each frame, each question, represents another vein of ore to mine. Most will run dry quickly, but a few will astonish you with their depth and richness. You never know until you start digging.

PROVOKE WITH PROMPTS

Crafting "How might we?" questions is a powerful way to stoke curiosity, but HMWs aren't the only approach worth trying when ideaflow wanes—especially when under pressure. Here are a few more tools to consider.

Subtract. The tool of subtraction introduces a simple but powerful constraint: Can we improve this idea solely by removing something from the picture? It's powerful in practice precisely because it goes against the grain.

The late American cartoonist Rube Goldberg's name is synonymous with elaborate and convoluted solutions to simple problems. For decades, Goldberg's drawings of hypothetical inventions were syndicated in newspapers across the country. The caption for Goldberg's illustration of a car "safety" device reads: "When jaywalker steps in front of car, he is scooped up and tossed into large, roomy funnel—as he slides into waiting cannon he hits ping-pong paddle, pulling lanyard and shooting him three blocks away where he won't bother you anymore." Jaywalking, solved. (Perhaps we should forward Goldberg's idea to Philippe Barreaud at Michelin.)

As absurd as Goldberg's overengineered contraptions are, they elicit chuckles of recognition because they reflect the usual approach to problem-solving. When there's a roadblock, the tendency is to design a suspension bridge before simply pushing the block off the road. In a paper published in

Nature, researchers confirmed this Goldbergian tendency: "People systematically default to searching for additive transformations, and consequently overlook subtractive transformations."

Leidy Klotz, an engineer and a coauthor on the paper, noticed this while building a LEGO bridge with his two-year-old son, Ezra. Since the bridge wasn't sitting evenly, Klotz decided to fix it. "I turned around to grab a block to add to the shorter column," he told an interviewer, "and by the time I turned around, Ezra had just removed a block from the longer column." The child had seen what the engineer had not. Less is more.

Crucially, we don't default to addition because subtraction is harder or more complicated. In the moment, it just doesn't occur to us. In a series of experiments, researchers found that "participants were less likely to identify advantageous subtractive changes when the task did not . . . cue them to consider subtraction."

It's odd that the brain leans toward addition since, if you think about it, less is more far more often than more is more. In fact, one of the most obvious markers of expertise is the ability to identify which steps in a process can simply be skipped. You'd think the brain would always steer toward subtraction, but the opposite is true, especially at work, where our perceived effort often correlates with our value to the organization. It's hard to win promotions by giving yourself less to do, even when the minimalist approach is more efficient or effective. Subtraction is just another area where innovation feels particularly uncomfortable in a work context.

Our instinct to add is especially powerful, Klotz and his colleagues found, when we're under pressure. This is why subtraction can be such a useful prompt when we're under a tight deadline. Think of being in a hurry and tugging on a door fruitlessly for far too long before noticing that "Push" sign. When you get stuck and the clock is ticking, paste the "Subtract" sign up and watch relief bloom on every face.

Run a retroactive. In chapter 5, we introduced retroactives for overcoming leadership objections to experimentation. In our experience, this tool is useful whenever we feel that sense of tunnel vision on a problem.

If you'll recall, running a retroactive involves projecting yourself into the future and looking back on your project from the perspective of having seen it fail. By asking yourself what went wrong from that mental vantage point, you can sidestep the brain's tendency to ignore or downplay tomorrow's problems in favor of reaching today's milestone.

To use a retroactive as a prompt, play a potential scenario out in the most pessimistic way possible. Start with a solution already on the table and imagine it operating under the full effect of Murphy's Law, with everything going wrong with clockwork regularity. Then get out a pencil and make an exhaustive list of each part of the idea that played out exactly as it shouldn't have (but clearly might if you're being honest with yourself). How did those metal bolts hold up under months of unexpectedly heavy winter rainfall? How did the big launch go when your celebrity endorser was publicly shamed? "Yes, and" is the innovator's mantra, but for this exercise, let everyone's inner critic out and shout "No, but" from the rooftops.

Once you've made your list, use these possible failure points as prompts to spur reflection. But don't fall for the addition trap. You can use a retroactive in tandem with subtraction by removing the failure-inducing elements and seeing if the main idea still works. If those bolts might cause unsightly rust marks under heavy rain, question whether they're even strictly necessary before investing in more metallurgical research. If pinning your brand to a fallible human being introduces a substantial risk in the rocky world of social media, question the need for such an endorsement before running background checks.

Think ahead and look back. A simple change in perspective can open your eyes to the obvious. If hindsight is 20/20, why not use it?

Generate un-ideas. Nolan Bushnell, founder of Atari, jump-started creativity by asking people to rank their ideas from best to worst and then selecting the *bottom* six: "How do we make them work?" By starting off with ideas labeled "bad," there was nowhere to go but up. "This process reversed people's normal mental dynamic," Bushnell wrote. "Instead of trying to figure out what's wrong with something, which triggers people's critical instincts, here they had to figure out what was right with something, which triggers people's creative instincts." According to Bushnell, every time they did this exercise at Atari, at least one of the six bad ideas became a successful reality.

When you're stuck in a loop on a given problem, the way out is to deliberately inject the unexpected. To find your wallet, don't just look in your pockets. Spill a certain number of marbles on the floor and don't quit until you've found each one. One way or the other, shake your brain out of its rut: "How is our logistics problem like an ultramarathon?"

Since divergence is valuable, try feeding yourself your problem's direct opposite. For an upcoming meeting, stop trying to think of ways to make it go well. Instead, reverse the polarity: "How does a meeting go badly?" Well, the coffee is cold. The A/V system has issues. People look at their phones instead of paying attention to the presenter. The list of "un-ideas" goes on and on.

Once you've assembled your un-ideas, use each one as a seed for further ideation. If the COO always arrives late, how can you make that late arrival a good thing? Leverage each of the problems you foresee and watch your brain bob and weave to regain its equilibrium. It's when things don't make sense to us that we become most creative.

To create un-ideas, create a frame for the very opposite of the problem you face. Not only will this spur fresh thinking, it will also be a mental relief after wrestling with the problem the same way you always do.

Observe, imitate, and diverge. There is no substitute for real-world exploration: Conduct Empathetic Interviews with your actual customers. Buy your own product on your own website. Eat in your own restaurant. One way or another, put yourself as close as possible to your customer's experience.

At one automobile manufacturer we worked with, the executives never visited a dealership or went through the buying process because each year's new model was automatically delivered to their doorstep. They barely had to stop for gas—their tanks were automatically topped up in the company parking lot.

"Stop insulating yourselves from the painful parts of your own customer experience," we told them. Ideas grow in the cracks *between* solutions, the areas of friction. Most people try to push through or otherwise ignore life's little frustrations. An innovator learns to recognize problems as opportunities.

Once you add something to your bug list, as suggested by the great Bob McKim back in chapter 4, look for solutions that may already exist. It's another Assumption Reversal: Convince yourself that a competitor has the right answer, then look for what that answer might be.

There's a reason so many businesses begin when someone experiences a problem for themselves and decides to solve it. You may want to build a food-delivery app because you've heard they're popular, but if you've never ordered food with an app yourself, you're going to waste a lot of time reinventing the wheel—and you'll never spot all the problems with the existing wheel that might be fixed.

Even if an ideal solution to your problem doesn't yet exist, people who also face it do *something* to deal with it. Talk to them about it. How do they manage with this problem today? Are they satisfied with their approach? What are its drawbacks? If possible, try it yourself. What are its strengths? Where does it fall short? As an exercise, try acting as a Salesperson for the Competition: Pitch the existing option to a potential customer and see if you can convince them of its outstanding merits. Even if you don't succeed, you'll learn something valuable about where the current option falls short . . . and what might work better instead.

We met Laura D'Asaro, the founder of cricket-protein start-up Chirps, back in chapter 2. When she saw how environmental concerns were driving demand for meat alternatives, she realized that insects represented an environmentally friendly protein source. The problem was, while people in other countries have long eaten grubs and crickets, Americans couldn't yet stomach crunchy critters. If someone wanted to switch from cows to caterpillars to minimize the environmental impact of their diet, their only existing option would be to try some caterpillar recipes. Sure, many Americans care about climate change, but enough to sample scorpion stir-fry? As we've learned, simply asking someone whether they'd eat Bug à l'Orange wasn't going to prove anything. Instead, D'Asaro went to the nearest pet store and bought some of every kind of edible insect in the reptile section. Then she cooked the bugs up in various ways—grilled and steamed, pepper and garlic—to see if she could convince friends and family to try some.

As D'Asaro suspected, there were no takers for her culinary creations. In exploring why people refused, however, she gained an insight. Unlike people in many other cultures, Americans don't eat identifiable animal parts in general. Unlike other cultures, we usually don't buy and eat whole animals—often, our meat arrives cut into strips. What Americans really love, D'Asaro realized, are foods that don't look like food at all: powders and supplements, for example. If she could hide environmentally friendly bug protein in a smoothie, she might have a product on her hands, both virtuous and palatable. Trying (and failing) to convince people to eat insects led D'Asaro to the idea that became Chirps cricket protein powder.

Again, this isn't about going down a rabbit hole of research, thinking, and planning instead of trying an idea out in real-world conditions. It's about getting the lay of the land. Note that D'Asaro had her insight only after cooking bugs and offering them to family and friends. The driving purpose of exploration is to generate ideas you can test. If you know how users or customers already solve the problem that bugs you, start there. If you don't, ask: "What did you do the last time you had this problem?" Build from there.

Basing your approach on an existing solution can seem like copying, but that's OK. Imitation is how we learn. Originality isn't about reinventing the wheel every time you go for a drive. Use the existing solution as a template and take it as far as it goes. When you arrive at the point where the existing solution disappoints or frustrates users, experiment from there. Innovation begins at the point of friction where things break down.

In short, immersing yourself in a problem isn't about business plans and market research. It's about finding the point of leverage where you can make the most valuable contribution. If you look closely, you can identify the seam between what's working and what isn't. The shape of that crack is the frame that will generate your best ideas.

~

Designing provocative questions that stoke curiosity is only one side of ideaflow. You can't generate hundreds or even thousands of divergent ideas without a steady diet of divergent inputs: new ideas, new approaches, new technologies. Consume the same stuff as everyone else does and expect your ideas to cluster closely around the expected and familiar.

In the next chapter, we will look at powerful techniques for gathering the kind of raw material that feeds truly original thinking.

10.

Encourage Creative Collisions

Fairchild Semiconductor once led the world in creative collisions. It also emerged from one.

In 1956, the American physicist William Shockley and two other scientists won the Nobel Prize for their work on the transistor, a crucial building block of the Information Age. That same year, Shockley left Bell Labs, an extraordinary hotbed of innovation, to found Shockley Semiconductor Laboratory in Mountain View, California.

Shockley chose Mountain View to be closer to his ailing mother, but it was another planet as far as technological innovation was concerned. Since none of Shockley's former colleagues would make the trek west with him, he had to recruit recent engineering grads. Hungry young talent collided with era-defining new technology. This influx of youthful energy played a pivotal role in establishing the creative culture that gave us the personal computer among many other technological innovations.

The Nobel wasn't good for Shockley, exacerbating the anger and paranoia of an already difficult man. Working at the lab was no picnic. Strange behavior was common, from Shockley's insistence on recording every company phone call to, on one occasion, a round of lie-detector tests to identify the "culprit" when someone at the company suffered an unexplained but minor injury. For all his failings as a leader, however, Shockley had a good eye for talent, assembling a world-class pool of young engineers.

Employees at Shockley Semiconductor Laboratory largely put up with the boss's autocratic management style, but when Shockley abruptly and inexplicably declared an end to silicon-based semiconductor research, the staff decided it was time to act. The true possibilities of this new technology had only just begun to reveal themselves. (People have a funny way of calling it quits right before a creative breakthrough.) In a way, what happened next was a creative collision, as Shockley's research ban ran headlong into a peerless group of young problem-solvers.

The young engineers knew they had lucked into a seat at the very cutting edge. Silicon-based transistors made vast leaps in electronic computation possible. Out in Mountain View, unconstrained by the beliefs of the mainstream physics and engineering communities, they might achieve almost anything. But this once-in-a-lifetime opportunity mattered only if they were allowed to pursue it. That's why a group of these employees, later dubbed "the traitorous eight," decided to leave the lab and start their own: Fairchild Semiconductor. William Shockley had inadvertently given birth to Silicon Valley.

Fairchild went on to play a pivotal role in the dawn of the Information Age, both as an innovation incubator as well as a source of serendipitous connection. Most of the founders eventually founded other key institutions, including the computer chip giant Intel. These companies came to be known as "Fairchildren," and together they were a major force in Silicon Valley in the 1970s and '80s. For all of Fairchild's impact on technology, however, the company itself settled into middle age as a relatively staid semiconductor manufacturing firm. By the time the company brought us in, Fairchild struggled as mightily to innovate as vacuum-tube manufacturers did in the face of the transistor. This wasn't because of a lack of expertise or insufficient investment in R&D. Technologically, Fairchild remained at the top of its game. Its focus had simply grown too narrow, hindering its ability to solve problems that didn't directly involve silicon.

Fairchild's sales organization catered to the needs of its largest customers, which made sense. A handful of enormous companies drove much of its business. A little effort with one of these customers went a very long way. Thanks to this emphasis, however, sales to small and midsize companies had slipped. With our help, the company wanted to "reinvent the customer experience for smaller customers."

While the two of us were thrilled to have the opportunity to collaborate with a storied institution like Fairchild, our work was cut out for us. Those small customers—including a quirky new automotive start-up called Tesla—had big problems. Assembling representatives from these companies, we conducted some Empathetic Interviews. To Fairchild's surprise, the interviews revealed that the endemic supply-chain disruptions in the semiconductor industry that hardly fazed large companies completely destabilized smaller ones. A routine delay of one shipment caused a well-capitalized start-up to miss a crucial earnings forecast altogether, as just one of many examples we gathered. To hedge their bets, smaller customers had taken to placing backup orders with Fairchild's competitors in the hope that at least one of these untrustworthy suppliers would deliver what was needed in time.

What struck us about this finding was Fairchild's reaction to it. The company acknowledged the problem but considered it intractable. Unexpected delays in production and distribution were simply a fact of life in the industry. Customers had the same issues with every vendor. There-fore, there was nothing to be done, no matter what the effect on Fair-child's reputation or bottom line. (This unfortunate tunnel vision is another example of the associative barrier that prevented Patagonia from seeing the opportunity represented by Under Armour in chapter 8.)

As you might suspect, ideaflow at Fairchild was at a low ebb. What would it take to get ideas flowing at Fairchild once again?

FEEDING THE FLOW

According to neurobiologist Morten Friis-Olivarius, "the brain is inca-pable of producing new material from scratch." He defines creativity as "taking something we already know and combining it in a new way." Or, as the novelist and intellectual Arthur Koestler theorized, it's the synthe-sis of two seemingly unrelated "frames of reference." Regardless of exactly how you define creativity, the key thing is that we never create out of whole cloth. Instead, we connect what we have, bringing together two or more elements in a new way. Abundant ideaflow requires enormous amounts of raw material to make more of these unexpected combina-tions.

Unfortunately, the act of gathering input doesn't look like traditional work to most leaders. The CEO of Stanza, Inc., a global manufacturer and distributor of sonnets, ballads, and villanelles, is frequently annoyed by the strange behavior he observes down in Poetry. Employees take walks during the workday. They spend hours perusing the work of painters, photographers, sculptors, and filmmakers. They read things *other than poetry*. That whole group needs to buckle down and get back to looking up rhymes. Next quarter's poetry isn't going to write itself!

Inputs are crucial. The more numerous and varied they are, the more valuable the subsequent combinations will be, whether your employees are crafting poems, chasing patents, or choosing a growth strategy. This is what professional creatives already understand, and it's why they're constantly feeding the Muse. They don't stop there, however. Once you've got your inputs, you've got to give them the opportunity to come together in a creative collision. As we'll see, this often requires stepping away from the problem to let the mind process what you've gathered in the background. This doesn't look like work to the CEO of Stanza, Inc., either.

The European Organization for Nuclear Research (CERN) in Switzerland runs the world's largest particle physics lab. At its enormous Geneva facility, scientists and technologists from around the world work tirelessly to unravel the secrets of the cosmos. CERN uses particle accelerators to smash atoms together at very high speeds. These collisions occur with terrific force, shattering tiny particles into even tinier particles and, in doing so, giving observers a momentary glimpse of reality's building blocks.

Though a creative collision isn't as violent as the atom smashing at CERN, the ideas one generates can be more powerful. For example, CERN incubated the World Wide Web. It was there that Tim Berners-Lee designed a tool to facilitate information sharing among its researchers. (Thankfully, Sir Tim's manager didn't order him back to his "real work" when he found him puttering with hypertext. Would you have been as patient?) The web itself went on to become an engine of creative collision on a scale never previously imagined.

Where an accelerator requires particles to function, ideaflow requires facts, patterns, inklings, experiences, perspectives, and impressions. CERN made the tunnel of the Large Hadron Collider sixteen miles long to leave room for particles to get up to speed. Any shorter, and the collisions wouldn't occur with sufficient force. Similarly, wildly diverse comparisons generate more interesting and useful intersections. When your ideas are stale, go wide.

With the help of programmer Ty Roberts, David Bowie designed the "Verbasizer" to carve up and rearrange text at random to spur ideas for new lyrics. Bowie didn't invent the literary technique known as *découpé,* which traces back at least as far as the Dadaists and was further popularized as the "Cut-Up Method" by William S. Burroughs. That said, Bowie was one of the first major pop artists to use computers to do the cutting and rearranging. "What you end up with," Bowie says as he taps on the keyboard, "is a real kaleidoscope of meanings and topics and nouns and verbs, all sort of slamming into each other."

Bowie's frequent collaborator Brian Eno developed an analog approach to inspiring divergent thinking. In the 1970s, Eno and a collaborator created a deck of cards featuring "Oblique Strategies": questions, instructions, and aphorisms to encourage lateral thinking. When encountering a roadblock, draw a card and follow its cryptic guidance: "Turn it upside down," for example, or, "What wouldn't you do?" Decades of popularity and many deck editions later, Oblique Strategies cards remain a favored tool of writers, artists, musicians, and business creatives around the world.

As you experiment with the input-gathering methods in this chapter, keep the central importance of diversity in mind. The further afield you go in your quest for unexpected inputs, the more interesting and valuable the resulting collisions will be.

So how do you make a practice of feeding your ideas? By deliberately exposing yourself to the new and the unexpected.

When you're young, this happens naturally. A five-year-old hasn't lived long enough to expect much of anything. *Everything* is new. Later in life, college is such a creatively fertile phase because, again, you are flung into new situations and inundated with unfamiliar ideas. Once you complete your education and enter the working world, however, this flow of divergent inputs slows. As you develop and follow routines, refine your approach to given tasks, and spend most of your time in a familiar environment, your brain stops paying such close attention to every detail of your day. There's a reason time seems to pass more quickly as we age. We take more for granted and *see* less.

This is especially true at large organizations. An organization is like a sphere. The larger the sphere, the smaller its surface area relative to its volume. You're inevitably insulated by its bulk and bureaucracy. Relative to a start-up or small business, there are vastly fewer connection points leading from any one employee to the customers, competitors, and vendors that could offer useful input.

In one study, forty scientists, including four future Nobel winners, were interviewed over the course of three decades. The researchers wanted to identify the factors that support problem-solving and creativity over the long term, from habits to working methods. In the end, they found a strong correlation between long-term success and the way these scientists spent their time *outside* the lab: hobbies, travel, artistic pursuits. More input, better output.

You don't innovate in the pickle business by eating cucumbers all day. The more "distant" the origins of your inputs, the more valuable and interesting the resulting combinations will be. Instead of trying to spot what is meaningful—which implies you'll know it when you see it— assume there is meaning to be found in everything. Study the world without judgment and let your mind create connections at its own pace.

WONDER WANDER

A Wonder Wander is the simple but life-changing practice of using your legs to feed your brain by taking a walk through a stimulating environment.

Studies show that walking alone is a powerful aid to creativity. Researchers at Stanford found that even walking on a treadmill increased creative divergent thinking for 81 percent of participants, a boost that persisted after sitting down. "Walking outside produced the most novel and highest quality analogies," the researchers concluded, but added that moving the body at all "opens up the free flow of ideas."

So, at a minimum, get up. If you can get out, do that, too. Then, to turn a walk around the block into a true Wonder Wander, choose a frame. A Wonder Wander begins intentionally, with a good question. As you move through a space, deliberately seek out connections to the prompt you've chosen. Imagine that your surroundings have been seeded with valuable clues. As you encounter each fresh stimulus, ask yourself: "What does this have to do with my problem?"

If someone is wearing Ray-Bans, or you pass by a Lululemon, ask yourself how the brand you've encountered might approach your prompt. The greater the distance between that brand's context and yours, the more fruitful this exercise can be. If a particular object stands out—fire hydrant, basketball hoop, mailbox—play with it as a metaphor. "What does a fire hydrant do on a fundamental level? And how might that apply to my problem? Is a 'hydrant' what we're missing?"

In a conference room, teams struggle to come up with more than a couple of potential analogies. Once they're exposed to divergent inputs on a Wonder Wander, however, possibilities forcefully present themselves. If you're trying to figure out who quickly creates trust, gosh, that's tough . . . until you leave the office: Preschool teachers, midwives, financial planners, artists, CrossFit trainers, and nutritional coaches are just a handful of answers that might spring to mind during a walk down a single city street.

Steve Jobs found inspiration for the original Macintosh in the appliance aisle at a department store. When he spotted a Cuisinart food processor on the shelf, something clicked. "He came bounding into the Mac office that Monday," Walter Isaacson recounts in his biography of the late Apple cofounder, "asked the design team to go buy one, and made a raft of new suggestions based on its lines, curves, and bevels."

On a Wonder Wander, volume is key. Write down questions and connections that come to mind and keep walking. Here's how one such walk might yield valuable prompts for idea generation:

- **A school playground.** A playground showcases other kids' toys. Where can we showcase our customers using the product so that others will see?

- **A luxury car.** Luxury car interiors can be made to order. Could we offer an "options package" for buyers to customize?

- **An Amazon delivery van.** Amazon shows its customers suggestions based on their viewing history. Could we adapt that technique to a physical location like ours?

- **A stoplight.** Could we show customers a "yellow light" warning before a product runs out?

- **A nail salon.** The rows of nail polish by the checkout counter are visually appealing. Could we leverage the color and variety of our products in this way?

During a Wonder Wander, you're trying out a slew of different mental models based on random inputs. The idea is to provoke insights in an uninhibited way. As the author and physician Edward de Bono wrote, "The natural inclination is to search for alternatives in order to find the best one." When you're seeking inputs, don't expect to stumble on the solution itself. Instead, according to De Bono, "the purpose of the search is to loosen up rigid patterns and to provoke new patterns."

Is walking essential to creativity? Many great thinkers, artists, and entrepreneurs throughout history, from Aristotle to Giacomo Puccini to, yes, Steve Jobs, would probably have agreed. Even so, there are ways to provoke wonder even when you're stuck on an airplane or waiting at the doctor's office.

- **Read.** Select a book or magazine at random. Examine the cover. Open to a random page. Imagine that someone flagged this particular page for you as a clue to solving your problem. Why?

- **Browse.** Go to Wikipedia.org and click "Random article" to be taken to one of the site's millions of crowdsourced entries—then pretend it wasn't random at all. What is Wikipedia trying to tell you? (Other online tools will send you to random websites, videos, and so on.)

Looking for "clues" in random places might feel like an occult practice. Unlike a Tarot card reading, however, we are simply leveraging the brain's pattern-matching ability to feed our ideas. To conserve energy, the brain prefers cognitive shortcuts—to look rather than see and hear rather than listen. To short-circuit this, begin the Wonder Wander with intention and continually seek relevance in the random inputs you observe. Assume the presence of connections and let the brain do the work of finding them.

ANALOGOUS EXPLORATION

A Wonder Wander is a convenient way to gather inputs and entertain an array of potentially useful analogies. You can do one any time you feel stuck and return to your desk with something valuable. Sometimes, however, a problem calls for deeper, more focused exploration. Rather than simply consider an analogy between your business and, let's say, a coffee shop, you go inside the store, buy a coffee, sit at a table, and even talk to customers and employees. Working with intention, you extract more and more information from the experience in the hopes of sparking a breakthrough with your own problem. In this way, a Wonder Wander can evolve into an Analogous Exploration.

We saw an opportunity to use this tool with Fairchild Semiconductor. Fairchild's leadership team was dubious that a solution for their disappointed small customers might lie somewhere outside their own heads. They were the experts on semiconductor logistics, after all.

We turned to an analogy to convince Fairchild of the value of analogies. While an idea may not be as tangible as a stick of computer RAM, you still need raw material to make one. You can't make a chip without silicon and you can't make an idea without input. When they reluctantly agreed to try our approach, we asked them to consider the following question: "How might we instill confidence among our small customers despite supply chain uncertainty?" To convert this into an Analogous Exploration, the question became: "Who instills customer confidence despite supply chain uncertainty?" The semiconductor industry hadn't licked this problem yet. Had anybody?

We led the team out of the building and onto the sidewalk for a Wonder Wander. Once their bodies were moving, their minds warmed to the task. We passed a Hyatt: "A hotel never knows which customers will actually show up for any given reservation," one leader said. Passing a restaurant, another chimed in: "A chef is never sure what the day's catch will be." More potential analogies revealed themselves: Florists. Spice markets. Coffee roasters.

Instead of simply returning to the office, we embarked on in-depth Analogous Explorations of the businesses that sparked our interest. In the hotel, we discovered that room inventory data is shared among competitors to ensure that travelers aren't left stranded when large events cause over-booking. Down the block, the florist told us how she communicated with the delivery company to know what to expect on each truck. She also talked to farmers about what they were cutting and even what they were planting. This transparency with supply-chain partners helped her plan for holidays and big events. Nearly every shop we explored offered an unexpected parallel or two that challenged the semiconductor industry's status quo.

As a result of these Analogous Explorations, Fairchild made instrumental changes to improve their small customer experience. For example, the hotel concierge inspired them to coordinate with competitors to ensure that critical components remained available to small customers during unexpected surges in demand. Since those customers were placing multiple orders as a hedge anyway, why not take the pain out of the process? Expanding on the florist's approach, Fairchild instituted a radical new information-sharing agreement with their largest distribution partner to get more transparency in their supply chain. They told us later that this was one of the largest supply-chain innovations in their industry in five decades. Not a bad haul for a walk around the neighborhood.

Fairchild's COO later told us that watching the competition so closely had been a trap. Those guys hadn't known how to solve the supply-chain problem, either. By deliberately seeking out unexpected sources of inspiration, Fairchild jump-started a series of innovations, all while reinvigorating its creative culture.

Over the years, we have used Analogous Explorations to help an Australian financial services organization learn from a tattoo parlor, an Israeli tech company learn from a farmers market, a New Zealand fishery learn from a tea shop, and a Japanese conglomerate learn from a rock-climbing studio, among many other surprising combinations. In each case, teams struggled to solve a problem because they lacked the requisite inputs to trigger fresh ideas.

Remember the importance of intention. Always begin with a frame. Before venturing out in search of inspiration, articulate the problem you're trying to solve as an HMW (How Might We) question. Then translate that into a prompt for Analogous Exploration by asking, "Who does X really well?" Now, get out of the conference room and start walking.

Rather than ask the people you encounter for advice, immerse yourself in the experience and see firsthand how they solve the problems. Become a customer if you can, or simply observe a customer interaction. For example, if you ask a barber how they create trust, they'll probably shrug, or just spout some answers that *sound* correct: "I guess I make eye contact and listen very carefully." The reality may be very different. We watched one barber give incredibly direct feedback ("No matter what I do to your hair, you're not going to look like Brad Pitt"). Instead of driving the customer out of the chair, it proved the barber's candor and earned the customer's trust. This was an unexpected but effective tactic, and one we never would have imagined if we hadn't seen it happen.

It bears repeating: Never forget your frame. Being out in the world during work hours can be invigorating, but it's easy to lose sight of your learning objective. Continually remind yourself and your collaborators of exactly what you're trying to learn before, during, and after each exploration to ensure that the pattern-seeking machine in everyone's head is tuned to the right frequency.

Once you've assembled a set of observations, create a new frame to inspire ideas you can test: "How might we use brutal honesty the way a barber does to build trust with new customers?" That's a much richer and more interesting prompt than "How can we build trust quickly?"

~

Ideaflow isn't something you crank up on the spot to tackle a single problem. To ensure a steady flow of new ideas when you need them, make a habit of exposing yourself to unexpected inputs. The solution won't appear when you're consciously trying to solve each problem but "out of nowhere," when you're taking a shower or driving to work. If you trace the solution that bubbles up, you may realize it stemmed from a conversation with your spouse, or something you read, or a podcast you listened to during your workout. That input had been percolating in the background, refusing to coalesce into a solution until the moment you were lightly preoccupied by another task. That's how ideas work. If you wait for the next crisis to gather your inputs, the output will never arrive in time.

If investing time in gathering inputs seems unprofessional, note that the greatest business leaders in history have made a discipline of doing so. Master innovators build the unexpected into their schedule. A busy manager can set aside an hour a week to walk around the neighborhood. A VP can aim for two. A CEO should shoot for five or more. In the early days of Amazon, Jeff Bezos did his best to leave Mondays and Thursdays unscheduled so he could spend the time "trawling for ideas, exploring his own site, sometimes just surfing the Web." If your job requires a vision for the future, today's ideas will determine tomorrow's bottom line. So read a book about a completely unrelated subject. See a movie in the middle of the day. Tour the local museum. Walk through downtown. Feed the machine if you expect it to function.

It also helps to change up your routine in small ways: Take a different route to work. Brush your teeth with the other hand. Even turning left instead of right when you enter the office can spark an insight. Make a habit of switching up your habits. Whatever it takes to throw your brain even a little bit off balance. This is how we force our thinking out of its comfortable groove. We are most creative when we are trying to restore our own equilibrium.

Why is there such determined resistance to gathering outside inputs? Comfort in the familiar. There's a reason we always turn right instead of left when we enter the office. Our rituals reassure us. Ironically, it's when we're under pressure and in need of new thinking that we cling most stubbornly to our routines. Though the groove feels safe, it's anything but. As innovators leapfrog your efforts, you'll realize that your groove was nothing but a rut.

11.

Untangle Creative Knots

The majority of business men are incapable of original thinking because they are unable to escape from the tyranny of reason. Their imaginations are blocked.

—DAVID OGILVY

A fter a while you will reach the hopeless stage," ad executive James Webb Young explained of the creative process. "Everything is a jumble in your mind, with no clear insight anywhere." You may know the feeling. According to Young, this overwhelming sense of fruitlessness is actually a necessary stage in the evolution of an idea, something you should expect. Even cherish.

That may be a bridge too far, of course.

Knowing you'll get stuck from time to time is one thing. Responding effectively is another. In this chapter, we'll explain why logjams are not only inevitable but crucial parts of the creative process, as well as what to do when, not if, you get stuck next.

Albert Einstein ran aground prior to a momentous discovery. The physicist had reached the point where he could no longer reconcile his theory of general relativity with the way light was understood to work. He knew better than to stare holes in the blackboard, however. Instead, the stymied thinker walked away from the problem. "[Einstein] went to visit his best friend Michele Besso, the brilliant but unfocused engineer he had met while studying in Zurich and then recruited to join him at the Swiss Patent Office," Walter Isaacson wrote in his biography of the famous scientist. Einstein told Besso he was stuck.

"I'm going to give it up," he announced.

Consciously surrendering the difficult problem invited Einstein's subconscious mind to step in. The next day, Einstein visited Besso again: "Thank you," he told his friend. "I've completely solved the problem." Only by stepping away from the knot could Einstein's mind finally unravel it. By taking a walk with a pal and giving the problem a break, Einstein intuited the leap from general to special relativity.

"You make absolutely no effort of a direct nature," James Webb Young advised the struggling thinker. "You drop the whole subject and put the problem out of your mind as completely as you can." When we encounter obstacles in other areas, the solution is usually to work longer, push harder, or just panic. When it comes to ideas, however, getting stuck is a natural part of the gestation process. Don't panic. Experienced creators learn to anticipate, even welcome, getting stuck as a sign they're at the cusp of a breakthrough. Singer, artist, and poet Patti Smith takes a particularly laid-back approach when she feels "out of sorts": "I try to take long walks and things like that, but I just kill time until something good is on TV." As a prolific artist with decades of work under her belt, Smith understands that "killing time" is anything but. Once you've ruled out the known approaches, you're left with only what the subconscious can assemble in the background, shuffling the inputs you've gathered into novel configurations until something clicks.

To move forward, step back: "You remember how Sherlock Holmes used to stop right in the middle of a case, and drag Watson off to a concert?" Young wrote. "That was a very irritating procedure to the practical and literal-minded Watson. But Conan Doyle was a creator and knew the creative process."

MAKING A TACTICAL WITHDRAWAL

As Michael Lewis relates in *The Undoing Project,* Israeli psychologists Daniel Kahneman and Amos Tversky coinvented behavioral economics in large part by taking long walks and joking around with each other. Some colleagues resented the two for having so much fun when they were supposed to be working. By walking, talking, and laughing together, however, the two men were incredibly productive. Over the years of their collaboration, they strolled their way through a series of sophisticated, insightful, and clever experiments that took the world of classical economics by storm and led to a Nobel Prize. "The secret to doing good research," Tversky once said, "is always to be a little underemployed. You waste years by not being able to waste hours."

Like Einstein, the French mathematician Henri Poincaré also knew when it was time to walk away. "I turned my attention to the study of some arithmetical questions apparently without much success," Poincaré wrote. Rather than beat himself up, he spent a few days by the shore. On a morning walk along the bluffs, a solution came to him with "brevity, suddenness and immediate certainty." Recognizing a roadblock and making the effort to let go of the problem at hand is a counterintuitive but essential creative skill.

In chapter 2, we urged you to make a habit of padding your schedule as a central creative strategy. Here we bring that strategic approach down to a tactical level. A Tactical Withdrawal is anything but procrastination. Procrastinating is the fine art of putting off until later what you know you should do now. You can't procrastinate if you don't know what to do. In fact, the real waste of time is persisting at a task past this sticking point. A single creative solution can remove the need for days, weeks, even months of effort. If you're too busy to call on your creative faculties, reexamine your priorities. No matter what your role, creativity is the highest value you bring to any endeavor.

So much advice around innovation and creativity amounts to *more*: more methods, more habits, more techniques. If we don't simultaneously carve away less important uses of our time to create space for reflection and contemplation—distance from the problem at hand—we only undermine the effort to boost ideaflow. Caught up in the day-to-day, our imaginations become blocked, just as David Ogilvy warned at the top of this chapter. To escape "the tyranny of reason," we must be as tactical about withdrawing from a losing battle as we are about gathering divergent inputs or vigorously testing our ideas. The "Father of Advertising" was an ace at the mental game of creative output. He intuitively understood that generating more ideas required doing a little less.

"I have developed techniques for keeping open the telephone line to my unconscious, in case that disorderly repository has anything to tell me," Ogilvy wrote. "I hear a great deal of music . . . I take long hot baths. I garden. I go into retreat among the Amish. I watch birds. I go for long walks in the country. And I take frequent vacations, so that my brain can lie fallow—no golf, no cocktail parties, no tennis, no bridge, no concentration; only a bicycle." Note that concentration here is the name of a card game, but in this case both meanings apply. Relax your concentration if you want ideas to flow.

Relaxation is a recurrent theme with top performers, and these are not individuals with unlimited time. In fact, our talks with CEOs and entrepreneurs reveal again and again just how deliberately they secure time and space for their minds to lie fallow. This isn't accomplished through week-ends away from email—or even the odd "retreat among the Amish"—but as a daily practice.

Mark Hoplamazian, whom we met in chapter 7, has been president and CEO of Hyatt Hotels for nearly two decades. Like any leader of a major corporation with tens of thousands of employees, meetings consume much of his day. His schedule is "pretty jammed," in fact. Keeping everything straight is a challenge, so Hoplamazian brings a notebook with him wherever he goes. Prior to a call or meeting, he will jot down three or four bullet points summarizing what he hopes to communicate, the gist of his thinking. Usually, this practice is sufficient to stay effective and on point. Now and then, though, he interrupts the busy course of his day to contemplate a particular problem in solitude. "I've come to several breakthroughs this way," he told us. "It's become a strategy."

But *when*, exactly? How does someone in the CEO seat decide it's time to say no to something that feels urgent and spend time in silent thought? Finding space must be incredibly difficult for someone with that degree of responsibility. It goes against Hoplamazian's wiring in particular: "Under pressure," he told us, "my default is, roll up my sleeves and work harder." But he knows that idea problems don't respond to sleeve rolling. "When I really get stuck," he said, "I need to take a giant step back and let my mind free."

Withdrawing to a quiet space and meditating on a tough problem sounds good in theory, but no one can afford to do that after every meeting, call, and email. Two signs tell Hoplamazian it's time to withdraw. First is tunnel vision: "I'm racking my brain, working on the problem to the exclusion of other stuff and unable to stop." Once the blinders go on, he realizes that he's become closed off to the very divergent inputs that might spark an insight. The second clue? When he opens his notebook to summarize his thoughts and comes up empty. "When I actually don't know how to organize my key points," he said, "it's because I'm unresolved. If I can't summarize, I have to take a step back."

It may sound obvious to distance yourself from a problem when stuck. In practice, however, how often do you actually do that? Most of the time, getting stuck on a problem gets us to struggle harder against the finger trap of rumination and tunnel vision. As we discussed all the way back in chapter 1, a classic sign of an idea problem is that brute force gets you nowhere. When you realize you're going in circles, turn to Tactical Withdrawal first. Find a quiet spot and spend a few minutes thinking or, better yet, doing something lightly distracting so your subconscious can do its work.

It's ironic that we must specify the use of withdrawal as a tactic. Why isn't this something that comes naturally? In our work with leaders, we find that stepping away from a problem runs so directly counter to the normal mode of operation that it becomes the last thing they're willing to try—*even when they know it's their best shot at a solution.* It just goes against the grain. Everything else responds to focus and directed effort. Only creativity differs. Creative breakthroughs arrive when we stop struggling. Once we've framed the problem properly, intuition functions best when we are lightly occupied with another task or just staring into space and taking a breather.

Taking a Tactical Withdrawal can be particularly hard within a team. In the wrong context, the behaviors that unblock ideaflow look like procrastination or laziness to others. If you're a leader facing a crisis, a pause can look like decision paralysis, something that saps team morale like nothing else. Rather than risk sending the wrong message, leaders blunder forward instead of taking the necessary time to allow a breakthrough to occur.

Innovations ranging from the double-helix structure of DNA to behavioral economics sprang up in moments of purposeful distraction. Rather than see this behavior in terms of retreat or even escape, reframe what you're doing as a Tactical Withdrawal. Bake the concept into the culture of the team so that everyone understands the purpose of a pause and its value to the larger mission. Encouraging and normalizing this begins by modeling it yourself.

WITHDRAWAL TACTICS

There are other ways to withdraw, many of which will sound familiar: Walking, alone or with someone else. Reading outside your discipline. Attending a lecture by an expert in another field. Playing a game. Even taking a nap. One way or the other, advances get made when we stop actively working on a problem and allow the subconscious mind to shuffle through the inputs it has collected in peace.

Some distractions are too distracting, however. Whipping out your phone for a few rounds of an addictive mobile game might feel like a relief, but it won't lead to a breakthrough. Nor will a mindless Netflix binge—when was the last time you had a great idea while watching television? Diving into something wildly engaging, colorful, and busy will only flush away the faint impressions we want circulating in the background of conscious thought.

The media theorist Marshall McLuhan made a distinction between "hot" and "cool" media. A hot medium like television is rich with information but creates a state of passive absorption. A cool one, like a book, is less overwhelming and requires more active involvement. As you might guess, a hot medium won't give your mind the necessary space to work.

You may already have a go-to withdrawal tactic for when you get creatively stuck. If so, go with what works for you. If not, we can recommend these alternatives:

> **Water.** When in doubt, get wet. Taking a shower or bath, or even heading out for a swim, provides just the right kind of distraction for creative problem-solving.

Of course, you could also hang ten. The American theoretical physicist Garrett Lisi turns to surfing to unlock his own creativity. Lisi made waves in the scientific community with his radical 2007 paper, "An Exceptionally Simple Theory of Everything," which proposed a novel way to reconcile particle physics with Einstein's theory of gravitation. Whether or not Lisi's theory is eventually validated by experiments, there is no question he took a thrilling conceptual swing at string theory. Surfing plays a crucial role in his creative process.

"Playing a lot allows me to have more mental flexibility when tackling hard problems," he told an interviewer. "There are times when you hit a wall, working on a tough problem, and nothing you try works. By throwing yourself into a different intense experience for a couple hours, you're able to come back and think about the problem with a fresh perspective and come up with a new approach that you might not have thought of if you had kept searching along previous lines."

Lisi isn't the only innovator who surfs to solve problems. As one senior leader based in Ireland told us, "I wish I could bring a notebook on my surfboard. So many breakthroughs happen as I'm paddling out."

Task switching. Immersing yourself in your work completely, without distractions of any kind, can be critical in some stages of the creative process. When you find yourself stuck, however, turning your attention to another task can release the logjam, particularly if it calls on a different mode of operation.

This task might involve another project entirely, or it might be something in your current project that calls on another skill. According to the American psychologist Howard Gruber, prolific creative workers pursue an interconnected network of related projects at any one time. He used the example of the poet John Milton, who worked on *Paradise Lost* for nearly thirty years but never let the epic poem consume all his creative energies. Over the years, Milton worked on shorter poems and prose as well as political efforts. This kept the flow of ideas open even as Milton struggled through his primary project. "When one enterprise grinds to a halt," Gruber concluded, "productive work does not cease." For Milton, the shift from long to short form or from poetry to prose gave him his Tactical Withdrawal. Likewise, as we saw in chapter 4, Bette Nesmith Graham was inspired to invent Liquid Paper correction fluid by her side gig as a sign painter.

"I like to have at least three defined projects going at any given moment," author Steven Johnson writes. "[Once] you define them, you're able to see those connections more clearly. You stumble across something and you're like, 'Oh, I know exactly where this goes.'"

Even more effective than switching to another demanding task—epic poem to prose piece, as in Milton's case, for example—is "an undemanding task that maximizes mind wandering." A group of psychologists found that, "compared with engaging in a demanding task, rest, or no break, engaging in an undemanding task during an incubation period led to substantial improvements in performance on previously encountered problems."

Turn to a hobby. Mervin Kelly, the celebrated president of Bell Labs, "supervised the arrangement of tens of thousands of tulip and daffodil bulbs" in his own backyard. The effort was "almost absurd in its meticulousness," according to Jon Gertner in *The Idea Factory,* a book about the legendary innovation hub. We can hypothesize, however, that it served an important function for Kelly, who repeated the feat every year. Your horticultural aspirations can, and probably should, be much more modest. "There's something about having your hands in the dirt that keeps you grounded," Claudia Kotchka, the innovation and strategy leader we met in chapter 7, told us. "Pulling weeds is the best. You're not really thinking about work per se, but ideas start to flow. People say they get their best ideas in the shower. I got mine in the garden."

If gardening isn't your thing, you might turn to a musical instrument, as Einstein did with his violin. Or a craft like woodworking. Writers play the guitar and keep one close to the keyboard. Scientists tinker with engines and assemble model trains. Entrepreneurs speed solve Rubik's Cubes. Mervin Kelly's Bell Labs colleague Claude Shannon would unicycle down the hallway while juggling four balls. Your work environment, interests, and, perhaps, knack for balancing will dictate your alternatives. The important thing is to let your conscious mind rest and recover while another part works on the problem.

Nap. In chapter 2, we discussed the importance of a good night's sleep to your creative performance. In addition to your evening slumber, an afternoon nap can help you attack a problem from a new angle. According to Dr. Jonathan

Friedman, director of the Texas Brain and Spine Institute, "emerging scientific evidence suggests that naps—even very short ones—significantly enhance cognitive function." Beyond that, naps may boost creativity specifically. According to one paper, napping increases your ability to connect facts you've learned into flexible frameworks and extract general principles. This process of abstraction is a crucial component of creativity. According to Andrei Medvedev, PhD at Georgetown University Medical Center, MRIs reveal unusually well-integrated and synchronized activity in the right hemisphere of the brain during a nap: "The brain could be doing some helpful housecleaning," he said, "classifying data, consolidating memories."

Creators ranging from Ludwig van Beethoven to Salvador Dalí to Thomas Edison have relied on naps to refresh their minds and spark insights. (Edison napped in what he called his "thinking chair.") While sleeping at your office may still be frowned upon where you work, more and more leaders are catching on to the value of this tool. Organizations from Google to Zappos to Ben & Jerry's to NASA make dedicated nap rooms available to their employees. Worse comes to worst, you could always lean your office chair back . . .

Seek a cool medium. If hot media are out, turn to a cool one. Reading a book, listening to a podcast, or looking at art can provide just enough absorption for a Tactical Withdrawal without completely sucking you in and wiping your problem away entirely. Unless you really, really love abstract expressionism.

"I read outside my discipline, as a discipline," Nathan Rosenberg, CEO of Insigniam, a global strategic consultancy, told us. "I subscribe to [the design magazine] *Wallpaper**, for example, just to push myself to see and think differently."

Talk. Brian Grazer, who, with his longtime partner Ron Howard, has produced a slew of hit films grossing over $15 billion at the box office, employs a full-time booker to schedule regular "curiosity conversations" with interesting people from all walks of life, from scientists to artists to politicians.

Grazer isn't gathering research material with these meetings in any traditional sense. His conversation partners have no specific connection to his ongoing film and television projects. Instead, he sees these talks as an opportunity to step outside the pressing problems of the day to perceive a wider vista. Naturally, Grazer can look back and see the impact these conversations have had on his subsequent creative output, but he goes into each one with the intention of getting away from his problems, not solving them.

If you find yourself going in circles, call a friend for a chat. Meet up with a former colleague for an impromptu cup of coffee. Or just put your phone down during dinner and have a real conversation with your spouse or kids. The only rule is, don't talk about your problem. Give that part of your mind an opportunity to rest and open yourself up to the unexpected.

Move. We've already made our case for the value of a stroll. There is no better bang for the buck in a creator's tool kit. Just remember to lean into boredom rather than avoid it by pulling out your phone. Experiencing the sudden urge to check email or scroll through social media is a sure sign that things are warming up in the back of your mind. Sadly, many breakthroughs are extinguished by the winds of digital distraction. If you keep moving forward despite that uncomfortable, antsy feeling, your brain will surrender. As you walk, it will turn its attention to your problem, shuffling inputs while you navigate the neighborhood.

If your phone is *really* calling you, pick up the pace. Even in her eighties, the enormously prolific Joyce Carol Oates considers running integral to her creative process: "If I don't go running every day, my writing doesn't work as well. It really depends upon this kinetic release of energy." For her part, Claudia Kotchka goes for a run when she needs to shake loose some new ideas, but she sometimes forgets her notebook: "My whole jog, I'm holding an idea all the way back."

~

Tactical Withdrawals require permission, not from others but from yourself. When we suggest this tool, people blame bosses or peers for the need to stay busy—or at least appear that way. In truth, the resistance to withdrawal is coming from inside. Clear, straightforward tasks can be completed with a minimum of uncertainty and emotional vulnerability, so we default to checking boxes off the to-do list first. Thorny idea problems bring up uncomfortable feelings instead. It takes courage to set today's concerns aside, even for a short time, and envision a larger tomorrow. The simple act of sitting in silence can feel like a radical act.

When you withdraw, you are investing in the highest value you bring to your work. If you give yourself permission to step away when you're stuck, your patience will be rewarded. Nothing compares with the relief of a creative solution arriving "out of nowhere," right when you least expect it. What these tactics share is that they offer at least some opportunity to muse, to daydream. With today's emphasis on the sprint, it's easy to lose sight of the central importance of gestation to our ideas. Staying completely focused on a problem narrows your field of view, leaving breakthrough solutions hidden just out of sight. To reveal them, relax that incessant focus.

In a 1970 appearance on *The Dick Cavett Show,* Paul Simon explained the process by which he wrote "Bridge Over Troubled Water." The song's opening was inspired by a Bach chorale. "I was stuck there," Simon said. "That was all I had of that melody."

"What makes you stuck?" Cavett asked.

"Well, everywhere I went led me where I didn't want to be," Simon replied. "So, I was stuck." The audience laughed, but Simon was being serious.

To give his subconscious mind the opportunity to devise a way forward, Simon set the unfinished songs aside and started listening to music outside his genre. He found himself absorbed by a particular gospel album.

"Every time I'd come home, I'd put that record on and I'd listen to it," he explained to Cavett, "and I think that must have subconsciously influenced me, because I started to go to gospel [chord] changes." An unexpected combination of musical influences—and a willingness to set his problem aside—led Simon to craft an enduring classic.

Conclusion

Innovate with Others

C reativity is the art of possibility. When facing dilemmas and deadlines, who doesn't experience the urge to just forge ahead in the usual way? The last thing you want to do when you're under pressure is consider more options. Yet, as that perceptive seventh-grader put it at the very beginning of this book, creativity is "doing more than the first thing that comes to your mind." That's exactly what's required of us if we want to achieve great things, in business or elsewhere. Creativity isn't just how we solve problems. It's how we contribute the very best of ourselves.

World-class creators and top-performing companies rely on these techniques to flood problems with ideas and achieve breakthrough outcomes. They resist the urge to converge and explore the full range of possibilities even when they're under pressure because they trust the process to make the effort worthwhile. This isn't because they love drama or welcome chaos. They know results matter and that timing is everything. Great innovators are often intensely pragmatic. They prioritize ideaflow because they like to win. The practices in this book take time and effort to implement, but they dramatically decrease *wasted* effort, reduce uncertainty, and multiply the odds of success by an order of magnitude. If these practices didn't deliver extraordinary results, none of the individuals and organizations we advise would use them more than once.

The risky move isn't investing time and energy in generating two thousand ideas. Flooding a problem with ideas and then winnowing them down through a rigorous validation process *lowers* the risk of trying new things. The riskiest move will always be starting with a handful of ideas and then settling on the one your boss likes the most. The bet-everything-on-red risk is running with that idea all the way to full-scale implementation. This approach—business as usual at most organizations—is motorcycle-without-a-helmet, even skydiving-without-a-parachute, risky.

We've watched thousands of experiments play out from beginning to end in nearly every business context imaginable. Believe us when we tell you: Very few "sure things" play out in real life the way they did in the conference room. This is why so many corporate initiatives and over-hyped new offerings result in expensive, embarrassing, demoralizing failures. Most companies play out their riskiest experiments as products, not prototypes.

Let's go back to ideaflow. Here's the formula again:

$$ideas \: / \: time = ideaflow$$

Low ideaflow: quiet conference room, eyes glazing over, minutes ticking away, two lackluster solutions scrawled on a whiteboard. High ideaflow: the effortless, even joyful, outpouring of surprising possibilities. Every single person in the room fully engaged in the process of imagination, variation, and integration. When the spigot is open, creativity becomes a delightful game, not a dreaded chore. You'll never have more fun at work. (Believe us, we've tried.) It takes practice, however, to reliably enter this effortless state every time you need it. Don't wait for a crisis to begin. Use these techniques in good times and in bad. Over time, you will develop a new mindset, a new, more effective way of responding to problems.

Reading this book alone won't do it. As with any other skill, you master the manual and then you throw the manual away. Develop and sustain a personal creative practice and rely on these techniques to consistently deliver next-level outcomes. One day, you'll look back at where you are now and wonder how you ever used to solve problems the old way.

For us as educators, nothing beats the moment someone finally gets it. When that stick-in-the-mud manager who has "never been very creative" and doesn't see the value in all this "extra" work finally sees the process pay off with a gem of an insight. Suddenly they're firing off a million possibilities with carefree abandon. *Look, I'm doing it!* The change doesn't stick unless they take the ball and run with it, however. If you don't maintain your own practice and model these behaviors as a leader, you can bet they won't propagate to the rest of the team and organization. Thankfully, it takes only a little regular maintenance to keep your creative capacity strong. If you do nothing else, incorporate the daily Idea Quota into your morning routine and build from there.

Assuming you've been doing your homework, let's measure your ideaflow again. Take out a pen and piece of paper. We'll do the same task from chapter 1 to compare apples to apples. Select an email in your inbox that needs a response. For two minutes, write down as many different subject lines as you can. No thinking, no pauses, no judgment, no revision. Just write subject lines as quickly as you can, serious or silly. All variations count. Focus only on quantity.

Now count them up. How many distinct subject lines did you generate? And how does that number compare to your first attempt? We'd bet that the number has gone up—your results should be proportional to the effort you've invested in boosting ideaflow. One way or the other, keep working at it. The more energy and intention you put into your creative practice, the easier it will be to solve all your other problems. That's because *every* problem is an idea problem. If you already knew how to solve something, it would just be *work*.

There's a difference between understanding how creativity works and practicing it yourself, between thinking and doing. Seize every opportunity to expand your toolbox and take your ideaflow to the next level. For example, Jeremy has never been a napper, but he became willing to experiment after assembling evidence of their associative benefits for this book. Naps appear throughout the literature on creativity. Artists, scientists, and philosophers routinely leverage the altered state right before and after a period of sleep to achieve greater insights. Clearly, naps do something interesting. There's a reason Edison called his recliner a "thinking chair" even though he only ever napped in it.

Recently, Jeremy was in the middle of a major workshop with only twelve minutes to go until he was supposed to introduce a speaker to a room of hundreds. Feeling foggy, he set a timer for a seven-minute nap. That would leave five minutes to reorient himself before returning to the hall. It felt a bit strange, but why not give this nap business a try?

Lo and behold, after drifting off for an instant at most, a potential solution to a problem from the d.school popped into his head. "Just like we say in the book," he thought to himself.

As of this writing, Jeremy naps on a regular basis. He also keeps a stack of Post-it notes nearby with the resolve to write down any ideas that arrive without judgment. The discipline of documentation must be maintained, even when you're on the verge of falling asleep or you wake up in the middle of the night.

This doesn't mean Jeremy isn't *tempted* to trade in the occasional inspiration for sweet slumber, though.

The other night, Jeremy came up with a potential solution to a problem right after turning off the lights. His first impulse was to roll over and go to sleep. Instead of writing the idea down, he'd just chant the idea a few times in his mind. Surely he'd still remember in the morning if he did that. Feeling hypocritical, however, he fumbled for a pen and scratched the idea down.

In the morning, Jeremy woke with the idea still at the forefront of his mind. He felt triumphant: "I *knew* I'd remember! Maybe I don't need to be quite so disciplined about documentation after all." Then he read what he'd scribbled on the Post-it note. As it turned out, he had written down a *totally different idea.* If he hadn't checked his note, he'd have been certain it was the same one. Go figure.

As for Perry, writing this book has made him even more aware of the value of analogous thinking. Today, a trip to Trader Joe's is no longer a chore but an opportunity. When Perry enters the store, he's shopping for analogies alongside the milk and eggs. Exploration can transform any aggravation, from waiting in line to watching a kettle boil. When he feels his impatience rising, Perry reframes the moment as an opportunity to bring a pressing problem to mind and seek out unexpected connections.

OWNERSHIP AND INNOVATION

We ardently believe that ideaflow—the capacity to generate novel solutions to any given problem—is the most crucial business metric of the twenty-first century. In our experience advising organizations, innovation capacity correlates directly to the success of teams and organizations. Therefore, leaders should monitor ideaflow as closely as any other key performance indicator. It isn't enough to simply watch the innovation pipeline, either. Leaders should invest time and effort in improving processes and incentivizing positive behaviors. Innovation drives market share, profits, and resilience. It's the ultimate competitive advantage.

Once you've solidified your own approach to creativity, it's time to bring it to your team and organization. As we've said, no one—not the founder, not the freelancer, not the "digital nomad"—operates entirely alone. To achieve greater ambitions, you must develop the capacity to innovate with others. Therefore, even if you don't lead a team or an organization, the information below applies.

Above all, innovation demands ownership. Closing the loop spells the difference between promising ideas and pipe dreams. It doesn't matter how many people are in the room when you tackle a problem. *One individual* must be given the mandate to follow through before the next meeting. If this isn't an established practice on your team, make it one.

What does a group of people usually do in the face of insufficient information about a problem? "Let's have another meeting." Without new information, however, you end up having the same conversation about the problem all over again, just with a shorter runway to solve it. That's where innovation stalls.

Break this cultural habit today. Hardwire follow-through into your process and be vigilant about it. It takes constant repetition and reinforcement to get everyone on board with the idea of ownership. Whenever you find the team resolving to have yet another discussion about the same problem, put on the brakes and get clarity about the data you'll need to have a *different* conversation next time. Then, commission and empower one person to ensure that the data gets gathered, ideally through real-world experimentation.

You'll recall Fairchild Semiconductor's visit to a local florist in chapter 10. That discussion about supply-chain transparency inspired the idea of sharing information with Fairchild's distribution partners. It worked for orchids, after all. When someone put the idea forward, you could feel the energy. Everyone saw the potential to help Fairchild's smaller customers. The question was, would the distributors agree to the arrangement? Fairchild couldn't move forward without that missing piece of information. *Oh, look at the time, only ten minutes until the next meeting starts.* Before someone could break the tension by pushing the issue off to a subsequent meeting, COO Vijay Ullal stepped in:

"Who's going to own this?"

Ullal assigned someone to call the company's distributors and ask them if they'd share information. Then, he put a dedicated follow-up meeting on everyone's calendar to review the results of that outreach. When that meeting happened, the problem's owner delivered an update: "I emailed ten distributors. Five agreed and the other five had the following three concerns." Now there was something new to discuss: addressing the concerns of the holdouts. Shepherded by its owner, the idea became an experiment. The experiment evolved into a new company process. That process dramatically improved Fairchild's small customer experience, solving the original problem.

Fairchild's COO didn't let the idea die. He assigned responsibility on the spot and scheduled the next milestone. This is a crucial discipline when creating with others. Every problem needs an owner. That owner needs to agree on a plan with the other stakeholders. What steps will be taken? What tests will be run? When will we review the results and decide how to proceed? Experiments are useless if, as so often happens in half-hearted innovation efforts, you don't review the findings with the decision-makers. Always carve out a specific time to follow up that includes everyone you'd need on board to move forward. Don't put that meeting too far into the future, either. Determine the information you'll need to take the smallest next step, whatever that may be. Then work backward to determine how much time the owner will need to get it.

When you make someone an owner, it's on you to remove a commensurate amount of work from their plate. Doing something new is hard. It requires substantially more bandwidth than an established task or routine. Before you close the meeting, decide on what that person will either stop doing or hand off to someone else to make room. Likewise, make sure that the owner is empowered with the necessary authority and resources to drive the project forward. They shouldn't have to reconvene with any stakeholders to get approval for what you're all already asking them to do.

At Amazon, they take this principle to its logical extreme: a "single-threaded leader" is "100% dedicated and accountable" for pushing one solution forward. "The best way to undercut a strategic initiative is to make it someone's part-time job," writes Tom Godden, an enterprise strategist at Amazon Web Services. "Yet this seems to be the preferred way of working. The CIO declares the initiative to be critical, but no one is empowered to make it happen end to end. Everyone expects someone else to do it. This is where the single-threaded leader steps in." While you may not have the freedom to assign one person's entire output to a particular problem, you must create some bandwidth to let them drive toward a solution.

Jasna Sims, head of innovation at Lendlease, established "exploration time" as a formal way of giving employees the bandwidth to focus exclusively on pushing ideas forward. If your organization doesn't have a similar mechanism in place, create one. People need time to try things out. If they don't have it, you won't get breakthroughs. Your future is at stake.

THE CREATIVE LEADER

The earlier you intervene in a project, the more impact you can have on its outcome. Seems obvious, right? Yet at most organizations, leaders get involved in projects only after many important decisions have already been made. If that's the case at your company, change this today by placing yourself as early in the innovation process as you can.

Getting there means normalizing the sharing of unfinished work and half-formed ideas—think back to Pixar's dailies meeting. If you demand polished perfection from employees, you'll never see anything until past the point where you can make the most effective contribution.

As the leader of a team or organization, effective innovation demands that you answer the following questions:

1. **Does your team or organization have a metric related to innovation?** Are you tracking the rate at which new ideas become products, services, and solutions? Are rewards and incentives influenced by those metrics? The lack of a metric around creative risk-taking sends a clear signal that innovation isn't valued as highly as other core functions like sales or customer service.

2. **Do you model creative behavior yourself?** Do you stick to a regular creative practice? Do you seek out inputs before generating outputs? Do you insist on generating many ideas *before* winnowing them down through experimentation? Practice what you preach, or the practices won't spread.

3. **Do you have a business strategy that makes new ideas not only welcome but necessary?** If you don't even admit the need for new ideas on a strategic level, you're only welcoming your own obsolescence.

4. **Do you create space for people to work in different ways and explore ideas outside of their regular work?** Can each employee dedicate a percentage of their time and bandwidth to exploration and experimentation? What mechanisms are in place to protect tomorrow's ideas from today's demands?

5. **Does participation in a failed innovation effort send someone's career up or down?** "We work hard at X to make it safe to fail," Astro Teller, head of X, Alphabet's R&D facility, explained in a TED talk. "Teams kill their ideas as soon as evidence is on the table because they're rewarded for it. They get applause from their peers. Hugs and high fives from their manager, me in particular. They get promoted for it. We have bonused every single person on teams that ended

their projects." Teller does this to send a message to everyone at X: If failure in an innovation lab is considered a personal failure, forget it. If moon shots that miss lead to *more* opportunities to explore, innovation skyrockets. Do you have a process that celebrates failure?

6. **Do people turn to you for *the answers*?** Your job as a leader is to empower them to seek the answers themselves. Unleash the *approach.* That's how you go from being a bottleneck to an amplifier. Lead people in their approach but let them find their own solutions.

At Michelin, Philippe Barreaud sought from the beginning to frame innovation as "just another muscle the company needs to operate." Innovation takes investment—of time, money, and energy. For Barreaud, justifying that investment as risk reduction through affordable losses moved the needle better than any other argument. Michelin expects its Customer Innovation Labs to get the company from where it is today to where it wants to be tomorrow.

At Logitech, CEO Bracken Darrell sticks to a simple seeds/plants/trees framework to ensure that the company is always growing, something it's been doing at an extraordinary pace for years. Seeds are new trends and opportunities being explored, plants are new businesses actively being nurtured, and trees are mature businesses. When Darrell started doing this, he'd have a dozen or so seeds going at any one time, with each one's leader reporting directly to him. As the company grew, he began allowing seeds to report to the business unit leaders. The challenge for these leaders is to fund seeds adequately on top of their core efforts. "So far," Darrell says, "they're doing it well." It isn't easy to balance innovation against execution, but what worthwhile effort ever is?

"Most of the seeds fail," Darrell says, "but they don't go away until I give up on them." Likewise, Darrell makes sure to "trim trees regularly." When this happens, Darrell celebrates failure by giving people a bonus and promoting them into other seeds, plants, or trees. "We never want association with a seed to appear to be a career-limiting move," he told us.

~

Whenever we introduce a new technique to a group, one participant will inevitably say, "This is something I've always done, but I could never justify why to other people. It just works for me." There are only so many ways you can tell your peers: "Trust me, guys, it may feel silly but do this and it will make you more creative." If you've experienced this internal resistance when introducing your own techniques to colleagues, hopefully this book will serve as a resource for explaining the underlying mechanisms of your creative approach and backing it up with research and examples. In many cases, people resist adopting a creative practice until they see it in a book by a couple of academics. Voilà. You're welcome.

For all the resistance to these techniques we encounter even as Stanford professors, you'd think we were asking people to invest in a timeshare, not carry a notebook or write down a few ideas each day. Where the weight of authority or anecdotal evidence fails us, a few statistics or a published paper will usually do the trick. What you really need to do is get people to try something once—results are more convincing than any formal study. Use this book to get others to give it a shot.

One way or the other, your goal isn't to memorize a bunch of facts about creativity but to increase your creative competence. This means not only knowing the techniques but also understanding how to diagnose a creative logjam and then select the appropriate tool from the toolbox. Is it time to diverge, or converge? Are we searching for better solutions right now, or should we seek out a better problem first? Creative competence grows with practice, so keep going. Over time, you'll reach for the right tool every time.

Creativity works pretty much the same way in every brain. Without a formal creativity curriculum for every student, however, we each intuit our own approach to problem-solving based on trial and error. Some stuff works, some doesn't, and it's hard to distinguish between the two. Hopefully, we've offered you a logical and memorable framework that validates your favorite methods while adding some powerful new techniques to your arsenal. The next time you get that feeling of dread in your stomach when a new problem arises, you'll remember something huge. You know exactly what you need—lots of ideas—and exactly where to get them.

If you've found value in this book, share it with friends, peers, colleagues, even competitors. Creativity is how we each bring out the best of ourselves and make the world a better place for everyone else. Creation is a magical process that works best with others. A common language of innovation makes it far easier to communicate and coordinate as you achieve breakthrough creative outcomes together. Let's get to work.

Acknowledgments

A book like this never comes to life without an entire community of support. Our project wouldn't even have gotten off the ground if it hadn't been for our remarkable literary agent, Lynn Johnston. Lynn deftly guided our journey as authors and saved us untold hours of wasted effort along the way. Our editor at Portfolio, Merry Sun, provided unflappable calm in the midst of the storm, her commitment to creating an outstanding book inspiring us in every interaction. Our collaborator David Moldawer masterfully coaxed our diverse experiences into a coherent structure. Heartfelt thanks from both of us to all three.

Thanks to Henrik Werdelin and Nicholas Thorne at Prehype, whose practical wisdom and bias toward action inspire us with every new collaboration. To Carl Liebert, for graciously inviting us into many adventures; his humility continues to impress. To Mark Hoplamazian, a leader worth following, for continually ringing the bell of purpose and empathy. To Philippe Barreaud, for always aiming for the moon. To Mike Ajouz, sparring with you pushes our thinking in new directions. To Tsuney Yanagihara and Julie Ragland, for making bold moves and taking big leaps of faith.

We'd like to acknowledge our collaborators at the d.school: Deb Stern, whose gracious counsel helped us navigate uncharted waters. Carissa Carter, for championing the evolution of the practice of design. Sarah

Stein Greenberg, for her wise leadership of the institution. Scott Doorley, for embodying the heart and soul of design. Dr. Kathryn Segovia, the quintessential design thinker and teacher. Bill Pacheco, alumnus cum collaborator—and Jeremy's perennial tennis partner against Perry. Bernie Roth, for his timeless wisdom and playful collaboration. David Kelley, whose insistence upon writing a book finally got us to see the light. Bob Sutton, who graciously cosigns many of our harebrained schemes. And Huggy Rao, who always has the perfect anecdote.

Thanks to all the incredible coaches and collaborators we've worked alongside over the years: Parker Gates, Anna Love, Logan Deans, LaToya Jordan, Josh Ruff, Saul Gurdus, Jess Kessin, Anja Nabergoj, Trudy Ngo-Brown, Scott Sanchez, Yusuke Miyashita, Scott Zimmer, Kelly Garrett Zeigler, Susie Wise, Adam Weiler, Whitney Burks, Kirk Eklund, Marcus Hollinger, Katherine Cobb, Jess Nickerson, Patrick Beauduoin, Neal Boyer, Daniel Frumhoff, Sarah Holcomb, Tom Maiorana, and Vida Mia Garcia.

Thanks to our publisher, Adrian Zackheim, and his amazing team at Portfolio for their effort, enthusiasm, and expertise: Niki Papadopoulos, Stefanie Brody, Veronica Velasco, Jessica Regione, Chelsea Cohen, Madeline Rohlin, Meighan Cavanaugh, Tom Dussel, Emilie Mills, Margot Stamas, and Heather Faulls. Special thanks to Jen Heuer for our magnificent cover and Alexis Farabaugh for our elegant interior. Design matters!

Thanks to Barbara Henricks, Megan Wilson, and Nina Nocciolino of Cave Henricks Communications for helping us share our message.

Finally, thanks to the many other incredible leaders, practitioners, and collaborators who directly or indirectly shaped this book: Andy Tan, Philippe Barreaud, Claudia Kotchka, Natalie Slessor, Jesper Kløve, Bracken Darrell, Lorraine Sarayeldin, Natalie Mathieson, Chris Aho, Linda Yates, Jacob Liebert, Lisa Yokana, Don Buckley, Andrew Tomasik, Charles Moore, Gabriela Gonzalez-Stubbe, Nobuyuki Baba, Bill Gibson, Ehrika Gladden, Brad van Dam, Casey Harlin, Dan Klein, Daniel Lewis, Nik

Reed, Erica Walsh, Greg Becker, Jasna Sims, Jay Utley, John Keller, Jon Beekman, Jooyeong Song, Ken Pucker, Kevin Mayer, Laura D'Asaro, Leticia Britos Cavagnaro, Linda Hill, Lisa Montgomery, Meghan Doyle, Miri Buckland, Ellie Buckingham, Reedah El-Saie, Tetsuya Ohara, Vijay Ullal, and Wolfgang Ebel.

Jeremy would like to express special appreciation to his family for the never-ending inspiration they provide: Michelle, Evie, Zelynn, Corrie, and Frances, I'm so happy I'm yours! Also Mom, Dad, Zacko, Rae-dio, Omayra, JP, the original Z and his better half—thanks for putting up with my shenanigans. And to my church family at NCCF—especially Bobby McDonald, Sandeep Poonen, and Zac Poonen—grateful for the continual reminder of what's truly important, and to "keep seeking the things above, looking unto Jesus."

Perry would like to thank Annie for her unwavering love and support during this project, and always, and Parker and Phoebe for letting him be their dad and for always asking questions.

Notes

EPIGRAPH

ix The truth is that: Marc Randolph, *That Will Never Work: The Birth of Netflix and the Amazing Life of an Idea* (New York: Little, Brown, 2019).

INTRODUCTION

xix Smart people are a dime: Jeff Bezos, *Invent and Wander: The Collected Writings of Jeff Bezos* (Boston: Harvard Business Press, 2020).

xx Steve Jobs credited: Tim Appelo, "How a Calligraphy Pen Rewrote Steve Jobs' Life," *Hollywood Reporter* (blog), October 14, 2011, www.hollywoodreporter.com/business/digital/steve-jobs-death-apple-calligraphy-248900.

1. MEASURE TOMORROW'S SUCCESS IN TODAY'S IDEAS

3 One resists the invasion: Victor Hugo, *The History of a Crime* (Tavistock, UK: Moorside Press, 2013).

10 Even before he founded: Brad Stone, *The Everything Store: Jeff Bezos and the Age of Amazon* (New York: Back Bay Books, 2014).

10 A randomized, controlled trial: Arnaldo Camuffo, Alessandro Cordova, Alfonso Gambardella, and Chiara Spina, "A Scientific Approach to Entrepreneurial Decision-Making: Evidence from a Randomized Control Trial," *Management Science* 66, no. 2 (February 2020): 564–86, https://doi.org/10.1287/mnsc.2018.3249.

15 When we feel safe enough: Amy C. Edmondson, "Strategies for Learning from Failure," *Harvard Business Review,* April 2011, https://hbr.org/2011/04/strategies-for-learning-from-failure.

21 According to a paper: Nicholas Bloom et al., "Are Ideas Getting Harder to Find?," *American Economic Review* 110, no. 4 (April 2020): 1104–44, https://doi.org/10.1257/aer.20180338.

2. AMPLIFY IDEAFLOW

23 The sole substance: Maria Popova, "How Steinbeck Used the Diary as a Tool of Discipline, a Hedge Against Self-Doubt, and a Pacemaker for the Heartbeat of Creative Work," *Brain*

Pickings (blog), March 2, 2015, www.brainpickings.org/2015/03/02/john-steinbeck
-working-days/.

29 **"Be regular and orderly":** Alan William Raitt, *Gustavus Flaubertus Bourgeoisophobus: Flaubert and the Bourgeois Mentality* (New York: P. Lang, 2005).

33 **sleep is essential for both:** Paula Alhola and Päivi Polo-Kantola, "Sleep Deprivation: Impact on Cognitive Performance," *Neuropsychiatric Disease and Treatment* 3, no. 5 (October 2007): 553–67.

33 **Likewise, Nobel laureate Otto Loewi:** Alli N. McCoy and Yong Siang Tan, "Otto Loewi (1873–1961): Dreamer and Nobel Laureate," *Singapore Medical Journal* 55, no. 1 (January 2014): 3–4, https://doi.org/10.11622/smedj.2014002.

33 **sleep improves our ability:** Ut Na Sio, Padraic Monaghan, and Tom Ormerod, "Sleep on It, but Only if It Is Difficult: Effects of Sleep on Problem Solving," *Memory & Cognition* 41, no. 2 (February 2013): 159–66, https://doi.org/10.3758/s13421-012-0256-7.

34 **What's more, sleep deprivation:** Alhola and Polo-Kantola, "Sleep Deprivation."

36 **"If, as a jazz musician":** Franziska Green, "In the 'Creative' Zone: An Interview with Dr. Charles Limb," *Brain World* (blog), August 22, 2019, https://brainworldmagazine.com /creative-zone-interview-dr-charles-limb/.

38 **Simply walking through:** Gabriel A. Radvansky, Sabine A. Krawietz, and Andrea K. Tamplin, "Walking Through Doorways Causes Forgetting: Further Explorations," *Quarterly Journal of Experimental Psychology* 64, no. 8 (August 1, 2011): 1632–45, https://doi.org /10.1080/17470218.2011.571267.

38 **"Everything ends up in print":** Mason Currey, ed., *Daily Rituals: How Artists Work* (New York: Knopf, 2013).

39 **Film director David Lynch:** David Lynch, *Catching the Big Fish: Meditation, Consciousness, and Creativity,* 10th anniversary ed. (New York: TarcherPerigee, 2016).

41 **"A link between a problem":** Diane Coutu, "Ideas as Art," *Harvard Business Review,* October 1, 2006, https://hbr.org/2006/10/ideas-as-art.

3. FLOOD YOUR PROBLEM WITH IDEAS

47 **A multitude of bad ideas:** Kevin Kelly, "99 Additional Bits of Unsolicited Advice," *The Technium* (blog), April 19, 2021, https://kk.org/thetechnium/99-additional-bits-of -unsolicited-advice/.

50 **For example, a 1987 meta-analysis:** Michael Diehl and Wolfgang Stroebe, "Productivity Loss in Brainstorming Groups: Toward the Solution of a Riddle," *Journal of Personality and Social Psychology* 53 (September 1, 1987): 497–509, https://doi.org/10.1037/0022 -3514.53.3.497.

50 **A study comparing solo work:** Runa Korde and Paul B. Paulus, "Alternating Individual and Group Idea Generation: Finding the Elusive Synergy," *Journal of Experimental Social Psychology* 70 (May 1, 2017): 177–90, https://doi.org/10.1016/j.jesp.2016.11.002.

51 **One of the pitfalls:** A. W. Kruglanski and D. M. Webster, "Motivated Closing of the Mind: 'Seizing' and 'Freezing,'" *Psychological Review* 103, no. 2 (April 1996): 263–83, https://doi.org/10.1037/0033-295x.103.2.263.

51 **The "equal-odds rule":** Dean Keith Simonton, "Creative Productivity: A Predictive and Explanatory Model of Career Trajectories and Landmarks," *Psychological Review* 104, no. 1 (1997): 66–89, https://doi.org/10.1037/0033-295X.104.1.66.

52 **Collaborating with a toy manufacturer:** Robert I. Sutton, *Weird Ideas That Work: 11½ Practices for Promoting, Managing, and Sustaining Innovation,* illustrated ed. (New York: Free Press, 2002).

53 **For example, Taco Bell's Insights Labs:** J. Bennett, "Behind the Scenes in Taco Bell's Insane Food Development Lab," *Thrillist,* March 2, 2017, www.thrillist.com/eat/nation /taco-bell-insane-food-development-lab.

54 **According to the inventor:** Madison Malone-Kircher, "James Dyson on the 5,126 Vacuums That Didn't Work and the One That Finally Did," *The Vindicated* (blog), November 26, 2016, https://nymag.com/vindicated/2016/11/james-dyson-on-5-126 -vacuums-that-didnt-work-and-1-that-did.html.

55 **"Isn't it a shame":** Frank Lewis Dyer and Thomas Commerford Martin, *Edison: His Life and Inventions* (original pub: New York: Harper & Brothers, 1910; Frankfurt: Outlook, 2019), 368.

57 **Another cognitive bias:** Brian J. Lucas and Loran F. Nordgren, "The Creative Cliff Illusion," *Proceedings of the National Academy of Sciences* 117, no. 33 (August 18, 2020): 19830–36, https://doi.org/10.1073/pnas.2005620117.

58 **A third limiter:** Amos Tversky and Daniel Kahneman, "Judgment under Uncertainty: Heuristics and Biases," *Science* 185, no. 4157 (1974): 1124–31, https://doi.org/10.1126 /science.185.4157.1124.

58 **first few suggestions in a brainstorming:** Justin Berg, "The Primal Mark: How the Beginning Shapes the End in the Development of Creative Ideas," *Organizational Behavior and Human Decision Processes* 125 (September 2014): 1–17, www.sciencedirect.com/science /article/pii/S0749597814000478.

59 **Merim Bilalić and Peter McLeod:** Merim Bilalić, Peter McLeod, and Fernand Gobet, "Why Good Thoughts Block Better Ones: The Mechanism of the Pernicious Einstellung (Set) Effect," *Cognition* 108, no. 3 (September 2008): 652–61, https://doi.org /10.1016/j.cognition.2008.05.005.

4. BUILD AN INNOVATION PIPELINE

69 **We are trying to prove:** Richard Feynman, *The Character of Physical Law,* with new foreword (Cambridge, MA, and London: MIT Press, 2017).

73 **General Motors saw early traction:** Laura Sky Brown, "GM's Car-Sharing Service, Maven, Shuts Down After Four Years," *Car and Driver,* April 22, 2020, www.caranddriver.com /news/a32235218/gm-maven-car-sharing-closes/.

78 **Research by our colleague:** Justin M. Berg, "When Silver Is Gold: Forecasting the Potential Creativity of Initial Ideas," *Organizational Behavior and Human Decision Processes* 154 (September 2019): 96–117, https://doi.org/10.1016/j.obhdp.2019.08.004.

79 **"It was fascinating":** Tim Ferriss, "Sir James Dyson—Founder of Dyson and Master Inventor on How to Turn the Mundane into Magic," September 2, 2021, in *The Tim Ferriss Show* (podcast), 1:35:57, https://tim.blog/2021/09/02/james-dyson.

85 **For example, Bette Nesmith Graham:** Zachary Crockett, "The Secretary Who Turned Liquid Paper into a Multimillion-Dollar Business," *The Hustle,* April 23, 2021, https:// thehustle.co/the-secretary-who-turned-liquid-paper-into-a-multimillion-dollar-business.

5. PUT YOUR IDEAS TO THE TEST

93 **"The first question of design":** Corita Kent and Jan Steward, *Learning by Heart,* 2nd ed. (New York: Allworth Press, 2008).

97 **A study of over a hundred:** Michael Leatherbee and Riitta Katila, "The Lean Startup Method: Early-Stage Teams and Hypothesis-Based Probing of Business Ideas," *Strategic Entrepreneurship Journal* 14, no. 4 (December 2020): 570–93, https://doi.org/10.1002 /sej.1373.

97 **Over the years, Wujec has:** Tom Wujec, "Build a Tower, Build a Team," February 2010, TED2010, Long Beach, CA, TED video, 6:35, www.ted.com/talks/tom_wujec_build_a _tower_build_a_team/transcript.

103 **"He was constantly sneaking":** Phil Knight, *Shoe Dog: A Memoir by the Creator of Nike* (New York: Scribner, 2016).

107 **Henrik Werdelin and Nicholas Thorne started:** Nathan Chan, "How Henrik Werdelin Built a 9-Figure Subscription Box Business for Dogs," June 9, 2020, in *Foundr* (podcast), 1:05:37, https://foundr.com/articles/podcast/henrik-werdelin-barkbox.

6. MAKE THE WORLD YOUR LAB

115 **Inspiration suggests the combination:** Robert Grudin, *The Grace of Great Things: Creativity and Innovation* (Boston: Mariner Books, 1991).

115 **According to the Alzheimer's Association:** *2021 Alzheimer's Disease Facts and Figures* (Chicago: Alzheimer's Association, 2021), 18–19, www.alz.org/media/documents /alzheimers-facts-and-figures.pdf.

121 **In 2021, Peloton:** "Peloton: Child Killed in 'Tragic' Treadmill Accident," BBC News, March 18, 2021, www.bbc.com/news/business-56451430.

7. MINE FOR PERSPECTIVES

143 **Many ideas grow better:** Oliver Wendell Holmes, *The Poet at the Breakfast-Table* (Boston: James R. Osgood and Company, 1872).

145 **Psychologist Heidi Grant:** David Rock and Heidi Grant, "Why Diverse Teams Are Smarter," *Harvard Business Review,* November 4, 2016, https://hbr.org/2016/11/why-diverse -teams-are-smarter.

150 **"One thing a person":** Ashton B. Carter, *Managing Nuclear Operations* (Washington, D.C.: Brookings Institution, 1987).

152 **When Mark Parker was CEO:** Ellen McGirt, "How Nike's CEO Shook Up the Shoe Industry," *Fast Company,* September 1, 2010, www.fastcompany.com/1676902/how-nikes -ceo-shook-shoe-industry.

155 **"They want a quarter-inch hole!":** Clayton M. Christensen, Scott Cook, and Taddy Hall, "Marketing Malpractice: The Cause and the Cure," *Harvard Business Review,* December 1, 2005, https://hbr.org/2005/12/marketing-malpractice-the-cause-and-the-cure.

156 **"No plan of operations":** Helmuth Graf von Moltke, *Moltkes militärische Werke: Die Thätigkeit als Chef des Generalstabes der Armee im Frieden* (Hamburg: E. S. Mittler, 1900).

157 **According to Duke University:** Martin Ruef, "Strong Ties, Weak Ties and Islands: Structural and Cultural Predictors of Organizational Innovation," *Industrial and Corporate Change* 11 (June 1, 2002): 427–49, https://doi.org/10.1093/icc/11.3.427.

157 **"After a bit I thought":** Richard P. Feynman, *"Surely You're Joking, Mr. Feynman!": Adventures of a Curious Character* (New York, London: W. W. Norton, 1997).

158 **Likewise, Bill Baker:** Jon Gertner, *The Idea Factory: Bell Labs and the Great Age of American Innovation* (New York: Penguin Books, 2012).

160 **IBM developed the revolutionary:** James W. Cortada, "Building the System/360 Mainframe Nearly Destroyed IBM," *IEEE Spectrum,* April 5, 2019, https://spectrum.ieee.org /building-the-system360-mainframe-nearly-destroyed-ibm.

162 **At Lockheed Martin's Skunk Works:** Ben R. Rich, *Skunk Works: A Personal Memoir of My Years at Lockheed* (New York: Little, Brown, 1996).

163 **The value of what psychology:** Kevin Dunbar, "How Scientists Think: On-line Creativity and Conceptual Change in Science," in *The Nature of Insight,* ed. Robert J. Sternberg and Janet E. Davidson (Boston: MIT Press, 1997), 461.

164 John Bardeen and Walter Brattain: Gertner, *Idea Factory.*

168 Pixar holds regular dailies: Ed Catmull and Amy Wallace, *Creativity, Inc.: Overcoming the Unseen Forces That Stand in the Way of True Inspiration* (New York: Random House, 2014).

8. SHAKE UP YOUR PERSPECTIVE

171 It is only afterward: Isaac Asimov, "Isaac Asimov Asks, 'How Do People Get New Ideas?':
A 1959 Essay by Isaac Asimov on Creativity," *MIT Technology Review,* October 20, 2014,
www.technologyreview.com/2014/10/20/169899/isaac-asimov-asks-how-do-people-get
-new-ideas.

174 Caught up in: Christopher Chabris and Daniel Simons, *The Invisible Gorilla: How Our Intuitions Deceive Us* (New York: Harmony, 2011).

185 As part of the Toyota Production System: Taiichi Ohno, "Ask 'Why' Five Times About Every Matter," Toyota Myanmar, March 2006, www.toyota-myanmar.com/about-toyota
/toyota-traditions/quality/ask-why-five-times-about-every-matter.

189 "[It] is possible": Ed Catmull and Amy Wallace, *Creativity, Inc.: Overcoming the Unseen Forces That Stand in the Way of True Inspiration* (New York: Random House, 2014).

189 "And the first thing I ask": Jennifer L. Roberts, "The Power of Patience," *Harvard Magazine,* October 15, 2013, www.harvardmagazine.com/2013/11/the-power-of-patience.

9. STOKE CURIOSITY

193 It is a familiar: John Dewey, *Logic: The Theory of Inquiry* (New York: Henry Holt, 1938).

195 The legendary artist and educator: Corita Kent and Jan Steward, *Learning by Heart* (New York: Allworth Press, 2008).

196 Ask yourself an interesting: Joe Fig, *Inside the Painter's Studio* (Princeton, NJ: Princeton Architectural Press, 2012).

198 Aerosmith, one of the best-selling: MasterClass, "Dare to Suck," January 9, 2020, Facebook video, 1:04, www.facebook.com/watch/?v=2544715345762983.

203 The caption for Goldberg's illustration: Jennifer George, ed., *The Art of Rube Goldberg: (A) Inventive (B) Cartoon (C) Genius* (New York: Harry N. Abrams, 2013).

203 In a paper published in: Gabrielle S. Adams, Benjamin A. Converse, Andrew H. Hales, and Leidy E. Klotz, "People Systematically Overlook Subtractive Changes," *Nature* 592 (2021): 258–61, https://doi.org/10.1038/s41586-021-03380-y.

204 Since the bridge wasn't sitting evenly: Nature Video, "Less Is More: Why Our Brains Struggle to Subtract," April 7, 2021, YouTube video, 6:19, https://www.youtube.com/watch
?v=1y32OpI2_LM.

206 "How do we make": Nolan Bushnell and Gene Stone, *Finding the Next Steve Jobs: How to Find, Keep, and Nurture Talent* (New York: Simon & Schuster, 2013).

10. ENCOURAGE CREATIVE COLLISIONS

214 According to neurobiologist: Morten Friis-Olivarius, "Stimulating the Creative Brain," June 20, 2018, TEDxOslo, Oslo, YouTube video, 14:00, www.youtube.com/watch?v=
hZCcVk8-RVQ.

214 Or, as the novelist: Arthur Koestler, *The Act of Creation* (London: Hutchinson, 1964).

216 "What you end up with": *Inspirations,* directed by Michael Apted (Clear Blue Sky Productions, 1997), 1:36.

217 In one study, forty scientists: Robert S. Root-Bernstein, Maurine Bernstein, and Helen Garnier, "Correlations Between Avocations, Scientific Style, Work Habits, and Professional

Impact of Scientists," *Creativity Research Journal* 8, no. 2 (April 1, 1995): 115–37, https://doi.org/10.1207/s15326934crj0802_2.

217 **Researchers at Stanford found:** Marily Oppezzo and Daniel L. Schwartz, "Give Your Ideas Some Legs: The Positive Effect of Walking on Creative Thinking," *Journal of Experimental Psychology: Learning, Memory, and Cognition* 40, no. 4 (2014): 1142–52, https://doi.org/10.1037/a0036577.

218 **"He came bounding":** Walter Isaacson, *Steve Jobs* (New York: Simon & Schuster, 2021).

219 **"The natural inclination":** Edward de Bono, *Lateral Thinking: Creativity Step by Step* (New York: HarperCollins, 2010).

224 **In the early days:** Chip Bayers, "The Inner Jeff Bezos," *Wired*, March 1, 1999, www.wired.com/1999/03/bezos-3/.

11. UNTANGLE CREATIVE KNOTS

227 **The majority of business:** David Ogilvy, *Confessions of an Advertising Man* (1963; repr., Harpenden, UK: Southbank, 2013).

227 **"After a while you will":** James Webb Young, *A Technique for Producing Ideas* (Victoria, BC: Must Have Books, 2021).

228 **"[Einstein] went to visit":** Walter Isaacson, *Einstein: His Life and Universe* (New York: Simon & Schuster, 2008).

228 **"I try to take long walks":** Mason Currey, *Daily Rituals: Women at Work* (New York: Knopf, 2019).

229 **"I turned my attention":** Dean Keith Simonton, *Origins of Genius: Darwinian Perspectives on Creativity* (Oxford: Oxford University Press, 1999).

233 **Taking a shower or bath:** Howard E. Gruber, "The Evolving Systems Approach to Creative Work," *Creativity Research Journal* 1, no. 1 (December 1988): 27–51, https://doi.org/10.1080/10400418809534285.

234 **"Playing a lot":** Greg Bernhardt, "Interview with Theoretical Physicist Garrett Lisi," *Physics Forums Insights* (blog), March 12, 2016, www.physicsforums.com/insights/interview-theoretical-physicist-garrett-lisi/.

235 **"I like to have":** Steven Johnson, "Dan Pink Has a Folder for That Idea," *Medium* (blog), January 31, 2018, https://medium.com/s/workflow/dan-pink-has-a-folder-for-that-idea-84252c35ddb.

235 **A group of psychologists:** Benjamin Baird et al., "Inspired by Distraction: Mind Wandering Facilitates Creative Incubation," *Psychological Science* 23, no. 10 (October 2012): 1117–22, https://doi.org/10.1177/0956797612446024.

236 **Mervin Kelly, the celebrated:** Jon Gertner, *The Idea Factory: Bell Labs and the Great Age of American Innovation* (New York: Penguin Books, 2012).

236 **According to Dr. Jonathan:** Amanda Gardner, "'Power Naps' May Boost Right-Brain Activity," *CNN Health*, October 17, 2012, www.cnn.com/2012/10/17/health/health-naps-brain/index.html.

237 **According to one paper:** Hiuyan Lau, Sara E. Alger, and William Fishbein, "Relational Memory: A Daytime Nap Facilitates the Abstraction of General Concepts," *PLOS ONE* 6, no. 11 (November 16, 2011): e27139, https://doi.org/10.1371/journal.pone.0027139.

237 **"The brain could be doing":** "Might Lefties and Righties Benefit Differently from a Power Nap?," *Georgetown University Medical Center* (blog), December 11, 2013, https://gumc.georgetown.edu/news-release/people-who-like-to-nap/.

238 **Brian Grazer, who:** Brian Grazer and Charles Fishman, *A Curious Mind: The Secret to a Bigger Life* (New York: Simon & Schuster, 2016).

239 **"If I don't go running":** Tim Ferriss, "Joyce Carol Oates—A Writing Icon on Creative Process and Creative Living," February 10, 2021, in *The Tim Ferriss Show* (podcast), 1:13:00, https://podcasts.apple.com/us/podcast/497-joyce-carol-oates-writing-icon-on-creative-process/id863897795?i=1000508500903.

240 **In a 1970 appearance:** "Paul Simon on His Writing Process for 'Bridge over Troubled Water,'" *The Dick Cavett Show,* uploaded January 27, 2020, YouTube video, 10:45, www.youtube.com/watch?v=qFt0cP-klQI&t=143s, originally aired April 9, 1970, *The Dick Cavett Show.*

CONCLUSION: INNOVATE WITH OTHERS

248 **At Amazon, they take:** Tom Godden, "Two-Pizza Teams Are Just the Start, Part 2: Accountability and Empowerment Are Key to High-Performing Agile Organizations," *AWS Cloud Enterprise Strategy* (blog), March 18, 2021, https://aws.amazon.com/blogs/enterprise-strategy/two-pizza-teams-are-just-the-start-accountability-and-empowerment-are-key-to-high-performing-agile-organizations-part-2/.

249 **"We work hard at X":** Astro Teller, "The Unexpected Benefit of Celebrating Failure," TED2016, February 2016, Vancouver, TED video, 15:24, www.ted.com/talks/astro_teller_the_unexpected_benefit_of_celebrating_failure.

Index